On the Margins

Roma and Public Services
in Romania, Bulgaria, and Macedonia

On the Margins

Roma and Public Services in Romania, Bulgaria, and Macedonia

WITH A SUPPLEMENT ON HOUSING IN THE CZECH REPUBLIC

A Call to Action to Improve Romani Access to Social Protection, Health Care, and Housing

By Ina Zoon

Edited by Mark Norman Templeton

A report to the

OPEN SOCIETY INSTITUTE

ISBN 1-891385-18-6 Paperback

Library of Congress Cataloging in Publication Data
A CIP catalog record for this book is available upon request.

Published by the Open Society Institute
400 West 59th Street, New York, NY 10019 USA

The Open Society Institute in New York funded the preparation and publication of this report. OSI is at the center of a network of foundations and programs committed to promoting the development and maintenance of open society by operating and supporting an array of initiatives in educational, social, and legal reform.

The report was researched and written by Ina Zoon, a Romanian human rights activist who has worked on Romani issues for much of the past decade. She currently lives in Madrid and works as a consultant to OSI and others. She is a member of the board of directors of the European Roma Rights Center.

The report was edited by Mark Norman Templeton, a 1999 graduate of the Yale Law School, a senior editor of the *Yale Law Journal,* and student director of the Allard K. Lowenstein International Human Rights Clinic. A 1999–2000 Robert L. Bernstein Fellow in International Human Rights, he spent the last year working on human rights issues in South and Southeast Asia, based in Bangkok, Thailand.

For More Information, Contact:
Ina Zoon
Tel: + 34 91 715 24 50
Fax: + 34 91 351 18 54
E-mail: inazoon3@worldonline.es

Deborah A. Harding
Vice President for National Foundations
Open Society Institute
Tel: (212) 548-0132
E-mail: dharding@sorosny.org

On the Margins online: www.soros.org/romaandpublicservices

Designed by Jeanne Criscola/Criscola Design
Map by Liz Pagano
Printed in the United States of America by Herlin Press, Inc.
Cover Photo: ©Rolf Bauerdick

Contents

Lack of Adequate Housing 115

Foreword

Mounds of garbage were piled along the narrow, rutted streets of Shuto Orizari, a Romani neighborhood in the capital city of Macedonia.

"When is the trash collected?" I asked my Macedonian companions.

"Every once in a while."

"When is the next bus?"

"There is no bus line."

"Hospital?"

"No hospital."

"Who lives here?"

"Just the Roma."

This was Skopje. But it could have been almost any city in any of the other countries of East Central Europe.

The visit to Shuto Orizari prompted me to ask Ina Zoon to begin work on this study of the Roma and their access to public services in Bulgaria, Macedonia, and Romania and housing in the Czech Republic—countries that, since the fall of communism in Eastern Europe, have been building democratic governments.

A democracy with deep roots strives to treat its minority group members as equals. But if the treatment of the Roma is used as a measure to judge the democratic credentials of the Eastern European states, they fail.

These democracies grew out of revolutions led by students, intellectuals, and dissidents who had high ideals. Their goals were freedom for themselves and their fellow citizens, without exceptions.

Once in power, however, the new leaders of these newly democratic states did not stand up for the Roma. They failed to defend the constitutionally guaranteed right of the Roma to equal treatment under the law. They implemented policies that further marginalized the Roma. These elected leaders did not fight societal discrimination, either direct or indirect. They did not dismantle the policies that continue to keep the Roma down.

Today, however, a valuable opportunity to bring about change is at hand.

The European Union is now considering increasing its membership by opening its doors to the countries of Central and Eastern Europe. It is scrutinizing each accession candidate's political commitment to equal protection, the rule of law, and the treatment of minorities. Romania, Bulgaria, and the Czech Republic are candidates for admission. Other countries, such as Macedonia, may one day be added to the roster of accession candidates. This report makes clear the work that lies ahead for each of these countries before their laws and the implementation of their laws are brought into accordance with EU standards.

Until now, scant attention has been paid to how the social policies of these new governments have affected the Roma. Human rights groups, international donors, and Western governments have largely focused on the treatment of Roma in the criminal justice system.

This report, an inside portrait of the Roma and their equal access to the public services of housing, health care, and social protection, lays down a challenge to the new leaders and their counterparts in the West. It outlines recommendations that must be adopted before these new democracies join the ranks of the European Union members.

Ina Zoon's report is a sobering account of how the Roma are excluded from public services. The report drives home the reality of Romani lives—the widespread discrimination that the Roma face each day—whether in policies, laws, indiffference, or hostility.

In the four countries under review, Roma are as much as 7 percent of the population. Most of them are semiliterate, unskilled, and unemployed. Government policies that stigmatize and exclude Roma are creating a permanent underclass that will burden the fragile economies of states in transition. Over the next decade, unless the policies are changed, this burden will become more onerous as these states suffer a deficit of skilled laborers in the work force.

The easiest, and perhaps least costly, solution to the lack of educated, skilled workers in the Romani population could be found in desegregation of schools. Romani children should be educated along with non-Romani children. This will be less expensive than having parallel school systems and would also help impede the development of two separate, unequal societies.

Antidiscrimination legislation should be enacted and implemented.

Roma should be allowed to compete in the labor market in order to bring the Roma in from the impoverished margins of society.

National leaders must also take clear stands against racism, intolerance, and exclusion. They should review and change national and local policies and laws that allow for discrimination.

These recommendations reflect some of the ideas that Ina Zoon presents in this report. They are first steps that can open the way to improving the status of Roma in these societies.

When I return to Shuto Orizari a decade from now, I hope to see citizens who have equal access to public services—whether garbage collection, hospitals, or public transport. This is not just a question of economic development. The woes of these societies will not be cured with the trappings of prosperity. On the contrary, the laws, their implementation, and government institutions must be strengthened—the framework of society built—for prosperity to spread.

Changing the status of the Roma could prove to be the single greatest challenge for these new democracies, the future members of the European Union.

Deborah A. Harding
Vice President for National Foundations
Open Society Institute

Acknowledgments

The idea for this report belongs to Deborah Harding, who supported in all possible ways each and every stage of it. The final version was structured by Mark Templeton, who provided overall supervision and invaluable guidance. The text has greatly benefited from the comments of Diane Orentlicher, Jim Goldston, Dimitrina Petrova, Andras Sajo, Maureen Lewis, Renate Weber, Vladimir Milcin, and Nina Schwalbe.

In Romania, Manuela Stefanescu, Florin Moisa, Mariana Buceanu, Maria Ionescu, Vasile Ionescu, Florin Buhuceanu, Vasile Burtea, Geza Otvos, Nicolae Bologa, Sorin Cace, Dana Costin, Emilian Nicolae, Violeta Dumitru, Ilie Dinca, Florin Cioaba, Gruia Bumbu, Adrian Moldovean, Istvan Haller, Rudolf Moca, Paustin Balan, Nicolae Ficuta, and Antonia Creteanu contributed significantly.

In Bulgaria, Savelina Danova, Rumyan Russinov, Yonko Grozev, Mihail Georgiev, Anton Karagiozov, Ivailo Turnev, Stefan Panayotov, Ilona Tomova, Vassil Chaprazov, and Nikolay Kirilov generously shared information and provided updates.

Elvis Ali organized the fact finding in Macedonia. Slavica Inzdevska, Dilbera Kamberovska, Jonuz Enver, Senaj Osmanov, Anifa Demirovska, Nezdet Mustafa, Meto

Jovanovski, Ramiza Sakip, Asmet Elezovski, Ahmet Jasarovski, Memedali Rahmani, and Azbija Memedova provided assistance and information on local Romani communities.

The chapter on housing in the Czech Republic was prepared with the generous assistance of the Counseling Center for Citizenship, Civil and Human Rights' team of Barbora Kvocekova, Pavla Bouckova, and Ladislav Zamboj, who gathered an impressive amount of regulations and other evidence. I am also indebted for information and comments to Petr Uhl, Marta Miklusakova, Emil Scuka, Ondrej Gina, Monika Horakova, Milena Hubshmannova, Kumar Vishwanathan, Klara Vesela, Ivan Vesely, Robert Olah, Markus Pape, and Michal Horak.

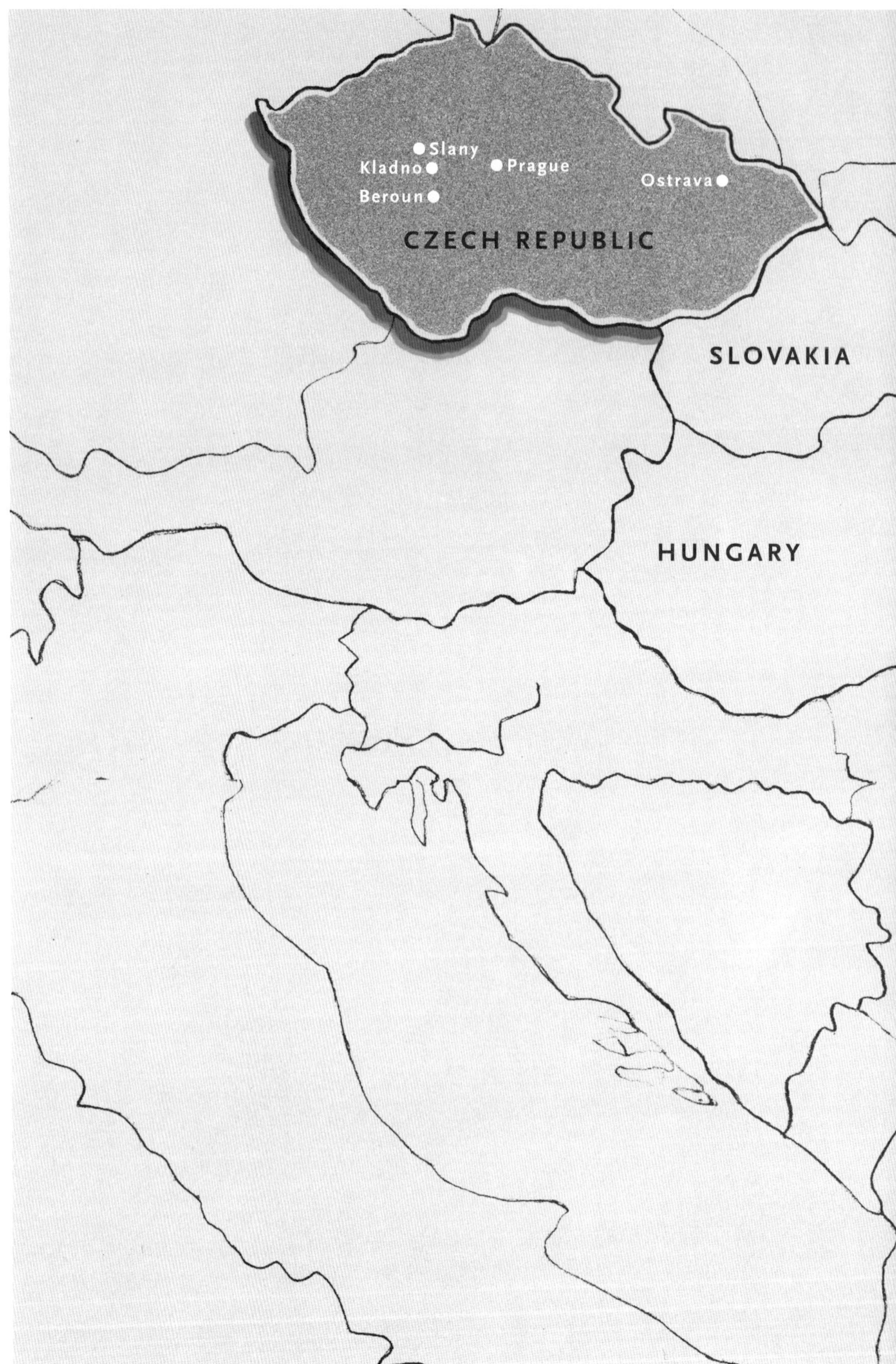
Slany
Kladno
Prague
Ostrava
Beroun
CZECH REPUBLIC
SLOVAKIA
HUNGARY

UKRAINE
MOLDOVA
Dej
Cluj-Napoca
Buhusi
Bacau
Targu Mures
ROMANIA
Focsani
Deva
Orastie
Sibiu
Mizil
Bucharest
Lom
UGOSLAVIA
Sofia
BLACK SEA
BULGARIA
Plovdiv
Kumanovo
Skopje
Stip
MACEDONIA
Prilep

"We give money to those who deserve it, old people who cannot work anymore, not to the Gypsies."

SOCIAL WORKER IN BUCHAREST

Executive Summary

The Roma, comprising between 2 and 7 percent of the populations of Romania, Bulgaria, and Macedonia, generally are the poorest of the poor with the lowest level of physical health and the most miserable accommodations. As the most vulnerable social group in these countries, Roma are overrepresented in all categories in need of social protection: the very poor, the long-term unemployed, the unskilled, the uneducated, members of large families, and individuals without residence permits, identity documents, or citizenship papers.

In all three countries, existing government programs to improve the lot of the unfortunate and the downtrodden, if implemented fairly and justly, would have to focus their efforts on the Roma. Social safety nets, applied without favor or prejudice, would catch the Roma at a rate proportional to the challenges that they face. At the very least, in a system devoid of ethnic bias, the Roma would benefit from these government programs at a rate similar to that of the rest of the population.

Instead, many of the social protection, health care, and housing programs in these countries effectively screen out the Roma from support they desperately need. Mobility patterns and practices can make it difficult for Roma to meet social protection requirements and to obtain or keep official documents such as birth certificates and identity cards—all of which governments may require for receipt of social support. Governments may define the family unit in such a way that those who are indigent and not married in a civil ceremony—which includes the vast majority of young Romani families—cannot qualify for family benefits under health care laws. Governments may characterize long-standing Romani dwellings as "temporary" because they are not part of the official city plan, which may result in Roma not establishing official residency and not receiving certain types of benefits.

Furthermore, some government officials and their representatives abuse their discretionary powers. Some social workers overestimate the true wealth of Romani clients, thereby disqualifying them from receiving social support. Some doctors and health care personnel refuse to accept Roma on their patient rolls and will not treat them, even under emergency conditions. Some municipal officials allocate less transportation and sanitation services to Romani neighborhoods than to others with similarly sized populations.

Governments, needless to say, can make choices about the types and levels of services that they will provide. They also may need to adjust those programs as they undergo transitions from one economic system to another. And they may need to change their policies in response to unexpected social and political challenges.

But government policies and government officials should not—and legally cannot—deprive Roma of access to public services that are available to the rest of the population. Indirect and direct discrimination in the provision of those benefits worsens the living conditions of Roma, who, as a group, are already most in need of social, health, and housing support. In the past few years, however, instead of helping, governments have withdrawn assistance and used their energies to keep the Roma on the margins of society.

This report documents the ways in which the Romanian, Bulgarian, and Macedonian governments and their representatives discriminate against the Roma in the provision of social protection benefits, health care, and housing. The supplement describes similar discrimination against the Roma in access to housing in the Czech Republic. The report shows how particular, facially neutral policies have a disparate impact on the Roma, and how certain government officials discriminate directly against Romani claimants requesting services.

1. Legal Standards

This study begins by outlining relevant international, regional, and national antidiscrimination legal standards and principles. It establishes that most forms of discrimination on the basis of race or ethnicity violate international and European law. It shows that with regard to the provision of social benefits, international treaty bodies have stated that governments should not distinguish among recipients on the basis of their race directly or indirectly. The report shows that the constitutions of the countries under review affirm the principle of equal treatment under law and incorporate ratified international human rights treaties directly into domestic law. Nonetheless, despite the clear international and regional standards and constitutional provisions, only Romania has developed general antidiscrimination legislation, and it remains to be seen how meaningful those laws will be.

2. Social Protection

The report assesses the extent to which governments discriminate against the Roma or fail to provide minimum support through social protection programs. It outlines the level of benefits provided under particular programs; reviews eligibility criteria for particular forms of support; discusses how these criteria relate to characteristics of the Romani population; reviews problems faced by Roma in complying with these procedures; identifies cases in which regional or municipal administrators appear to have used their power in an arbitrary and discriminatory manner; and reviews administrative and legal appeals processes.

The key findings with regard to social protection are:

- Poverty and unemployment rates in Romania, Bulgaria, and Macedonia are two to two-and-a-half times higher for Romani families than for the rest of the population.
- Governments provide a variety of benefits to persons in need, including social support, food pantry distributions, monthly assistance for the payment of rent, support for heating, emergency help, child allowances, additional benefits for families with children, maternity benefits, and birth grants.
- The amount of each benefit is insufficient to cover the overall needs of the beneficiary.
- In determining eligibility for benefits, governments impose a number of criteria, most of which have a disparate impact on the Roma. These criteria include: a means test; a domicile requirement; work responsibilities; identification documents; limitations on the size of living quarters; and bans on foreign travel, corporate ownership, and housing sales.
- There are a variety of additional barriers for Roma in obtaining social protection benefits, including difficulties in accessing government facilities; forced choices between types of social support; allocation of funds by the government to other socially disadvantaged groups; delay or nonallocation of funds; time limits on the receipt of benefits; poor relations between Roma and social workers; and lack of knowledge about these programs in the Romani community.
- Administrative and legal appeals processes are seldom used and rarely result in redress.

3. Health Care

The study assesses the extent to which governments or private persons discriminate against Romani patients and interfere with their ability to obtain adequate health care. It reviews the general status of Romani health in each of the three countries; highlights the relative cost of medical care and discusses health insurance plans; describes the view of Romani patients put forth by the media; identifies cases of direct discrimination against Romani patients by doctors and other medical personnel; discusses how legal provisions impede the ability of Roma to receive health care; outlines other barriers to Romani access to health care; shows problems that Roma confront in obtaining emergency care; and discusses general levels of staffing, equipment, and facilities in Romani neighborhoods.

The key findings with regard to health care are:

- The health of the Roma is generally worse than the health of the population at large. Their life expectancy is many years shorter than the life expectancy of the majority. Their children have a higher infant mortality rate and a higher rate of vitamin deficiencies, malnutrition, anemia, dystrophy, and rickets than their non-Romani peers.
- Governments have health care and health insurance systems designed to provide treatment to persons who receive social support benefits or are otherwise in need.
- Many Roma, however, do not receive the medical treatment they need due to direct and indirect discrimination.
- The media has created an image of Romani patients as people who cannot follow doctors' directions or respect the rights of other patients.
- Some health care professionals and facilities discriminate directly against the Roma. They may decline to accept Romani patients and may subject Romani patients to verbal abuse and degrading treatment. They may segregate patients on the basis of race and decline to provide medical certificates documenting injuries inflicted during racist attacks.
- Health insurance systems predicate coverage on eligibility requirements that may have a disparate impact on the Roma, such as marital and citizenship status, family size, and level of educational achievement.
- There are a variety of additional barriers for Roma in accessing health care services. These barriers include lack of information in the Romani community, unlawful practices of the local authorities that lead to loss of health insurance or the impossibility of obtaining health insurance without payment of a contribution, and abuse of power by social workers.
- Roma do not have equal access to emergency medical facilities. Emergency center operators often refuse to send an ambulance when they assume the

request is for a Romani patient, and they give priority to calls from non-Romani neighborhoods. Doctors and nurses avoid, postpone, or refuse to attend to patients in remote Romani communities, especially at night.

- If they exist, health care facilities in Romani neighborhoods are understaffed and underequipped as compared to the facilities serving non-Romani neighborhoods.

4. Housing

This report assesses the extent to which governments discriminate against the Roma or fail to address the inadequate housing available to the Roma. It mentions the national strategic plans for improving housing conditions for the Roma; outlines the types of housing conditions for Roma in a given country; reviews issues involved in property ownership; examines particular communities that suffer from segregation, such as those separated from other areas by walls or displaced en masse; details differential treatment in the provision of basic municipal services; and describes harassment of Roma in their homes and apartments.

The key findings with regard to housing are:

- Poverty, overcrowding, and lack of infrastructure dominate Romani neighborhoods. In many places, twice as many Roma live in half the amount of space as the rest of the population. The housing itself is often decrepit and barely inhabitable.
- Government strategies to address Romani housing problems are nonexistent or lack substance.
- A large number of Romani families do not own the land on which their houses are built and do not have building authorizations or proper property contracts for their houses.
- An equally large number of Roma do not reside legally in the apartments that they occupy.
- Roma have not received a fair share of the agricultural land returned to those who once owned or worked it.
- A significant number of Roma live in segregated communities. Some of the people in these communities were forcibly displaced from better neighborhoods; others took up residence because they had no place else to go. Many Romani communities are located near garbage dumps. In other places, walls or other physical barriers separate the Romani communities from the majority population.
- Some Romani settlements lack electricity. The houses may have been built illegally, the residents do not have clear legal status, or the electric company

and local authorities failed to introduce electricity into the Romani area while providing it to nearby non-Romani dwellings. Local electric companies have installed antitheft devices in Romani, and only in Romani, neighborhoods.

- Municipal transportation networks do not reach many Romani settlements. Buses often stop at the edge of Romani neighborhoods. Where there is public transportation, the buses often do not run as frequently and are of lower quality than those that serve other neighborhoods.
- Most garbage collection is less frequent in Romani neighborhoods than in non-Romani areas. Public health problems arise frequently from insufficient solid waste disposal.
- In some Romani communities, people are forced to drink contaminated water, to share one source of water among dozens of families, or to travel considerable distances to reach the water source.
- Authorities and private gangs frequently invade Romani houses and destroy Romani property.

5. Recommendations

The study concludes with a set of recommendations that call on the countries to develop and implement meaningful legislation to protect the Roma and other groups from public and private discrimination. The report urges the governments to allocate appropriate funds to the social protection, health care, and housing needs of their Romani populations. It encourages government leaders to foster and strengthen their relationships with Romani community leaders. And it calls on the international community to lend technical expertise, financial support, and monitoring mechanisms to bring about equality for the Roma.

6. Supplement and Appendix

The supplement on housing in the Czech Republic confirms that similar living conditions and discriminatory policies and practices exist wherever there is a significant Romani population. The research on Romani housing in the Czech Republic is part of an effort to study access to public services by the Roma in other Central European countries.

The study focuses on racial segregation practices, systematic evictions, and the increasing ghettoization of Czech Roma. It documents direct discrimination in the rental of municipal apartments. It also documents the existence of dozens of local regulations that bar access to housing to people without clean criminal records, without a university education or without permanent residence. It argues that the implementation of these regulations has a disparate impact on Czech Roma, leading to indirect discrimination.

The appendix attempts to show, in descriptive rather than analytical terms, what it is like to live in several types of Romani settlements in Romania.

7. Methodology

This study is based on interviews that the author conducted in Romania, Bulgaria, and Macedonia from October through December 1999. Subsequent trips in 2000 to these three countries and the Czech Republic, during which the author spoke with government officials, legislators, social workers, Romani activists, and Romani residents, verified and expanded on the information initially gathered. The report also draws and builds on the work of several recent studies, including Dena Ringold's report for the World Bank, *Roma and Transition in Central and Eastern Europe: Trends and Challenges*, and the OSCE High Commissioner on National Minorities' paper, *OSCE Report on the Situation of Roma and Sinti in the OSCE Area*. The report, except where noted, covers legal developments through August 2000.

Although the author undertook significant efforts to determine which discriminatory practices occurred in which countries, it was impossible to gather sufficient evidence about all types of practices across all of the countries. Therefore it is important to note that just because the discussion of a particular country does not establish that a specific discriminatory practice takes place there, it does not mean that Roma do not suffer from that practice in that country. This written report focuses on what the author documented during her trips to these regions, not on addressing the status of every problem faced by the Roma in the countries under review.

Although the report presents the problems confronting the Roma in the relatively neat categories of social protection, health care, and housing, the reality is complex. The typical Roma faces all three types of challenges—and more—every day. In the end, the only way to improve the lot of the Roma is if Romani communities, national governments, and the international community together take on the massive problems of discrimination and poverty that beset the Roma.

"Citizens are equal before the law and public authorities, without any privilege or discrimination."

ROMANIAN CONSTITUTION

"All persons are born free and equal in dignity and rights."

BULGARIAN CONSTITUTION

"All citizens are equal before the Constitution and law."

MACEDONIAN CONSTITUTION

Legal Standards

International, regional, and domestic legal standards firmly espouse the principles of non-discrimination and equal protection. These principles hold that most instances of discrimination on the basis of race or ethnicity infringe on universal human rights, violate basic moral principles, and impede positive social interaction and the functioning of political institutions. International, regional, and domestic bodies and courts have stated clearly that antidiscrimination and equal protection provisions apply not only to civil and political rights, but also to economic, social, and cultural rights.

This section of the report aims to elucidate the relevant international, regional, and national standards in order to analyze the claims of discrimination in the provision of social protection, health, and housing benefits to the Roma. In general, international and regional standards prohibit discrimination on the basis of race, ethnicity, and a variety of other criteria unless "the criteria for such differentiation are reasonable and objective and if the aim is to achieve a purpose which is legitimate" under the international human rights conventions.[1] International and regional standards prohibit most forms of direct and indirect discrimination. Direct discrimination takes place when "one person is treated less favorably than another is, has been, or would be treated in a comparable situation on grounds of racial or ethnic origin."[2] Indirect discrimination occurs when "an apparently neutral provision, criterion, or practice would put persons of a racial or ethnic origin at a particular disadvantage compared with other persons, unless that provision, criterion, or practice is objectively justified by a legitimate aim and the means of achieving that aim are appropriate and necessary."[3] This section explores these legal standards in depth.

The following discussion frames the analysis of discrimination claims in the subsequent sections. The rest of the report consists of the presentation of a practice or provision, a showing that the practice or provision affects Roma directly or indirectly, and an inquiry as to whether the government may be able to justify that practice or provision. In some cases, no official has stated why the government is acting, or not acting, in a particular manner. In such instances, it is necessary to guess the government's intent. In almost all cases, even if one gives the state the benefit of the doubt, it is impossible to justify the discriminatory practice against the Roma. This method of analysis flows directly out of the legal standards and approaches reviewed in this section.

The legal analysis in this work emphasizes the international and regional antidiscrimination principles rather than the domestic standards, because Romania, Bulgaria, and Macedonia have only recently begun to articulate their own national antidiscrimination rules. In fact, as of January 2001, Romania was the only one of the three countries to have adopted specific antidiscrimination legislation. The question of implementation looms large; it is unclear whether Romanian state agencies will modify policies so as to comply with this antidiscrimination ordinance, whether existing procedural and evidentiary rules will prevent courts from effectively enforcing the rights and providing meaningful remedies, and whether the ordinance will have any real effect on relations between different people. This section and the report emphasize the relevant international and regional standards, because interpretive bodies have devoted greater efforts over a longer period to articulating them than these three countries have. Furthermore, the Romanian, Bulgarian, and Macedonian constitutions directly incorporate the international human rights standards into their domestic legal systems, and these countries are expected to adopt relevant European standards as part of their bids to join the European Union. Therefore, it is appropriate to emphasize the international and regional standards.

1. International Standards

The definition of racial discrimination in the International Convention on the Elimination of All Forms of Racial Discrimination (ICERD) serves as the starting point for analysis by many international bodies and observers.[4] The Convention states that "the term 'racial discrimination' shall mean any distinction, exclusion, restriction or preference based on race, color, descent, or national or ethnic origin which has the purpose or effect of nullifying or impairing the recognition, enjoyment or exercise, on an equal footing, of human rights and fundamental freedoms in the political, economic, social, cultural or any other field of public life."[5] The UN Human Rights Committee, among others, has drawn on this definition when articulating what constitutes impermissible behavior under other international treaties.[6]

International standards regarding antidiscrimination impose several positive duties on states. Those governments that have ratified the ICERD, for example, have agreed to "undertake to pursue by all appropriate means and without delay a policy of eliminating racial discrimination in all its forms" by not engaging in any "act or practice of racial discrimination against persons, groups of persons or institutions," by ensuring that "all public authorities and public institutions, national and local, shall act in conformity with this obligation," by taking "effective measures to review governmental, national and local policies," by "amend[ing], rescind[ing] or nullify[ing] any laws and regulations which have the effect of creating or perpetuating racial discrimination wherever it exists," and by "prohibit[ing] and bring[ing] to an end, by all appropriate means, including legislation as required by circumstances, racial discrimination by any persons, group or organization."[7]

States that have ratified the International Covenant on Civil and Political Rights (ICCPR) have agreed "to respect and to ensure to all individuals within its territory and subject to its jurisdiction the rights recognized in the present Covenant, without distinction of any kind, such as race."[8] And states that have ratified the International Covenant on Economic, Social and Cultural Rights (ICESCR) have agreed to guarantee that "the rights enunciated in the present Covenant will be exercised without discrimination of any kind as to race. . . ."[9] Other international agreements contain similar obligations for state parties, even though they may not elaborate on the responsibilities to the same extent. Through these provisions, governments promise that they and their agents will not discriminate on the basis of race.

International instruments also distinguish between and prohibit direct and indirect racial discrimination. For example, ordinances that openly deny social benefits, access to state-sponsored medical clinics, or the opportunity to live in particular housing units to a person because he or she is a member of an ethnic group would constitute direct discrimination and are prohibited under international law. Indirect discrimination occurs when governments adopt policies that adversely affect a protected group without mentioning that group by name, regardless of intent. For example, a government might choose to close state-owned health clinics that are not "profitable." But if the facilities in minority neighborhoods are the only ones that are not profitable, and the effect of the government policy is that minorities will have significantly less access to health care than the majority, then the government may have engaged in impermissible race-based discrimination. The Committee on the Elimination of All Forms of Racial Discrimination (CERD) has stated that indirect discrimination violates international human rights standards as much as direct discrimination. To demonstrate impermissible discrimination, groups may show that a policy or policies have a disproportionate impact on a minority group. "In seeking to determine whether an action has an effect contrary to the Convention, [the Committee] will look to see whether that action has an unjustifiable disparate impact upon a group distinguished by race, color, descent, or national or ethnic origin."[10] Policies that indirectly discriminate against groups violate the international norm as much as policies that discriminate directly.

International standards protect a wide range of individual and group liberties. Signatories to the International Convention on the Elimination of All Forms of Racial Discrimination, for example, have agreed to guarantee the particular civil, economic, social, and cultural rights of all persons, regardless of race or ethnicity. The civil and political rights include freedom of movement and residence within the state and the right to leave any country and to return to one's own country, among others.[11] The economic, social, and cultural rights include the rights to work, free choice of employment, just and favorable conditions of work, protection against unemployment, equal pay for equal work, and just and favorable remuneration; to public health, medical care, social security, and social services; and to housing, among others.[12]

With regards to the provision of social benefits, international treaty bodies have stated that governments should not distinguish among recipients on the basis of their race directly or indirectly. The Committee on Economic, Social and Cultural Rights (CESCR) has said that governments may not discriminate on the basis of race "in access to food, as well as to means and entitlements for its procurement,"[13] and that "health facilities, goods and services must be accessible to all, especially the most vulnerable or marginalized sections of the population, in law and fact, without discrimination on any of the prohibited grounds."[14] The Committee has also stated that governments should provide remedies for those who suffer from discrimination in "allocation and availability of access to housing," regardless of whether private persons or public entities are responsible for the discrimination.[15]

States party to the International Covenant on Economic, Social and Cultural Rights may not depart from the core obligation of nondiscrimination and minimum services, even when they face severe resource constraints. For example, in General Comment 14 on the right to health, the CESCR stated the core obligations as follows: "to ensure the right of access to health facilities, goods and services on a non-discriminatory basis, especially for vulnerable or marginalized groups," "to ensure access to the minimum essential food which is sufficient, nutritionally adequate and safe, to ensure freedom from hunger to everyone," "to ensure access to basic shelter, housing and sanitation, and an adequate supply of safe and potable water," and "to ensure equitable distribution of all health facilities, goods and services."[16] The Committee continued: "If resource constraints render it impossible for a State to comply fully with its Covenant obligations, it has the burden of justifying that every effort has nevertheless been made to use all available resources at its disposal in order to satisfy, as a matter of priority, the obligations as outlined above. It should be stressed, however, that a State party cannot, under any circumstances whatsoever, justify its non-compliance with the core obligations set out in paragraph 43 above, which are non-derogable."[17] The Committee has affirmed similar principles in its General Comments on food[18] and housing,[19] among others. State parties to the ICESCR may not engage in impermissible discrimination and may not reduce services significantly, even during times of hardship, according to the Committee, which monitors compliance with the Covenant.

Although some international treaties say that state parties may discriminate on the basis of citizenship, an emerging norm is that governments should not do so with regard to fundamental rights. The International Convention on the Elimination of All Forms of Racial Discrimination indicates clearly that the instrument does not prevent governments from distinguishing among persons on the basis of their citizenship. "This Convention shall not apply to distinctions, exclusions, restrictions or preferences made by a State Party to this Convention between citizens and non-citizens."[20] However, a state party to the International Covenant on Civil and Political Rights agrees to ensure the rights of "all individuals within its territory and subject to its jurisdiction"—citizens and noncitizens alike—although it does not prohibit discrimination on the basis of citizenship.[21] "Thus, the general rule is that each one of the rights of the Covenant must be guaranteed without discrimination between citizens and aliens," the Human Rights Committee has stated. The Committee has expressed its concern that governments discriminate against noncitizens impermissibly on too many occasions and that they do not inform aliens sufficiently of their rights under national and international law.[22] Thus the emerging norm is that governments may, but should not, treat aliens differently from their own citizens, especially with regard to fundamental human rights.

It is critical to note that international standards do not prohibit all forms of differential treatment on the basis of race. International treaties and the bodies that interpret them have stated that governments may justify distinguishing among persons on the basis of race for particular reasons, that certain circumstances may justify positive treatment for a previously disadvantaged group for a limited period of time, and that the discrimination principles apply only to rights enumerated in the international charters.

The UN Human Rights Committee has indicated that some government may be able to articulate valid reasons for treating persons differently because of their race. In General Comment 18, "Non-discrimination," the Committee stated that "not every differentiation of treatment will constitute discrimination, if the criteria for such differentiation are reasonable and objective and if the aim is to achieve a purpose which is legitimate under the Convention."[23] The General Comment, which serves as an encapsulation of the Committee's understanding of the international standards based on its determinations as of the time of the General Comment, did not elaborate further on which criteria are reasonable and objective and which aims are legitimate. The Committee's concluding observations on country reports help by giving some concrete examples of legal and illegal differentiation, but the Committee does not appear to have fixed on any particular definitions.

Some international agreements and bodies that interpret discrimination have observed that governments may adopt affirmative action programs for particular groups for fixed periods of time. The International Convention on the Elimination of All Forms of Racial Discrimination, for example, states that "special measures taken for the sole purpose of securing adequate advancement of certain racial or ethnic groups . . . as may be necessary in order to ensure such groups or individuals equal enjoyment or exercise of human rights and fundamental freedoms shall not be deemed racial discrimination, provided, however, that such measures do not, as a consequence, lead to the maintenance of separate rights for different racial groups and that they shall not be continued after the objectives for which they were taken have been achieved."[24] The UN Human Rights Committee has observed that a state may grant preferential treatment to a particular group for a particular period as part of the general pursuit of equality.[25] These programs would benefit groups that had lacked access to or had been denied their civil, political, economic, social, and cultural rights in the past.

Some, but not all, conventions limit the nondiscrimination provisions to the rights enumerated in the treaties. For example, Article 2 of the International Covenant on Civil and Political Rights requires state parties not to engage in discrimination, but only "for the rights recognized in the present Covenant." Article 26, however, requires states to ensure equal protection of the law for all persons, regardless of their racial or ethnic background. In general, the international conventions and the committees that interpret them do not limit their protections to the enumerated rights only. The Committee on the Elimination of Racial Discrimination has stated that the rights and freedoms mentioned in the treaty "do not constitute an exhaustive list." The Convention requires states to prohibit racial discrimination with regard to all rights contained in the Universal Declaration of Human Rights and other international human rights conventions.[26] Furthermore, the treaties themselves contain so many rights, covering so many subjects, that the agreements protect most areas in which persons can suffer from racial discrimination.

The international prohibitions against discrimination are binding on the legislative, administrative, and judicial apparatuses in the countries covered in this report. First, these governments or their predecessors signed and ratified most of the international treaties that prohibit racial discrimination to a greater or lesser extent. Romania, Bulgaria, and Macedonia have signed and ratified the International Covenant on Civil and

Political Rights, the International Covenant on Economic, Social and Cultural Rights, the Convention on the Rights of the Child (CRC), the Convention on the Elimination of All Forms of Discrimination Against Women (CEDAW), and the International Convention on the Elimination of All Forms of Racial Discrimination.[27] As discussed below, the constitutions in each of these countries state that international treaties are the law of the land. Second, the Universal Declaration of Human Rights contains an antidiscrimination provision that is binding on all states as a matter of customary international law. Therefore, the international prohibitions are binding on the legislative, administrative, and judicial apparatuses in these countries.

Although most treaties prohibit racial and ethnic discrimination, they generally do not elaborate on the type of proof that is required to prove illegal differential treatment, aside from mentioning that persons can prove discrimination through showing disparate impact. It is helpful to look to the emerging European standards to understand how to determine whether a policy or practice discriminates impermissibly.

2. European Standards

Various European agreements, joint statements, and directives prohibit discrimination on the basis of race and ethnicity. In recent years, European governments and intergovernmental bodies have attempted to clarify which policies and procedures constitute impermissible discrimination and how a person or group proves it. Treaties regarding social and economic rights contain antidiscrimination provisions, which have particular relevance for understanding how governments differentiate wrongly in the provision of public services.

2.1. European Convention for the Protection of Human Rights and Fundamental Freedoms

All countries covered by this report have ratified the European Convention for the Protection of Human Rights and Fundamental Freedoms,[28] which prohibits discrimination on the basis of race and ethnicity, but only for the rights and freedoms contained in the Convention. Article 14 states that "the enjoyment of the rights and freedoms set forth in this Convention shall be secured without discrimination on any ground such as . . . race, color . . . national or social origin, [or] association with a national minority. . . ."[29] The treaty does not ban all forms of discrimination; rather, it prohibits differential treatment only with regard to the "enjoyment of the rights and freedoms" set forth in the Convention. Member states agree to "secure to everyone within their jurisdiction the rights and freedoms defined in . . . this Convention."[30]

Despite the general prohibition of race-based distinctions, states may discriminate on the basis of race with regard to the fundamental rights and freedoms contained in the Convention, if they make appropriate showings. The European Court of Human

Rights, which has the authority to interpret and apply the European Convention's provisions, has stated that some kinds of distinctions are permissible. "A difference in treatment is discriminatory if it 'has no objective and reasonable justification,' that is, if it does not pursue a 'legitimate aim' or if there is not a 'reasonable relationship of proportionality between the means employed and the aim sought to be realized.'"[31] Therefore, a state may differentiate among persons of different racial backgrounds if it has an objective and reasonable justification for its policy—in other words, if it is pursuing a legitimate aim through reasonably proportional means.

The Committee of Ministers of the Council of Europe recently approved and opened for ratification a new convention protocol that expands and clarifies the Convention's antidiscrimination protections significantly. Optional Protocol 12 states that "[t]he enjoyment of any right set forth by law shall be secured without discrimination on any ground such as . . . race, color, . . . association with a national minority . . . or other status. No one shall be discriminated against by any public authority on any ground. . . ."[32] Drafters intended to expand protection for those who suffer from discrimination in at least four ways: "in the enjoyment of any right specifically granted to an individual under national law; in the enjoyment of a right which may be inferred from a clear obligation of a public authority under national law, that is, where a public authority is under an obligation under national law to behave in a particular manner; by a public authority in the exercise of discretionary power (for example, granting certain subsidies); and by any other act or omission by a public authority (for example, the behavior of law enforcement officers when controlling a riot)."[33]

Although the new protocol primarily imposes an obligation on state parties not to discriminate, it also contains affirmative duties for states to prevent some forms of discrimination among private persons. The explanatory report says that a state's responsibility to "secure" rights may include a duty to intervene if the discrimination takes place in a sphere that the law regulates—"for example, arbitrary denial of access to work, access to restaurants, or to services which private persons may make available to the public such as medical care or utilities such as water and electricity, etc."[34] States that sign and ratify the protocol may, therefore, have a duty to prevent private discrimination in health services and basic utilities, two of the three types of public services reviewed by this report.

As stated earlier, all states covered in this report have signed and ratified the European Convention for the Protection of Human Rights and Fundamental Freedoms.[35] The existing antidiscrimination provisions of the convention apply to these countries. Some of the topics discussed in this convention, such as the right to an effective remedy,[36] right to respect for private and family life,[37] and the prohibition of forced labor[38] are relevant when considering poor delivery of public services. But, so far, none of the countries has ratified Optional Protocol 12. If they do, each country will need to implement the protocol's broad-based antidiscrimination principles with regard to all human rights, which will bear directly on the provision of social protection, health care, and housing.

2.2. Council of the European Union Directive 2000/43/EC of 29 June 2000

The Council of the European Union has issued a new directive for member states that requires them to prohibit and punish racial discrimination. Council Directive 2000/43/EC of 29 June 2000 states that "the principle of equal treatment shall mean that there shall be no direct or indirect discrimination based on racial or ethnic origin."[39] The directive bans discrimination because it interferes with the enjoyment of many civil, political, social, economic and cultural rights.

The directive prohibits two forms of discrimination, the first of which is direct discrimination. The directive states that "[d]irect discrimination shall be taken to occur where one person is treated less favourably than another is, has been, or would be treated in a comparable situation on grounds of racial or ethnic origin."[40] To analyze whether a person, group, organization or institution has discriminated against a person or group of people directly, it is necessary to gather data about how the alleged discriminator treated the person or group asserting discrimination and others similarly situated. Then it must be shown that the alleged discriminator treated the person or group claiming discrimination worse than others in a like position because of the race or ethnic origin of that person or group asserting unfair treatment.

The directive also bans indirect discrimination. The text states, "[I]ndirect discrimination shall be taken to occur where an apparently neutral provision, criterion, or practice would put persons of a racial or ethnic origin at a particular disadvantage compared with other persons, unless that provision, criterion or practice is objectively justified by a legitimate aim and the means of achieving that aim are appropriate and necessary."[41] A government that implements a policy or practice that provides fewer services to or lowers the social status of one racial or ethnic group relative to another must show that it does so for lawful reasons through the least-restrictive methods.

The directive forbids discrimination by public and private actors in the provision of basic social services and economic transactions. The decree applies to "all persons, as regards both the public and private sectors" in relation to employment,[42] social protection "including social security and health care,"[43] and to "access to and supply of goods and services which are available to the public, including housing,"[44] among others.

In sum, the directive bans direct and indirect discrimination by public and private actors in the public sphere in social security, health, and housing, unless the party making the differentiation does so for a legitimate purpose using appropriate and necessary means. The regulation speaks to the provision of social services to minority groups, which is the focus of this report.

The directive requires states to reverse any legislation or administrative rules that discriminate impermissibly. "Member states shall take the necessary measures to ensure that . . . any laws, regulations, and administrative provisions contrary to the principle of equal treatment are abolished."[45] Legislatures and administrative agencies should act of their own accord, without any prompting by the courts, to eliminate discrimination from the state's policies and practices. The directive states that an instruction to discriminate is impermissible, presumably even if no person acts on that instruction.[46] Governments that do not overturn existing discriminatory laws may violate the decree.

States must give a great deal of weight to the claims made by the party alleging inappropriate differential treatment, according to the new directive. After the alleged victim of the discriminatory practice provides evidence that suggests direct or indirect discrimination, the burden of proof is on the alleged perpetrator to prove that his, her or its actions did not violate the directive. "[W]hen persons who consider themselves wronged because the principle of equal treatment has not been applied to them establish . . . facts from which it may be presumed that there has been direct or indirect discrimination, it shall be for the respondent to prove that there has been no breach of the principle of equal treatment."[47] The presumption, more or less, lies in favor of the plaintiff, once he or she has made a prima facie showing of discrimination. The directive permits, but does not require, states to introduce rules of evidence that are even more favorable to those alleging wrongful treatment.[48]

This directive may soon apply in three of the countries covered by this report. Romania, Bulgaria, and the Czech Republic are not members of the European Union, but they have sought to join the intergovernmental entity. The EU enlargement process favors those countries that adopt measures to bring their internal legal orders into compliance with the European Union directives. Therefore, although the directive does not apply to these states yet, they will need to adopt and implement similar policies and practices to increase their chances of acquiring membership. Romania has taken a first step wth the passage in August 2000 of the Antidiscrimination Ordinance (see "3. National Standards" below).

2.3. Framework Convention for the Protection of National Minorities

All countries covered by this report have signed the Framework Convention for the Protection of National Minorities, which articulates antidiscrimination provisions for national minorities.[49] The Framework Convention states that "[t]he Parties undertake to guarantee to persons belonging to national minorities the right of equality before the law and of equal protection of the law."[50] Signatories "undertake to take appropriate measures to protect persons who may be subject to threats or acts of discrimination"[51] and "undertake not to interfere with the right of persons belonging to national minorities to establish and maintain free and peaceful contacts across frontiers with persons lawfully staying in other States. . . ."[52] The Framework permits states to engage in affirmative action programs in order to promote equality between minority and majority groups.[53]

According to the preamble, signatories agree to "implement the principles set out in this Framework Convention through national legislation and appropriate governmental policies." States are to report on their progress to the Council of Europe on a periodic basis. Since all the states in this report have signed the agreement, they have consented to implement these policies and principles and to hold themselves publicly accountable for their action or inaction.[54]

2.4. Organization for Security and Cooperation in Europe: Statements and Standards

All states covered by this report are members of the Organization for Security and Cooperation in Europe (OSCE), which has noted that governments should assist the Roma and protect them from differential treatment on the basis of race. At the Istanbul Summit in November 1999, leaders declared, "We deplore violence and other manifestations of racism and discrimination against minorities, including Roma and Sinti. We commit ourselves to ensure that laws and policies fully respect the rights of Roma and Sinti and, where necessary, to promote antidiscrimination legislation to this effect."[55] They also noted in the Charter for European Security "the particular difficulties faced by Roma and Sinti and the need to undertake effective measures in order to achieve full equality of opportunity, consistent with OSCE commitments, for persons belonging to Roma and Sinti. We will reinforce our efforts . . . to eradicate discrimination against them."[56] The heads of states or governments produced statements in Copenhagen[57] and Helsinki,[58] among other places, which affirm the principles of nondiscrimination. OSCE expert groups have called on participating states "to undertake effective measures in order to achieve full equality of opportunity between persons belonging to Roma ordinarily resident in their State and the rest of the resident population."[59]

Although these OSCE statements do not have the same legal force as the international and European treaties described above, they are another mechanism through which the governments bind themselves morally, and perhaps under customary international law, to prevent discrimination against the Roma. Since the countries covered in this report participated in the OSCE discussions, the principles that emerged from the meetings obligate the countries, particularly if their governments did not dissent on these issues.

2.5. European Social Charter and Revised European Social Charter

Major European treaties regarding the provision of public services prohibit discrimination. Perhaps the most important treaty in this area is the Revised European Social Charter. Article E of the Revised Charter states that "the enjoyment of the rights set forth in this Charter shall be secured without discrimination on any ground such as race, color, sex, language, religion, political or other opinion, national extraction or social origin, health, association with a national minority, birth or other status." As is true for the other treaties described above, states may differentiate among persons on the basis of race if they are pursuing legitimate objectives: "A differential treatment based on an objective and reasonable justification shall not be deemed discriminatory." The report to the Charter explains: "An objective and reasonable justification may be such as the requirement of a certain age or a certain capacity for access to some forms of education. Whereas national extraction is not an acceptable ground for discrimination, the requirement of a specific citizenship might be acceptable under certain circumstances, for example for the right to employment in the defense forces or in the civil service."[60]

The Revised Charter covers a wide range of rights. Social benefits include safe working conditions,[61] benefits for pregnant women and new mothers,[62] social security at least to the level of the European Code of Social Security,[63] social welfare services,[64] social, legal, and economic protection for the family,[65] support for the welfare of young children,[66] and programs for migrant workers.[67] The Charter also promotes dignity at work[68] and antipoverty and social exclusion measures.[69] Health benefits include the right to protection of health[70] and the right to social and medical assistance.[71] Housing policies include promotion of access to housing of an adequate standard; prevention and reduction of homelessness with a view to its gradual elimination; and provision of affordable housing.[72] Antipoverty measures also speak to the provision of social, health, and housing services.

When signing the Charter, state parties affirm which of the Charter's provisions apply to them. Signatories must agree to uphold the right to work, the right to organize, the right to bargain collectively, the right of children and young persons to protection, the right to social security, the right to social and medical assistance, the right of the family to social, legal, and economic protection, the right of migrant workers and their families to protection and assistance, and the right to equal opportunities without discrimination on the grounds of sex. State parties then bind themselves to an additional seven articles or twenty-two paragraphs, which include the rights discussed in the previous paragraph. To understand which provisions apply to which states, it is necessary to review each signatory's ratification, acceptance or approval.

All states covered in this report have signed the European Social Charter or the Revised European Social Charter,[73] but not all have ratified all of the provisions. Nonetheless, the convention's antidiscrimination provisions apply to the state parties, which all of the countries in this report are.

3. National Standards

Each country reviewed in this report prohibits discrimination to a greater or lesser extent. Each country's constitution incorporates ratified international human rights treaties directly into domestic law. Despite these protections, most of the countries have not yet passed general antidiscrimination legislation or included detailed antidiscrimination provisions in other legislation.

All countries reviewed in this report have constitutional antidiscrimination provisions of greater or lesser scope. All constitutions affirm the notion of equality before the law, although some draw distinctions between citizens and all persons. The Romanian Constitution, for example, holds that "[c]itizens are equal before the law and public authorities, without any privilege or discrimination,"[74] and the Bulgarian Constitution states that "all persons are born free and equal in dignity and rights."[75] The Macedonian Constitution proclaims that "[c]itizens of the Republic of Macedonia are equal in their freedoms and rights, regardless of sex, race, color of skin, national and social origin, political and religious beliefs, property and social status. All citizens are equal before the Constitution and law."[76]

According to the constitutions of each of these countries, ratified international human rights treaties are incorporated into domestic law and are directly binding on the state. The Romanian Constitution states: "Constitutional provisions concerning the citizens' rights and liberties shall be interpreted and enforced in conformity with the Universal Declaration of Human Rights, with the covenants and other treaties Romania is a party to."[77] The highest law of the Romanian land also indicates that international standards trump domestic principles when conflicts arise. According to the Romanian Constitution, "Where any inconsistencies exist between the covenants and treaties on fundamental human rights Romania is a party to, and internal laws, the international regulations shall take precedence."[78] The Bulgarian Constitution reads: "Any international instruments which have been ratified by the constitutionally established procedure, promulgated, and come into force with respect to the Republic of Bulgaria, shall be considered part of the domestic legislation of the country. They shall supersede any domestic legislation stipulating otherwise."[79] The Macedonian Constitution states that internal law cannot change the country's properly ratified international legal obligations.[80]

The domestically incorporated international and European human rights standards provide an additional source of antidiscrimination protection for persons in these countries. Each of the countries has ratified major international human rights treaties that prohibit discrimination on the basis of race. Each of the countries has constitutional provisions that make those ratified treaties binding on the legislative, executive, and judicial branches. Therefore, those who wish to press discrimination claims can draw on international and European standards as well as domestic constitutional provisions.

While these countries' constitutions contain antidiscrimination clauses, to date only Romania has passed general antidiscrimination legislation. In August 2000, the Romanian government adopted an Ordinance on Preventing and Punishing all Forms of Discrimination.[81] The Antidiscrimination Ordinance states that certain acts constitute offenses: any threats, constraints, use of force or any other means of assimilation, colonization or forced movement of persons with a view to modify the ethnic, racial or social composition of a region or of a locality;[82] any behavior forcing a person belonging to a race, nationality, ethnic group or religion, or a community, respectively, to unwillingly leave their residence, to be deported or to lower their living standards with a view to make them leave their traditional residence;[83] any behavior aimed at forcing a person or group of persons to move away from a building or neighborhood or aimed at chasing them away on account of their belonging to a race, nationality, ethnic group, religion, social category or to a disadvantaged category, or on account of their beliefs, sex or sexual orientation.[84]

The ordinance, which is now in force,[85] provides that the exercise of the right to housing is based on the principle of equality among citizens without privilege or discrimination. Regulations and orders, as well as active or passive behavior, that unjustifiably favor or disadvantage a person, a group of persons or a community trigger contraventional liability.[86] The refusal to sell or rent a plot of land or building for housing purposes, to grant a bank credit or to conclude any other kind of contract with a person or group of persons on account of their belonging to a race, ethnic group, a social or a disfavored category constitutes an offense.[87]

The targets of discrimination are entitled to claim damages proportional to the prejudice; they are also entitled to claim the reestablishment of the situation prior to the discrimination or to the annulment of the situation created by discrimination, in accordance with common law.[88] The claim for damages is exempted from judicial taxes.[89] Upon request, the court can order that the competent authorities withdraw the license of legal entities that significantly prejudice the society by means of a discriminatory action or that repeatedly violate the provisions of the Antidiscrimination Ordinance, even if they have only caused a minor prejudice.[90]

Human rights nongovernmental organizations (NGOs) can appear in court as parties in cases involving discrimination pertaining to their field of activity, when a community or group of persons have been subject to prejudice[91] or in cases where a person was discriminated against and that person delegates to the NGO the right to act on his or her behalf.[92]

Members of the National Council for the Prevention of Discrimination determine when sanctions should be applied. The council is a specialized, public administration body, subordinated to the government, which should have been established at the beginning of November 2000, that is, within sixty days from the publication of the antidiscrimination law.[93]

The question of implementation looms large; it is unclear whether Romanian state agencies will modify policies so as to comply with the Antidiscrimination Ordinance, whether existing procedural and evidentiary rules will prevent courts from effectively enforcing the rights and providing meaningful remedies, and whether the ordinance will have any real effect on relations between different groups. But if successfully applied, the Romanian law will set an important precedent for how other countries can punish and prevent discriminatory behavior and protect the Romani minority population.

> "We eat from the garbage. We pick up empty bottles and sell them. Nobody in this neighborhood receives social support. They say there are no funds."
>
> ROMANI WOMAN IN ALBA IULIA, ROMANIA

Barriers to Social Protection

This section examines access of Roma to social protection in Romania, Bulgaria, and Macedonia. It identifies policies and practices that discriminate directly or indirectly against the Roma. It also relates cases in which public officials and private citizens have treated Roma poorly.

International and European law recognizes the need for states to provide minimum amounts of social support to their citizens. The Universal Declaration of Human Rights provides for the right to an adequate standard of living, "including food, clothing, housing and medical care and necessary social services, and the right to security in the event of unemployment, sickness, disability, widowhood, old age or other lack of livelihood in circumstances beyond his control."[1] The International Covenant on Economic, Social and Cultural Rights (ICESCR) holds that state parties "recognize the right of everyone to social security, including social insurance"[2] and that "[s]pecial protection should be accorded to mothers during a reasonable period before and after childbirth."[3] In the Convention on the Rights of the Child (CRC), signatories "recognize the right of every child to a standard of living adequate for the child's physical, mental, spiritual, moral and social development"[4] and "recognize for every child the right to benefit from social security, including social insurance, and shall take the necessary measures to achieve the full realization of this right in accordance with their national law."[5] The Revised European Social Charter has several provisions on the right to adequate social protection.[6]

Antidiscrimination clauses are always present, integrated in the text of the relevant articles, described in the general comments of the committees that oversee reporting under the conventions, or provided by separate human rights instruments. The International Convention on the Elimination of All Forms of Racial Discrimination (ICERD) prohibits racial discrimination in "the enjoyment of the right to . . . social security and social services,"[7] while the Convention on the Elimination of All Forms of Discrimination Against Women (CEDAW) requires state parties to eliminate discrimination in "the right to social security, particularly in cases of retirement, unemployment, sickness, invalidity and old age and other incapacity to work, as well as the right to paid leave."[8] The Committee on Economic, Social and Cultural Rights (CESCR) has stated that governments may not discriminate on the basis of race "in access to food, as well as to means and entitlements for its procurement,"[9] among other necessities. The Revised European Social Charter also affirms freedom from discrimination.[10]

Within the context of these international standards of social protection, this section of the report discusses the most common forms of transfers that are present in all three countries and that correspond to the needs of Romani communities. The report focuses on the social assistance system and additional provisions for children and families. The social assistance system is the primary source of government aid for the very poor, a category into which the bulk of the Romani population falls. The provision of additional support for families with children has greater financial significance for large families, such as Romani families, which, on average, are larger than others.

This report does not address other major social protection programs such as pensions or short-term unemployment benefits. As demonstrated in the following country sections, the Romani population on the whole is young, with a relatively small number of pensioners. The majority of Roma without regular jobs belong to the ranks of the long-term unemployed.

To assess the extent to which governments discriminate against the Roma or fail to provide minimum support through their social protection programs, the report:

- presents the level of benefits provided under particular programs;
- reviews eligibility criteria for particular forms of support;
- discusses how these criteria relate to characteristics of the Romani population;
- reviews problems faced by Roma in complying with these procedures;
- shows opportunities for discretion by local officials;
- identifies cases in which regional or municipal administrators appear to have used their power in an arbitrary and discriminatory manner;
- and reviews administrative and legal appeals processes.

Romania

1. The State's Obligations under International, Constitutional, and National Law

Romania is a party to all United Nations conventions relevant to the right to social welfare: the International Covenant on Civil and Political Rights (ICCPR),[11] the International Covenant on Economic, Social and Cultural Rights (ICESCR),[12] the Convention on the Rights of the Child (CRC),[13] the Convention on the Elimination of All Forms of Discrimination Against Women (CEDAW),[14] and the International Convention on the Elimination of All Forms of Racial Discrimination (ICERD).[15] At the European level, Romania has ratified the European Convention for the Protection of Human Rights and Fundamental Freedoms (ECHR),[16] the Revised European Social Charter,[17] and the Framework Convention for the Protection of National Minorities.[18]

In the 1991 Constitution, the Romanian state pledged to fulfill in good faith its treaty obligations.[19] Lawfully ratified treaties are part of national law.[20] Constitutional provisions concerning citizens' rights and liberties must be interpreted and enforced in conformity with the Universal Declaration of Human Rights, in addition to the covenants and treaties to which Romania is a party.[21] When any inconsistencies exist between the covenants and treaties on fundamental human rights and the country's internal laws, the international regulations take precedence.[22]

Romania's Constitution establishes the state's obligation to ensure a decent standard of living for its citizens.[23] It also establishes the rights to food, clothing, adequate housing, reasonable living conditions, and their continuous improvement.[24] Children and young peope enjoy special protection and assistance in the exercise of their rights.[25] The state provides allowances for children and benefits for the care of sick or disabled children; other rules and regulations provide additional forms of social protection for children and young people.[26]

2. Poverty in Romania

The total population of Romania is approximately 22.8 million persons. Based on voluntary self-identification, ethnic Romanians comprise 89.4 percent of the population, Hungarians 7.1 percent, Roma 1.8 percent, Germans 0.5 percent, and others 1.2 percent.[27] The Romanian government estimates that the country contains one and a half million Roma,[28] while experts on the Roma believe that two million is a more accurate approximation.[29]

The World Bank says that roughly 30 percent of the population of Romania lived in poverty in 1998, and that nearly 12 percent lived in extreme poverty.[30] Forty-five percent of the population lives in rural areas. Twelve percent of the families have three or more children. Of this 12 percent, two-thirds of the families with three children are poor, as are five-sixths of the families with four or more children.[31]

Poverty disproportionately strikes Romania's Roma. According to the Romania Integrated Household Survey (RHIS),[32] in 1997 the Romani poverty rate was 79 percent, compared to the national poverty rate of 31 percent.[33]

3. National Strategies for Romani Integration and Social Support

The government's program for 1998–2000 established three priorities for the protection of minorities: (i) creation of an Inter-Ministerial Commission,[34] (ii) elaboration of a national strategy to improve the situation of the Roma, and (iii) allocation of financial resources to support projects and programs created by national minority organizations. In 1998, the government established an Inter-Ministerial Commission for National Minorities and a subcommittee for Romani issues. Representatives of eight ministries cooperate with experts on the Roma through the Department for the Protection of National Minorities or DPMN (Departamentul Pentru Minoritati Nationale) in formulating strategies for different sectors.

In the second part of 1999, the "Improvement of the Roma Situation" program was launched with cofunding by the PHARE National Program and the Romanian Government. The program (RO9803.01) allocates 1.1 million euro for the elaboration of a national strategy for protecting the Romani population and 900,000 euro for the implementation of several pilot projects.[35] The national strategy is expected to be completed in 2001. Romani organizations are participating in the development of the national strategy. In the area of social protection, the Working Group of Roma Associations (GLAR)[36] recommended, inter alia, an evaluation of the legal norms governing social benefits. The Inter-Ministerial Subcommission for Roma and the Inter-Ministerial Commission for National Minorities approved the GLAR recommendations in September 2000.[37]

4. Social Protection Programs

The Romanian social protection system includes social assistance for persons and families with little or no income and for families with children. It also provides unemployment benefits, social health insurance, and additional benefits and institutional services to children in difficulty.

4.1. Social assistance for persons and families with little or no income

The main transfers for the indigent in Romania are social support, food pantries, and emergency help.

4.1.1. Social support

Social support is a means-tested cash transfer to the poorest of the poor. Beneficiaries of social support are families and persons who earn less than the monthly minimum basic income (MBI) established by law. Regulations set the amount of support equal to the difference between the MBI and the monthly income of the family.[38]

The main procedure for establishing eligibility is the "social inquiry"[39] or assessment of a family's financial situation by a social worker. Applicants must comply with real estate and personal property requirements, and they must have permanent resident status in the place where they apply for benefits. Romanian citizens and foreigners legally residing in Romania are eligible for support.

The Law on Social Support[40] and other governmental decisions[41] govern the distribution of social support. Local government budgets finance this benefit.[42]

4.1.2. Food pantries or "social canteens"

Food pantries or "social canteens" provide means-tested, in-kind transfers. Different food pantries provide different services. They may sell low-priced agricultural products. They may prepare food and distribute it through mobile centers. Food pantries may not even exist in rural areas, since local councils often assume that those living in rural areas can obtain sufficient food for themselves and their children.

Seven categories of persons may qualify for assistance from food pantries: a) minors, b) students up to a certain age, c) beneficiaries of social support, d) pensioners, e) persons under retirement age who are socially isolated, or have a low income, or do not have any relatives legally required to support them, f) disabled and chronically sick people, and g) any person who temporarily has no income.[43] Those who fit into one of these categories and earn less than the MBI for a person living alone[44] qualify to receive food free of charge; others who do not meet the income test but are otherwise eligible must contribute 30 percent of their monthly income, up to the value of the meals served in one month.[45]

Government regulations set the amount of money that should be spent for food per eligible person per day.[46] The regulations also state that food pantries should distribute two portions every day.[47] In practice, only pantries in big cities such as Bucharest or Cluj comply with the "two meals a day" requirement; most of the pantries in the rest of the country distribute, at best, hot food once a day, or, at worst, bread once a week.[48]

In general, the food pantries do not provide sustenance to most of those who qualify for their services. In some cities, such as Orastie, it is estimated that only 5 to 10 percent of eligible persons receive food. According to the municipality, in October 1999 there were 2,600 social support cases, out of which 2,000 were Roma; the food pantry served one hundred people, and the majority of beneficiaries were non-Roma.[49] In other cities, such as Buhusi, all eligible persons received food, but the level of the service was minimal—one portion of bread per person per day.[50]

The Law on Food Pantries governs the provision of food through food pantries. The Ministry of Labor and Social Protection has responsibility for the legality of the food pantries' operations.[51] Local budgets provide the financial resources and materials.[52] The municipal accounting department verifies whether the funds allocated for food pantries are lawfully spent; however, the law does not establish an effective mechanism to check the quality of the services. Regardless of the number of poor persons living in any given administrative unit, the law permits, but does not require, the local authorities to organize food pantries.[53]

4.1.3. Emergency support

The national government and mayors may grant additional emergency support to families or persons in need due to natural disasters, arson, or "other justified reasons." Local budgets and a special fund of the Ministry of Labor and Social Protection cover these costs.

Officials have a significant amount of discretion in determining award recipients, because Article 22 of Law 67/1995, which regulates eligibility, financing, and distribution of emergency support, does not define the terms "families and persons in need" and "other justified reasons." Local leaders also have the right to determine the amount of emergency support. The law does not explicitly require the local councils to allocate a certain amount of money in order to ensure the payment of emergency support in case of need. Obtaining emergency help can have less to do with the law and more to do with the local council's budgetary policy, the mayor's benevolence, and his interpretation of legal terms such as persons "in need" and "justified reasons."[54]

4.2. Social assistance for families with children

Family protection includes several types of cash transfer including child allowances, additional benefits for families with children, and birth grants.

4.2.1. Child allowances

Romania awards a 65,000 lei (less than U.S. $4) allowance per child per month to families.[55] Every child, born in or out of wedlock, adopted or placed into foster care, has the right to receive the same amount of money regardless of the number of children in the family. Romania protects all Romanian children and foreign children living with parents who are legal residents of Romania.

The Law on Child Allowances[56] established the universality of the right to receive support for children, regardless of the parents' employment or economic status.[57] Children between seven and eighteen receive allowances if they remain in school.[58] The regulations punish failure to attend school for any reason except a medical excuse, by removing the child allowance.[59]

Romani leaders have supported the "school attendance requirement" from the very beginning as a way to encourage the education of Romani children. Scholars note that linking the child allowance to school attendance transformed a protective social assistance measure into an educational incentive.[60]

However, from the perspective of the family budget, the low level of child allowances can only be a modest incentive for teenagers to attend school. Boys are able to work and, eventually, might earn more than the benefits offered by the state.[61] For Romani girls, the situation is more complicated, as the custom of early marriages has greater influence on the continuation of their studies than does qualification for child benefits.[62]

The state pays child allowances to the mother or the father, according to the parents' agreement. If there is no agreement, the parent with whom the child lives or the parent who has custody of the child receives the allowances.[63] With the agreement of their legal representative, children above the age of fourteen may receive allowances themselves.[64] These allowances come directly from the state budget.[65]

In Romania, the families of more than five million children receive child support payments every month.[66] For many low-income Romani families, these allowances are the main, or a very important, source of income.[67] The 1993 legislative changes, which extended coverage to unemployed parents, resulted in tremendous support for large, indigent families.

The existing plan works well because it protects children of employed and unemployed parents equally, offering a certain degree of protection to the children of the working poor. Financing from the state budget, rather than from local budgets, ensures regular payment. And, unlike the Macedonian or Bulgarian systems, the Romanian child allowances program—which provides a flat sum for every child—does not discriminate against children belonging to large families. The extremely low amount of the child allowance, however, does not ensure effective protection for children living in poverty.

The universality of child benefits—although adopted by many European countries—poses a dilemma. The egalitarian approach provides child allowances to some families that do not really need them while those who need them to survive receive insufficient funds. Yet such a trade-off might be necessary to ensure popular support for continuing the program.

4.2.2 Additional benefits for families with children

In 1997, the government introduced additional benefits for families with children.[68] The law distinguishes between families with two, three, and four or more children, and it establishes a lump sum for each. In autumn 1999, the state set the benefits at 50,000 lei (U.S. $2.70) for two children, 100,000 lei (U.S. $5.40) for three children, and 125,000 lei (U.S. $6.75) for families with four or more children. Eligibility is independent of family income. The National Solidarity Fund and the national budget cover the program's costs. In 1998, more than one million families received additional benefits.[69]

Studies on the alleviation of poverty emphasize the relationship between large family size and the risk of poverty.[70] Consequently, the introduction of additional benefits would make sense if they would be proportional with the number of children and targeted toward the working or nonworking poor. In this case, they are not.

Although outwardly neutral, the program has a disparate impact on the Roma. The average number of children per family within the Romani population is much higher than within the majority. In 1992, for example, Romani women between the ages of thirty-five to thirty-nine were responsible for five children on average, while women of the same age in the population at large had responsibility for only 2.1 children.[71] Limiting additional benefits to a fixed amount for families that have more than four children disproportionately affects Romani families as compared with non-Romani families. The Council of Europe noted the lack of political will of the postcommunist governments to support large families:

"The history of Romania is quite specific, but demonstrates the unintended consequences of social authoritarian intervention by the state. Post-war, most former communist and state-socialist countries experienced declining birthrates and subsequent pro-natalist policy (also evident in the French family benefit system). However, in Romania, the totalitarian pro-natalist policy withheld family planning services, and offered financial support to mothers of large families. According to Zamfir, this had the effect of creating a u-shaped birth curve by income. Better-off people continued to control their family size, while the poorest increased them, resulting in a polarization of family size not only by income, but by group, including Roma and residents in specific regions. Following the collapse of employment incomes and of support for children, large low-income families are suffering very severe poverty. This polarisation has now resulted in a popular view concerning the irresponsibility of such families and groups. Consequently, there has been a lack of political support for . . . cash transfers towards families with children after 1989."[72]

4.2.3. Birth grants

Mothers receive one-time grants[73] for each child they have after the first child.[74] The state directs funds to local administrations to pay for the grants, based on the mother's residence.[75] The law provides that authorities may only withhold birth grants in order to recover unlawfully obtained benefits or to pay the legal obligations of family members.[76] Romani NGOs allege that local authorities use birth grants to cover family debts, such as administrative fines, court costs, and rent, that are beyond the bounds of their authority. Romani mothers receive only what remains after the debts are paid.[77]

5. Impact on the Roma of Eligibility Requirements and Recipient Responsibilities

Persons who receive social support must fit certain eligibility criteria and comply with additional responsibilities imposed by government officials. The rules and regulations set clear standards in some areas, while in others administrators have a great deal of discretion in applying the directives.

Some eligibility requirements have a disparate impact on the Roma. If evidence of a disparate impact exists, government officials must show that those policies are reasonable and objective and pursue a legitimate aim. In general, there is enough anecdotal evidence to suggest that lawmakers and administrative officials discriminate against the Roma, but more research would be helpful. Some Roma also claim that officials directly discriminate against them on the basis of race in applications for social services. If verifiable, such behavior is unjustifiable, indefensible, and illegal.

5.1. Means test

The government grants social support to persons who do not have property other than what is "necessary for family needs."[78] Local councils have discretionary power to decide what possessions are not strictly necessary for the needs of the family (e.g. TV sets, radios, refrigerators, bicycles, etc.)[79]

Local authorities estimate the value of property that the owner cannot use to produce income, such as paintings, art objects, jewelry, and ornaments in precious metals. The owner has no right to social support for a period equal to the number of months that result from dividing the price of the object by the MBI. The law presumes that the person will sell the property to cover living costs. Those who use property, such as cars, tractors, motorcycles, cows, goats, chickens, rabbits, etc., to produce income must declare the revenues obtained. They may retain their property and remain eligible for social support if their income remains under the MBI.

The means test does not discriminate against Roma on its face, nor should its provisions discriminate against the Roma in practice. However, Roma allege that administrators use their investigative powers, under a "social inquiry" provision, to find reasons to exclude Roma from benefits rather than to validate their claims.

One social worker in Bucharest sees her mission as reducing the number of Roma who qualify for social support under the means test: "The law [67/1995] required us to give all Gypsies social support without checking their eligibility. They had cars and TV sets and still dared to claim social protection, and we could not reject their claims. By the end of 1995, in my sector alone, we were paying social support to 1,800 families. We wrote to the ministry and described how the Gypsies are taking advantage of the system. Soon after this, the social inquiry requirement was introduced through HG 125/1996. Since 1996 we have succeeded in reducing the number of beneficiaries from 1,800 families to 200. We give money to those who deserve it, old people who cannot work anymore, not to the Gypsies."[80]

More research is necessary to determine how widespread these practices are and whether social workers treat the Romani population differently from other similarly situated persons. If social workers do treat Roma differently, then they are engaging in illegal discrimination.

5.2. Domicile requirement

Social support payments are made at the place of permanent residence (or permanent domicile) of the beneficiaries. The system is rigid: Those who live far from the municipality where they are registered do not have effective access to social assistance.

The domicile requirement, although outwardly neutral, has a disparate impact on the Romani community. The Roma are overrepresented in almost all categories of persons who have difficulty complying with this regulation, such as those who do not have identification documents, who live in substandard housing, barracks, ghettoes, or unlawfully built structures, or who have a high level of mobility. If persons lack identification documents, they cannot register as permanent residents because they have no legal identity.[81] If they live in ghettoes, they may live in "uninhabitable" structures, so officials will not register them as residents.[82] Bureaucrats deny agricultural workers permanent residence because they live in barracks. Since social assistance payments are made only at the place of residence, any form of mobility results in de facto loss of access to social benefits.

The number of Roma affected by the domicile requirement is sizeable. Experts on the Roma suggest that 25 percent of Roma from the Hunedoara district, for example, fall into this category.[83] Since the 1970s, fifteen families, with five to six children each, have lived in barracks lacking water and electricity near the village of Mintia (Hunedoara). The adults worked on a nearby construction site. When the project ended, Romani families remained in the barracks.[84] Local authorities have never registered them as permanent residents. In Mangalia, ninety-three Romani families, comprised of 628 persons, who lived in the city for periods between twenty-five and forty years, are not registered as permanent residents. Before 1989, they were employed as agricultural workers. They lived in barracks owned by the state agricultural enterprise. After 1989, they were told that, although they had lived there for decades, they could not register as permanent residents in a company house. The net result is that they are effectively barred from social assistance and health care.[85]

Government officials may assert that these policies are reasonable. They may argue that it is inappropriate to register persons who live in temporary housing or whose dwellings are not "habitable." They may argue that these rules exist so that persons do not claim and receive benefits in more than one place.

These concerns are not compelling in light of the problems that the policies create. The fact is that people live in the dwellings, regardless of whether the structures meet the building codes. Many have lived there for a long time. In addition, it would be possible for the state to implement other means of tracking which persons receive benefits in which locations, rather than requiring them to receive assistance only in the place where they are registered. The government should recognize and address the realities of housing conditions and mobility patterns in the provision of benefits.

5.3. Work requirements

Local councils may require food pantry beneficiaries to participate in public work "assignments" (activitati gospodaresti). While such requirements do not discriminate directly against the Roma, the law is vague and open to abuse in practice.

The law does not specify what kind of activities officials may require of claimants, thus permitting the imposition of all types of work, from peeling potatoes to digging ditches. Romani women state that administrators require them to perform exhausting, unsanitary, or humiliating work, such as cleaning toilets, collecting garbage, or even, as in Buhusi, performing agricultural work on private property. In Dej, adults who qualify for food pantry benefits must work in municipal extermination services without receiving any training or information about the harmful substances they handle.[86] In Buhusi, the city fired the majority of the municipal employees of the street cleaning and garbage collection services; officials now deploy food pantry beneficiaries instead.[87]

Local Romani leaders allege that the administrators assign work along ethnic lines. They state that officials give Roma the so-called "dirty work," while non-Roma receive less onerous tasks—or no assignments at all.[88] Several Romani women reported at least two incidents in which, seeing them working on the streets, a senior municipal official yelled from his car: "Clean well, crows, or I'll cut off your bread."[89]

The law does not establish the maximum number of workdays that local councils may require. Governments in Orastie and Bacau demand from three to five days per month, in Bucharest eight days per month.[90] Significant regional variations raise questions of fairness and proportionality regarding the work requirement.

Governmental officials engage in illegal discrimination if they assign Romani beneficiaries to work more frequently or in more difficult or more dangerous conditions than non-Romani beneficiaries. There appears to be no legitimate reason, such as a special skill set that the Roma have and others do not, for differentiation of treatment. More research about the relative handling of these groups is needed in order to determine whether the anecdotes reported above describe the discrimination problem fully and accurately.

5.4. Lack of identification documents

The existence of identification documents is the sine qua non for accessing social welfare benefits, health services, or public housing. Not having such documents seriously affects the exercise of many other rights by placing a person's freedom in danger, jeopardizing his or her participation in community life, and barring access to employment and education. The lack of documents is one of the most important problems confronting a large segment of the Romani population in Romania. The Working Group of Roma Associations (GLAR) considers that any strategic approach to Romani issues in Romania must prioritize support for obtaining identity documents.[91]

The most frequently mentioned missing documents are birth certificates and identification cards. The lack of civil marriage certificates raises difficult legal issues but also sensitive cultural ones related to the acceptance of the civil institution of marriage within the Romani community.

A recent report of the Romanian Ombudsman indicates that some hospitals refuse to issue birth registration papers to mothers who cannot pay medical costs. Birth certificates may also be missing because children are born at home, and parents neglect or postpone registering the newborn. Legal provisions that provide high fines for delays in registering children, neglect by social workers, and administrative corruption[92] are additional obstacles to obtaining birth certificates.

Experts describe the lack of birth certificates, identity cards, and civil marriage certificates as a "mass phenomenon."[93] Thousands do not have legal documents that reflect their family relationships and legal status correctly. Recent studies report that approximately 5 percent of Roma living in Romania do not possess a birth certificate, and approximately 4 percent do not have an identity card.[94]

5.4.1. Birth certificates

The debate over the absence of birth certificates started in 1995 when the authorities responsible for the protection of minors reported that more than 2,500 institutionalized children each year did not have identity documents. The children, whose ethnic identities officials did not reveal, may never have had birth certificates. Or their documents were lost while they were transferred from one institution to another.

Romani community leaders state that the percentage of Romani children without birth certificates is particularly high in certain regions and within certain groups. The problem occurs frequently in seminomadic groups of Kalderash from Moldova, large families that returned to Romania after long stays in other countries, and communities living in miserable conditions near garbage dumps or in ghettoes.[95]

Particularly difficult issues arise in connection with children born outside of Romania. Some of them have no identity document whatsoever; others have a document issued by health authorities certifying the birth, but no civil registration. There are also many cases of children who have birth certificates issued by the appropriate authorities in a foreign country, but their parents gave false names because they entered the country illegally or stayed longer than legally allowed. Finally, a number of adults do not have birth certificates. Some have lived for decades without them, whereas others lost or destroyed the documents during attacks against Romani communities in recent years.

5.4.2. Identity cards

The state issues identity cards based on birth certificates. It is therefore reasonable to think that a significant percentage of those who do not have birth certificates cannot obtain an identity card. However, the number of persons without birth certificates is not necessarily equal to the number of persons without identity cards. Some lost their birth certificates after obtaining an identity card, others did not renew identity cards before they expired, and others misplaced their documents while traveling. Sometimes thieves stole the identity documents. Other times, identity cards disintegrated after being stored in damp houses with leaky roofs and no heating.

5.4.3. Marriage certificates

Couples who do not marry in a civil ceremony—and their children—have huge administrative problems. If the parents are married under civil law, the state presumes that the husband sired the child. If the parents are not so married, the name of the biological father appears on the child's birth certificate only if he acknowledges the child before a notary and pays a fee. Those fathers who do not have money for the fee or who do not understand the legal consequences of their actions do not go through the process. The child takes the mother's name instead. For administrative purposes, the state considers the father unknown, and as a result, the father loses de jure and de facto parental rights. This can cause a number of problems later, particularly if the father tries to collect the child allowance, to obtain housing for himself and the child, or to transfer property to the child.

5.4.4. Statelessness

One academic researcher estimates that between 1,200 and 6,000 stateless Roma live in Romania.[96] Most renounced their Romanian citizenship at the beginning of the 1990s before Parliament adopted a new citizenship law.[97] They had hoped to increase their chances of receiving asylum from Western countries; however, foreign governments rejected their applications, and the Roma returned to Romania—without Romanian citizenship.

5.4.5. Addressing the lack of identification documents among the Roma

The DPMN, the Inter-Ministerial Commission, and the GLAR have placed the lack of documents issue on their agenda. The draft strategy for Romani integration prepared with the Ministry of Interior includes a program aimed at filling the gap. Such a program will require the cooperation of the local authorities, including administrative departments and the police; the Department for the Evidence of the Population (DEP), a national citizen registration bureau; Romani NGOs and the Romani community; and funding organizations. If funding becomes available, the DEP could organize meetings with the leaders of all fifty district offices and local authorities to discuss the national strategy and to monitor its implementation.[98] For now, however, the program faces significant problems, ranging from questions of political will to community sensibilities and from lack of funds to legal assistance issues.

Poverty is often the reason for not replacing lost or destroyed identity cards. For example, for a lost, destroyed, or expired ID, the person concerned must pay an issuing fee of 800 lei (U.S. $0.04), a 12,000 lei (U.S. $0.65) fine for losing it, and 23,500 lei (U.S. $1.27) for a new, codified ID. These sums may seem small to those who live in industrialized countries, but it represents a quarter of the monthly Minimum Basic Income for a person in Romania. Persons who live in severe poverty find it difficult to spend this amount of money for documents. In 1999 alone, 270,000 Romanian citizens (approximately 95,000 of whom were traveling abroad) failed to renew their expired IDs. Each year the police issue 300,000 "provisional identity cards"[99] for persons who, accused of a crime, declare that their identification papers were lost, destroyed, or stolen.[100]

Several Romani organizations are already involved in specific programs to address these problems. In October 1999, the city government of Turda, together with the Romani foundation Sindy Humanitas, launched a program funded by the Open Society Foundation–Romania called "Romani Integration into Society through Issuing Civil Status Documents."[101]

It is difficult to predict how various Romani groups, particularly the seminomadic groups, will respond to these programs. To increase the acceptability of these ventures, police participation should remain minimal, and DEP representatives should perform their work within city halls. Programs should avoid unrealistic deadlines, fines, and other punitive measures.

Organizing such a program on a national scale requires clear political will, interdepartmental action, and the commitment of time and resources by local authorities. Unfortunately, the majority of local governments in rural areas or small cities do not yet have computers or communications facilities to obtain or process information, and they do not possess the financial resources, staff, or expertise to acquire computer networks.

More research is necessary to determine whether the percentage of the Romani population that does not have identity documents is greater than the percentage of the population at large. One would suspect that it is indeed the case, just as one would suspect that a lack of identity documents affects the poor more than the wealthy. Since the Romani community has a greater percentage of poor than the general population, these burdens are likely to fall disproportionately on the Roma. The bottom line is that poor Roma—the ones most in need of social assistance—are the ones least likely to comply with the legal requirements for social protection.

6. Additional Barriers to Social Protection

6.1. Difficulties in accessing government facilities

Access to government facilities is critical for those who depend on direct support from the government. In most, if not all cases, persons who seek social support must apply for benefits at a municipal building. They visit government facilities to establish residency, to provide evidence of unemployment, and to receive payments.

Many Roma report that officials deny them physical access to city halls. Local NGOs report that Roma "are not permitted" to enter city halls in Deva, Hunedoara,[102] and Ungureni (Bacau).[103] In Orastie, Romani women linger in the street while the non-Roma wait inside.[104] "They do not let us in," said a woman waiting in front of city hall, "because they say, 'Gypsies are dirty and smell.' The Romanians are all inside, where it is warm, and we are waiting out here in the cold."[105]

Officials sometimes claim that Roma are disruptive in public offices. However, problems caused by a few do not justify discriminatory treatment of an entire race. Government officials engage in illegal discrimination if they block Romani beneficiaries from accessing government facilities at a greater rate than non-Romani beneficiaries. To the extent to which a particular person poses a safety problem, the government could and should provide additional security personnel so that social workers can do their jobs. Government officials could even reasonably prevent that person from entering public facilities, provided that he or she has other ways of applying for and receiving benefits.

6.2. Forced choice between sources of support

Many poor persons in Romania qualify for more than one form of social support. They may meet the requirements for social support, access to food pantries, social assistance for families with children, and health benefits.

However, in many localities, social workers require individuals and families who qualify for both social support and the food pantry to choose one and to give up the other. The practice is unlawful,[106] but, in the regions of Moldova and Transylvania, it appears to be widespread in small and medium-sized cities such as Cluj, Alba Iulia, and Dej.[107] Knowing that social support is rarely, if ever, provided, most people opt for the food pantry. One of the most severe consequences of giving up social support is the loss of public health insurance under the requirement that persons must prove they receive social support before they can obtain subsidized health benefits.[108]

More research is necessary to determine whether social workers make non-Roma choose between types of benefits. Research is also needed to determine if the requirement is part of an effort by national, regional, or municipal governments to reduce the amount of support provided to those who are legally entitled to it, or if certain social workers are acting in an inappropriate manner on their own authority.

Regardless, forced choices between sources of support are unfair to Roma. These actions are illegal and an abuse of administrative authority. There appears to be no legitimate reason for continuing these practices.

6.3. Allocation of limited funds to other needy groups

As documented in section 4.1.2., some local councils do not allocate sufficient money to the food pantries to support all eligible persons. Many of those councils develop additional criteria for determining which persons will receive support.

These additional requirements tend to exclude the Roma. For example, a local council may give priority to providing social support to old persons living alone, while Roma, as a rule, live in extended families and do not allow their elderly to live alone. The council may decide to allocate all the money to support the functioning of a residence for the elderly, to which Roma generally do not have access, and not to pay social support for the very poor, a group in which the Roma are overrepresented.

According to the local authorities, in Geoagiu commune, Huneadoara, 164 families qualify for social support. Of these families, 108 are Roma. In 1999, social support was paid only once, in April. "There is no money for social support because all the funds have been allocated for residences for the elderly," the city hall secretary said.[109] The local Romani leader, Nicolae Bologa, claims that the local council explicitly voted "not to give money to the Gypsies."[110]

According to international standards such as the ICESCR, even if a government has limited resources, it may not discriminate directly or indirectly because of race in the allocation of social benefits. Governments certainly have the right to set their own priorities and to allocate more benefits to some groups rather than others. However, a government may not discriminate on the basis of race when determining which groups will receive assistance.

6.4. Delay or nonallocation of funds

It is impossible to ignore the scarcity of financial resources in Romania. Communes, small cities, and medium-sized cities hit hard by economic crises face real financial problems. They do not have sufficient budgetary resources of their own. The budgetary structure gives them control over only 40 percent of their income, with the rest going to national and district budgets. This may partially explain why, except in the capital and in several big cities, social support is not paid, is partially paid, or is paid with significant delays. A World Bank study revealed that in 1997, social support was delayed in 72.7 percent of the analyzed cases; two-thirds of the delays were due to lack of funds.[111] There are no indications that the situation has since improved.

The law requires local councils to evaluate needs and to "contribute to the achievement of social aid and protection measures."[112] The local council has the discretion to determine the content and the extent of its "contribution."[113]

Romani leaders claim that the payment of social support is a lower priority for the authorities in localities where the majority of the potential beneficiaries are Roma. They say that local councils attend to other administrative expenditures first, allocating support for the Roma from what remains. As a rule, nothing is left for the Roma.

Romani leaders in Buhusi estimate that more than 75 percent of the claimants for social support are Roma and that is the reason why the local council does not allocate money for social support.[114] Roma from Moruzeni, a large Romani neighborhood in Marasesti, receive social support only twice a year, for Easter and Christmas. In 1999, the city government reportedly rejected new applications, stating it has no money to pay the requests already approved.[115]

In Alba Iulia's largest Romani neighborhood, "the Industrial Zone," people are convinced that racism, not lack of funds, is the main reason for the suspension of payments: "We have eight children, my husband and me. He is employed and earns 500,000 lei every month," one resident states. "The social assistance department told me that we have the right to social support, but we received nothing because the city has no money. But they spend money on celebrations and on new furniture for city hall and on traveling abroad. We eat from the garbage. We pick up empty bottles and sell them. Nobody in this neighborhood receives social support. They say there are no funds. If we were Romanian, they would find funds."[116]

Orastie is a small Transylvanian city with 25,000 inhabitants. Industry and commerce are languishing, and the unemployment rate is 29 percent. According to the deputy mayor, out of 380 families eligible for social support, more than 300 families are Roma, each of them with four to seven children. The municipality suspended payments between April and October 1999, because there were insufficient funds[117] and the authorities did "not want to pay social support anymore to people who do nothing."[118]

Many, if not most, municipal governments claim lack of funds to justify systematic nonpayment of social support. However, these governments are not penniless; they do allocate funds to other projects instead of social support. Although established by law, the right of those eligible for social support to receive benefits is continuously eroded by the discretionary decisions of local councils not to allocate funds, to allocate less than needed, or to delay the distribution of benefits for the protection of the very poor.

International standards such as the ICESCR specify that a government may not discriminate directly or indirectly because of race in the allocation of social benefits. Governments may not discriminate on the basis of race when determining which legally qualified persons will receive assistance. Governments may not curtail benefits in a discriminatory manner. Local councils that do so violate the rights of the people.

7. Existing Legal and Extra-legal Remedies

Roma and non-Roma have few avenues for seeking redress for rights violations. They can submit complaints to the national ombudsman, or they can attempt to have government prefects intercede to challenge local council acts. Romani leaders report, however, that they will have only limited success in these efforts until the government effectively implements the antidiscrimination law, setting clear standards and penalties.

The ombudsman can have an important role to play in promoting social protection rights; he defends individual rights and freedoms against violations by public administrators. However, he cannot reverse administrative decisions. He intervenes only in relation to unlawful acts or facts.[119]

The Office of the Ombudsman has four departments and a staff of forty persons with legal training. In 1998, the ombudsman created a special department for the protection of children, women, and families, but he also abolished the department designed to deal with minorities (Department for Minorities, Cults, and Mass Media) which was included in the initial structure of the office.

The overall number of complaints rose from 1,168 in 1997 to 3,000 in the first months of 1999, but the ombudsman ruled than more that 90 percent were outside his office's jurisdiction. To date, the office has issued decisions in over 200 cases and recommended a few cases to the authorities.[120] The office regularly receives complaints of racial discrimination, the majority of them related to prohibiting Roma from bars, restaurants, or supermarkets. A significant number of complaints relate to social protection, but in general, they do not raise allegations of racial discrimination.

The government, through its prefects, controls the legality of the local council's acts. When called upon to implement a decision of the local council that they deem illegal, mayors have a legal obligation to inform the prefects.[121] In certain cases, the prefects may challenge local council acts in the administrative court. The court may dissolve the local council if the court finds that the municipal governing body has repeatedly made unlawful decisions.[122]

Bulgaria

1. The State's Obligations under International, Constitutional, and National Law

Bulgaria has ratified the International Covenant on Civil and Political Rights (ICCPR),[123] the International Convenant on Economic, Social and Cultural Rights (ICESCR),[124] the Convention on the Rights of the Child (CRC),[125] the Convention on the Elimination of All Forms of Discrimination Against Women (CEDAW),[126] and the International Convention on the Elimination of All Forms of Racial Discrimination (ICERD).[127] At the European level, Bulgaria has ratified the European Convention for the Protection of Human Rights and Fundamental Freedoms (ECHR),[128] the Revised European Social Charter,[129] and the Framework Convention for the Protection of National Minorities.[130] Bulgaria accepted the collective complaints procedure as a part of its ratification of the Revised European Social Charter.

The Bulgarian Constitution establishes the obligation of the state to protect the family, motherhood, and childhood.[131] Moreover, the Constitution recognizes citizens' rights to social security and social welfare.[132] The state must provide social security for the temporarily unemployed and must offer special protection to disabled persons and to the elderly without relatives.[133] Constitutional norms are directly applicable.[134] Lawfully ratified international instruments are part of the domestic law and take precedence over national norms that stipulate otherwise.[135]

2. Poverty and Unemployment in Bulgaria

Approximately 8.5 million people live in Bulgaria. According to the 1992 census, the main groups are Bulgarians (85.5 percent), Turks (9.5 percent), and Roma (3.7 percent). The European Commission report on 1999 notes that the Romani share of the Bulgarian population is 5 percent,[136] and the Council of Europe in 1998 has indicated the Romani share to be approximately 7 percent.[137]

The Roma have much higher rates of unemployment than the rest of the population. Romani leaders told the Council of Europe's rapporteurs that unemployment in the Romani community was between 80 and 90 percent in 1998,[138] while the European Commission reported that overall unemployment in Bulgaria was 16 percent.[139] Unemployment for women in general in 1999 was around 68 percent, while the percentage of unemployed Romani women was estimated to be approximately 98 percent.[140]

The Roma also suffer higher rates of poverty. The World Bank reported that 84 percent of the Roma were poor in 1997, compared to 36 percent of the total Bulgarian population.[141] The government classifies as "poor" those who have a monthly income between 40 and 90 leva (approximately U.S. $21 to U.S. $47). "Extreme poverty" starts under 40 leva per month.[142] In 1998, according to the Ministry of Labor and Social Policy, between 50 and 60 percent of the beneficiaries of social welfare were Roma.[143] In some municipalities the percentage was even higher (e.g. 75 percent in Lom).[144]

3. National Strategies for Romani Integration and Social Support

On 22 April 1999, the Bulgarian Council of Ministers approved the Framework Program for Equal Integration of Roma in Bulgarian Society, a policy document prepared by Roma organizations in cooperation with the National Council on Ethnic and Demographic Issues (NCEDI). The document states: "Roma in Bulgaria are the group which occupies the lowest level in the social hierarchy. They are not adequately represented in the political life and in the Government of the country. In the social economic aspect as a whole, the status of the Roma is dramatically lower than the Bulgarian average, marked by high unemployment rates, deplorable living conditions, bad health, high illiteracy rates, etc. This stable characteristic in the situation of the Romani community is the external manifestation and direct consequence of discriminatory treatment."[145]

The adoption of the Framework Program, the goal of which is the "elimination of the unequal treatment of Roma in Bulgarian society,"[146] was a significant success for the Romani human rights movement. The program emphasizes that "the elimination of discrimination against Roma is one of the main political priorities of the Bulgarian state"[147] and envisages the inclusion of antidiscrimination clauses in a number of laws, such as the Penal Code and laws on education, health care, and territorial development. It also calls for the establishment of a National Committee for Prevention of Discrimination.

The paragraph on social protection calls for (i) amending the Law on Social Assistance so as to create "vulnerable ethnic minorities" as a protected subcategory of "socially vulnerable groups;" (ii) training for social workers who work in Romani communities; and (iii) the monitoring role of NGOs. The NCEDI working group on Romani issues elected twenty-four experts and organized a seminar on "teamwork" in September 1999. The experts are expected to develop strategies for sector reform.

The initial successes, however, have not had sufficient follow-up, according to Romani NGOs and outside observers. In January 2000, Romani Baht reported that, in practice, implementation of the strategy had not yet started.[148] In March 2000, the representatives of seventy Romani NGOs declared that the government had not done anything to accomplish any of the tasks put forward in the Framework Program and that Roma continue to be excluded from the decision-making processes in matters of their interest.[149] In June 2000, U.S. Helsinki Commission Chairman Representative Christopher H. Smith decried the Bulgarian government's failure to "even draft such an [antidiscrimination law], let alone pass it."[150]

The 1999 PHARE Program allocated 500,000 euro to "Promoting the Social Integration Support System (SISS) for the Roma Minority in Bulgaria." The grant, aimed at supporting the implementation of the Framework Program, focuses on access to education, infrastructure development of Romani areas, and training Romani representatives to work in public administration. The program has awarded approximately 100,000 euro for access to education, approximately 300,000 euro for infrastructure development of Romani areas, and approximately 100,000 euro for training Romani representatives to work in public administration and on policy issues.[151]

4. Social Protection Programs

The Bulgarian social safety net includes social assistance and family benefits.[152] Social assistance benefits include monthly social support, energy allowances, and one-time support; family benefits include child allowances, birth grants, and benefits for the care of children under the age of three. Out of the total sum allocated for income transfers and labor market programs, pensions take 75 percent of available funds. Child allowances, social assistance, and labor market programs receive 12 percent, 7 percent, and 6 percent of the budget, respectively.[153]

The National Welfare Council designs the country's social policy, and the Ministry of Labor and Social Policy implements the policy through its National Social Assistance Service, a separate legal entity based in Sofia, which coordinates the activities of territorial Social Work Centers (SWCs). The Social Work Centers make the payments from funds they receive from municipal revenues and national budget subsidies. The national budget pays for other benefits for families in need, such as child allowances, birth grants, and maternity benefits.

The state pays unemployment benefits for a period of four to twelve months after the loss of employment, depending on how long the person had worked.[154] After this period, those who are still unemployed may apply immediately for social assistance.

4.1. Social assistance for persons and families with little or no income

The main forms of cash transfer within the social assistance programs examined by this report are monthly social support, monthly assistance for the payment of rent, one-time support, and support for heating. Access by Roma to monthly social support has particular importance, because it is the condition sine qua non for access to noncontributory health insurance.[155]

The Bulgarian Parliament adopted the Social Assistance Act at the beginning of 1998.[156] The Ministry of Labor and Social Policy issued implementation regulations in November 1998, which it further amended in the spring of 1999.[157] The act establishes the criteria and the functions of social assistance and social services, sets up partnership rules between central and local government authorities in the financing and management of the programs, and provides for increased participation of nongovernmental organizations in the social services area. The act also enables affected parties to appeal the decisions of the Regional Social Work Centers to a court.[158]

The Social Assistance Act contains an antidiscrimination clause which establishes the responsibility of the administration to provide welfare benefits to all those in need without restrictions or privileges based on race, nationality, political or ethnic affiliation, country of origin, sex, age, religion, beliefs, or social status.[159] With regard to the first few months under the new legislation, the National Social Work Service "has not so far received any complaint or report of alleged discrimination based on ethnic or other origin with regard to the payment of social assistance."[160]

4.1.1 Monthly social support

To receive monthly support, applicants must pass two types of financial tests. Examination of the tests indicates that the program targets families living in extreme poverty and not the poor in general.

First, recipients may not earn more than the "differentiated minimum income," a figure determined by multiplying the minimum basic income (MBI) and a coefficient specific to each category of beneficiaries.[161] For example, the coefficient is 0.5 for children between seven and sixteen, if not at school;[162] 0.9 for spouses living together;[163] 1.0 for persons living alone;[164] and 1.2 for persons over seventy living alone, the disabled, and orphans.[165] The Council of Ministers has set the MBI at approximately 60 percent of the minimum monthly wage. In 1999, the MBI was 30.875 leva (U.S. $19.30) per month. Therefore, to qualify for monthly support in 1999, a claimants' level of income must have been below 15.437 leva (U.S. $9.64) per month per family member for the most disadvantaged category—unemployed parents whose children do not attend school—and below 37.050 leva (U.S. $23.15) per month per family member for protected categories such as the elderly, the disabled, and orphans.

Second, recipients may not have more than 200 leva per person in deposits, shares, and interest,[166] and may not own movable or immovable property that could be a source of income—except for belongings for normal family use.[167]

Eligibility depends on other criteria as well. To receive monthly social support, a person must have been registered with the unemployment office for at least six months.[168] The following do not qualify for monthly social support: persons whose relatives are legally required to support them,[169] full-time, part-time, and evening students in higher education institutions (save for disabled students), children who attend private schools,[170] and able-bodied persons who refused land settlements or the tilling of municipal land for the respective year.[171]

4.1.1.1 Benefits in kind

As a rule, benefits are provided in cash. However, the law sets up two cases when monthly social benefits may be paid in kind: when parents fail to look after their children[172] and when cash benefits are not used according to their purpose.[173] These are individual cases and require individual determinations.

In the spring of 1999, a government decree stipulated that municipalities may distribute 30 percent of monthly support in food.[174] The municipalities decide when, where, and what kind of food is distributed. According to two local officials, the government adopted in-kind benefits to create and preserve jobs for employees of the canned food industry, and not to satisfy any particular dietary needs of the poor.[175] Those who do not accept in-kind assistance live without support for the month.[176]

The practice is common throughout the country. Romani NGOs report that in some cities, such as Lom, the Social Work Centers provide not only part of the monthly support but also a part of child allowances and maternity benefits on an in-kind basis.[177]

4.1.2. Monthly assistance for the payment of rent

Unemployed individuals may also qualify to receive social assistance for monthly rent. Included among those eligible, if they have an income under 150 percent of the MBI, are: (i) orphans under age twenty-five who graduated from vocational training courses, (ii) people over seventy years old or disabled persons (assisted first or second disability grade) who live alone, and (iii) single parents who live in municipal or state-owned housing. In order to receive aid, the person concerned must present a receipt showing that he or she has already paid the rent.[178]

4.1.3 One-time support

The Social Work Center may pay, once a year, a lump sum not bigger than five times the basic minimum income, to families that need it for unforeseen health, educational, communal, or other necessities. The center's director decides whether to grant or to reject an application for this type of support.[179] The law does not establish any other specific criteria for assessing requests.

Abuses and discretionary and discriminatory practices have been frequently reported in connection with the one-time support. The fact that welfare officials have the discretionary power to decide, with almost no legal constraints, who is entitled to this type of aid leads to "constant protests and anger in the [Romani] community," according to the World Bank.[180]

4.1.4. Support for heating

At the beginning of 1997, the Bulgarian economy suffered a period of hyperinflation. Without external support, the collapsing national economy could not have assisted low-income households. PHARE initiated the Emergency Social Assistance Program,[181] aimed at helping to meet expenditures for electricity and central heating during the November to April cold season. Although PHARE no longer provides funding, the program was, and continues to be, one of the most important components of the social assistance program in Bulgaria.

In 1997–1998, all families living under the poverty line qualified for support. They received a flat sum per family member,[182] multiplied by various indexes, but not more than a total of 20 ECU.[183] In 1998–1999, when the Ministry of Labor and Social Policy (MOLSP) funded the effort, new regulations were adopted, which provided heating support only for the families that met a special income test[184] and eligibility requirements otherwise identical to those for monthly support.[185]

The new regulations had a disparate impact on the Romani community, reducing dramatically the number of Romani beneficiaries of heating support. The situation in Fakulteta, Sofia, illustrates the disastrous effect of the facially neutral regulations. National coverage of the program slightly increased from 18 percent in 1997–1998 (according to PHARE and MOLSP) to 19.4 percent in 1998–1999 (according to MOLSP), while in Romani-inhabited Fakulteta the number of beneficiaries dropped by at least 68 percent.

In the spring of 1998 in Fakulteta, 7,842 households received "urgent social aid for heating."[186] The adoption of the 1999 regulation, in Fakulteta alone, excluded more than 5,000 Romani families from the heating support plan. According to the authorities, in the spring of 1999 only 2,454 households received support for heating in all Krasna Poliana, the district that includes Fakulteta.[187]

There is no evidence that the economic or social conditions of the Roma in Fakulteta improved so much in one year as to justify the precipitous drop-off in Romani participation in the program. While the Bulgarian government certainly has the right to decide how to allocate benefits to different groups in the community, it cannot discriminate against groups on the basis of their race, particularly during times of economic hardship. The stark change in coverage and its impact on the Roma merits further investigation.

4.2. Social assistance for families with children

The state protects families through benefits such as child allowances, birth grants, and maternity benefits, all governed by the Decree on Encouragement of Childbearing (DEC).[188] All Bulgarian citizens are entitled to benefits under DEC whether or not otherwise insured by other schemes. In fact, DEC might be seen as yet another form of social assistance.[189] The Social Security Fund, municipal funds, and educational institutions' budgets cover the payments.[190]

4.2.1. Child allowances

The main form of family support is universal child allowances provided monthly for children up to the age of sixteen, or eighteen if attending school.[191] The state awards 15 leva

(U.S. $7.89) for the first child; 30 leva (U.S. $15.80) for the second child; 55 leva (U.S. $28.95) for the third child; 15 leva (U.S. $ 7.89) for a fourth and each additional child.[192] Short-term unemployed parents receive an extra 10 percent of their unemployment benefits for each child under eighteen. Single mothers who alone provide for the maintenance of their children are entitled to increased amounts: 40 leva (U.S. $21.05) for the first child; 60 leva (U.S. $31.58) for the second child; 110 leva (U.S. $57.89) for the third child; and 30 leva (U.S. $15.78) for a fourth and each additional child.[193]

In general, the employed and insured parent receives the allowances. Where both parents have jobs, mothers have priority. If both parents are unemployed—and registered as such—child allowances are paid from the state budget through local offices exercising jurisdiction over the parents' residence.[194]

The issues related to the equal access to social protection of single mothers are particularly important for the Romani community[195], where, according to Bulgarian authorities, the number of women in this situation is particularly high.[196] Of special concern is what appears to be a pattern of denying Romani women access to single mother benefits. For example, a recent study carried out in Sliven and in three surroundings villages notes that "in most of the cases the social workers refuse to allow the status of single mother to young Romani women."[197]

Credible sources report that Romani single mothers from the Fakulteta neighborhood in Sofia are also denied access to increased allowances. A "single mother group claim" was registered with the Social Program of Romani Baht, when the social workers from the Social Work Center refused to give several Romani women single mother application forms, although they fulfilled the legal requirements.[198] Under the law, women who receive court-awarded alimonies, live within the same household with the child's father, or are legally married to another person are not entitled to single mother increases.[199]

Other reports mention denial of child allowances to mothers under sixteen years old.[200] This type of denial has a disparate impact on Romani women because they constitute the overwhelming majority of very young mothers.[201]

4.2.2. Maternity benefits

The Decree on Encouragement of Childbearing establishes an entitlement to maternity benefits, such as monthly aid for pregnancy and childcare benefits for children under the age of three. Although the right is universal and all mothers and children should receive them, the available information indicates low coverage of the Romani community. For example, Romani Baht reports that, although approximately 3,000 children under the age of three live in Fakulteta, only 402 received childcare benefits in 1998.[202] In 1999, in Istucen, Plovdiv, 991 mothers received childcare benefits while at least 5,000 Romani and Turkish families live in Stolipinovo alone.[203] More research needs to be conducted to determine the extent to which qualified members of other ethnic groups receive these benefits to determine whether there is a disparate impact on Roma in the implementation of the program.

4.2.3. Birth grants

All Bulgarian women are entitled to a flat sum after giving birth. If the mother has a job, the government pays the grant to her directly; if she does not, the state gives the money to the child's father. When both parents are not insured, the municipal budget pays the grant to the mother.[204] For the first child, the payment equals one minimum monthly wage; for the second, two minimum wages; for the third, two-and-a-half minimum wages; and for the fourth and subsequent children, one minimum wage.[205]

4.2.4. Childcare benefits for children under the age of two

Employed or student mothers[206] receive 60 leva per month, for a period of time that starts forty-five days before the birth of the child and ends when the child reaches the age of two.[207] The government also pays a 10 leva per month benefit to unemployed mothers,[208] if they register as such and the termination of their employment took place within a six-month period preceding the birth. Therefore, any pregnant woman who is employed with a work contract, even for only one month, during the final six months of pregnancy, qualifies for full childcare benefits for the next two years. Unemployed mothers, the category in which Romani women are overrepresented, receive only one-sixth of the monthly amount that employed mothers do, although they do receive it from the baby's birth until the child is three years old.

Social workers state that they are willing to help pregnant non-Romani women find short-term employment so that they can qualify for the higher level of benefits. According to Rumiana Panova, director of the "Triaditza" Unemployment Office, "it is very easy for us to arrange with an employer for a pregnant woman to work for one month just to give her access to maternity benefits."[209] Romani women, who suffer from a 98 percent unemployment rate, do not receive similar help from social workers.

The recently adopted Social Insurance Code did not bring any improvement for those excluded under the previous system. Rather, it increased the required period of employment before giving birth from one to six months, and claimants must pay social insurance for at least six months before the birth of the child in order to receive benefits.

5. Impact on the Roma of Eligibility Requirements and Recipient Responsibilities

Persons who receive social support must fit certain eligibility criteria and comply with additional responsibilities that government officials impose on them. The rules set clear standards in some areas while in others administrators have considerable leeway in how they apply the regulations. Several of these policies and practices discriminate against the Roma. The introduction of extremely severe eligibility requirements and other barriers to access particularly affect Roma "both because they are at a higher risk of poverty and because they face unique circumstances that limit their ability to access services."[210]

5.1. Means test

One of the legal requirements for accessing monthly social support is not to have "movable or immovable property that may be a source of income—except for belongings for normal family use."[211] Social workers determine the fulfillment of this requirement through periodic inquiries. Because the law does not provide further guidance, the Social Work Centers can decide "what may be a source of income" and which objects are necessary for the "normal use of the family." In 1998, a study by the International Labor Organization (ILO) noted that the wording of this particular requirement is "prone to very subjective interpretation and results in large variances, from region to region, in decisions on entitlement to assistance."[212] The study called for the strengthening of the legislation in order to remove, or at least to reduce, the degree of subjectivity in the application of the rules.[213] Bulgarian researchers also mention the social workers' discretionary powers and their tendency to reduce local expenditures by interpreting "in more restrictive ways the means-test criteria."[214]

Romani NGOs maintain that local officials use the means test in a discriminatory manner to exclude Romani applicants from support. Romani Baht reports that the majority of the approximately 7,000 Romani families in Fakulteta, Sofia, live in severe poverty. Approximately 95 percent of families do not have regular income. However, less than 2 percent, or 128 families, have access to monthly support.[215] In some villages, the ownership of an animal is reportedly sufficient to deny access to benefits; in others, officials reject applications for monthly support from Romani women if they grow medical herbs—in a plot as small as one square meter—because the herbs "might bring income."[216]

Credible reports maintain that, in an abuse of their discretionary powers, some officials do not even perform the means test for certain categories of persons, thereby denying them the opportunity to receive any benefits. In the district of Sliven, the municipal and regional Social Work Centers reportedly "decided not to allow monthly social help to families with both parents unemployed in the villages."[217]

Government officials should not apply the means test in a manner that discriminates against a particular group of people because of their race. The incidents documented above suggest a pattern of discrimination. It would be helpful for researchers to gather more data about how social workers treat non-Roma and Roma in order to establish the extent of the illegal abuse of discretionary authority by these social centers.

5.1.1. Alleged discrimination in distribution of food

Some Roma claim that food distribution centers give higher quality food to non-Roma. Romani families in Nadezhda, Sliven, state that they receive canned food and almost never meat, milk, sugar, flour, or oil like non-Romani families who do not live in the ghetto.[218] They also say that because the government replaced part of the monetary assistance with food, they have less capacity to buy other necessities:

"It is ridiculous to force us and our children to eat canned tomatoes in a country which is famous for the quality of its fresh vegetables and where the fresh tomatoes are still cheap. We need detergent and soap, not peppers in a can. The government knows that people are throwing away this food. The reality is that a significant part of the social support was simply cut. Private owners of canned food factories, and their friends and relatives in the government and parliament, sell their products to the state. The government, without asking us, wrote a decree and now forces us to swallow whatever they want, because we cannot say no. It is simply corruption and we pay for it with our health."[219]

The Council of Europe has criticized this type of practice, noting that in transition economies with incomplete safety nets the replacement of cash benefits with benefits in kind "is a further reduction in autonomy, and may be a threat to human dignity."[220]

It is inappropriate and illegal to allocate different types of food to different ethnic groups because of their race. The only imaginable exception would be if a certain group had unique nutritional needs, and that does not seem to be the case for the Roma. It appears that government officials treat Roma differently from non-Roma when distributing foodstuffs; more research will help document and establish a strong discrimination claim.

5.2. Travel ban

The government does not pay monthly social support to persons who traveled abroad at their own expense during the last twelve months, except to receive medical treatment or in connection with the death of a family member.[221] The country of destination, the number of trips, or the frequency of the journeys is irrelevant. The claimant must demonstrate compliance by presenting his or her passport to social welfare officials.[222] If the person declares that he or she does not have or has lost the passport, and the social workers have reason to believe that this is not true, the Social Work Center may request police assistance to clarify whether the person traveled abroad in the last twelve months or not. All family members must comply with the requirement, not just the person formally entitled to financial support.[223]

Bulgarian law imposes a travel ban only on those seeking monthly social support. According to employees in Social Work Centers in Sofia, Plovdiv, Sliven, and Chirpan, the government introduced the requirement in response to the growing phenomenon of Romani border commerce with Turkey, Greece, Romania, and especially Serbia.[224] The provision affects the poorest of the poor by requiring them to choose between social support and important travel. If they desire social support, they can no longer participate in family events such as weddings or baptisms that take place in other countries. They cannot visit their relatives abroad when they are sick. They have to wait for a funeral to cross the border without losing social support.

Although many NGOs and private persons mentioned this requirement as particularly unfair, monitoring programs do not yet exist. Information on Romani family ties across the borders in the Balkans is almost nil. Data on the mobility of social support beneficiaries and the reasons for their travels is scarce. For example, 11 percent of the people interviewed by sociologists in the Nikola Kocev neighborhood in Sliven declared that they had traveled to neighboring countries on private business. Only 1 to 3 percent of the rural Roma and 8 percent of the inhabitants of Nadezhda have ever been abroad.[225]

It is not yet clear what kind of impact the travel ban has on Romani applicants for monthly support and in which way, if any, it affects poor Romani families more than Bulgarian or Turkish families. More research is necessary to determine whether the policy has a disparate impact on the Roma. Evidence is also needed on whether the ban is performing its stated objective of preventing wealthy persons from claiming social support.

Nonetheless, it is worth noting that the requirement may violate other constitutionally protected rights. Bulgarian citizens have the right to leave and enter the country freely. The state may limit this right only for reasons of national security, public health, or protection of rights and freedoms of other citizens.[226] The travel ban may also interfere unjustifiably with a person's private life, another constitutionally protected sphere.[227]

5.3. Work requirements

The municipality grants monthly support only if a claimant agrees to participate for at least five days a month in a work program organized by the city.[228] The municipality denies the month's support to those who refuse.[229] The regulations exclude persons with a diminished capacity for working, women with children under the age of three, and those who take care of a gravely ill family member.[230] The implementation of the five-day work requirement is, as a rule, administrated by the Social Work Centers.[231]

There appears to be a divergence between the program's stated intention and its effect. The community work programs based on the five-day work requirement are supposed to give the poor a sense of participation in community life, to occupy a portion of their time, and to promote proactive behavior in chronically unemployed people.[232] However, NGOs and Romani interviewees state that government officials implement the work requirement in a discriminatory manner, creating injustice, tensions, and frustration.

In Sliven, Romani women reported that the Social Work Center requires them to work, but that it does not make non-Roma work. "For almost three years I have been on monthly support and every month I have to clean the streets," one woman said. "I am not illiterate, I have ten years of education. But how educated we are is irrelevant. What matters is that we are Roma. When we go to the social center we always see Bulgarian women waiting in the same line with us to receive the money. But when we clean the streets, we never see a non-Romani woman. This is not about work; this is about fairness. The mayor fired our husbands from municipal services and now they use us for free. We do not mind doing something for the money we get. But the social workers send only Roma into the streets. This is their way of telling us that we are good at nothing else. There is no rotation system, no control, no fairness in the distribution of work."[233] A fifty-two-year-old father of three from Sliven reiterated the discrimination allegation: "Only Gypsies have to work for five days to be granted social assistance. And we work for five days, but they don't give us assistance!"[234]

In July 1998, the press reported that the authorities in the small village of Borovan decided to peg payments of social welfare to Roma in the winter to forced work in the summer. "Those who work won't steal! . . . Today every poor able-bodied male is invited to sign up and earn his living," official announcements stated. "Gypsies in Borovan can choose between working on 7.5 hectares of tobacco fields or 5.1 hectares of vegetable fields. The lazy have nobody but themselves to blame, since those who refuse to work in the field are automatically, and lawfully, disentitled from government relief. . . ."[235]

Governmental officials engage in illegal discrimination if they make Romani beneficiaries work more frequently than non-Romani beneficiaries, or if the ethnicity of a person determines the type of work that he or she is assigned. More research is needed about the relative treatment of these groups in order to determine the extent of discriminatory practices.

5.4. Ban on corporate ownership

The government does not pay monthly social support to claimants who have registered a company under the Commercial Code.[236] Authorities look only at the registration of the company without taking into consideration the company's viability as reflected by its income—or lack of it.

NGOs from Sofia, Lom, and Plovdiv note that a significant number of unsuccessful Romani entrepreneurs genuinely believed in market economy opportunities and enthusiastically registered small companies at the beginning of the 1990s, immediately after the law permitted it. Many of them failed. Three or four years later, the majority had given up any attempt to work on their own. Today, the law excludes them and their families from receiving monthly support. Among them are many women with dependent children.[237]

Although persons in this position could formally close down their companies, that solution is not practical for many. The complexity of the commercial procedure requires legal assistance, and legal and administrative fees might be as high as 150 leva (approximately U.S. $80), a sum that, as a rule, is beyond the reach of persons in need of social protection.[238]

The government may have at least two legitimate objectives for excluding people with registered companies from obtaining social support. The aim may be to exclude from the social assistance system persons and families who have sufficient financial resources. Or it may be to encourage unsuccessful entrepreneurs to close companies that exist only on paper.

However, the requirement places an unfair and senseless burden upon the truly poor. The government uses a means test as a part of its general determination of a person's wealth and income. If the state applies the means test in a professional manner, then there is no need for the registered companies requirement to serve as a proxy for the wealthy, which the government can verify in other ways. If clearing the government rolls of nonfunctioning corporations is a high priority, then the state can waive the administrative fees for the truly poor.

Systematic monitoring is needed in order to gather more information about individual cases and general trends to prove that the corporate ownership requirement has a disparate impact on the Roma. If the policy does, then government officials will have difficulty justifying the requirement, since it has other means by which it can achieve the same objectives, such as an effectively administered means test, without treading on a particular ethnic group.

5.5. Ban on sale of housing within the past five years

Selling a house or an apartment automatically excludes a family from monthly social support for five years.[239] The director of a Social Work Center from a district with a large Romani population said the government introduced the requirement in response to an increase in the number of Roma selling their apartments in Bulgarian or mixed neighborhoods and moving into their relatives' houses in Romani neighborhoods or mahalas.[240]

A significant number of Romani workers lost their jobs during recent years due to economic crises and structural reforms. Families became further impoverished. People who rented municipal apartments and were unable to pay the rent were evicted. Many of those who owned apartments found themselves unable to pay household expenses. They were forced to sell their apartments and return to live with relatives in their neighborhoods.[241] Some used the money to start small private businesses. When successful, families pulled themselves out of poverty. Unfortunately, many attempts failed. Money obtained for apartments was gone well before five years, and the families were not richer but poorer.

The phenomena is well known and well documented throughout many postcommunist countries. The High Commissioner on National Minorities noted this practice in his 2000 report on Romani living conditions.[242] Bulgaria is no exception: Many families sold their apartments located in other districts of the capital city, because they felt threatened by the anti-Romani hostility of the majority and moved into Romani-dominated areas where they felt safer.[243] The result was a continuous increase of the size of the population of Fakulteta in recent years.[244]

In general, Romani apartments were very small, placed in the poorest areas and with substandard facilities. The amount of money obtained, for example, in 1995 for such an apartment hardly justifies a five-year exclusion from social support. The exclusion is automatic, without any other assessment of the real income of the family during the five years.

While it is clear that the housing sale disqualification affects Roma since many of them sold their dwellings to pay debts, more information is needed on how the policy has affected the non-Romani poor. If the policy does have a disparate impact on the Roma, then government officials will have difficulty justifying the requirement, since they have other means by which they can achieve the same objective of preventing false claims, such as by administering a means test effectively.

5.6. Limitations on size of living quarters

The Ministry of Labor and Social Protection issued regulations in 1998 that restrict the size of the dwelling that claimants and their family members can occupy and still qualify for monthly social support. The regulations provide that a single person may have one room;[245] families with two or three members, two rooms;[246] families with four members, three rooms;[247] and families with five or more members, four rooms.[248] Every person who does not belong to the family yet lives in the same dwelling is entitled to one room.[249] The provisions do not take into account how many square meters each person has or the size of the dwelling in absolute terms.

For example, a family of eight living in a five-room apartment is not eligible for monthly support. To receive monthly support, they must sell the apartment and move into a smaller one, with a maximum of four rooms. However, as explained in the previous section, if they sell, they lose the right to social benefits for five years.

The policy would appear to have a disparate impact on the Romani population. Romani families are much larger than non-Romani families, on average. This policy discriminates based on family size by capping the number of rooms to which a family is entitled. To build a case against this policy, more data on families forced to move to new quarters is needed. It is difficult to imagine a reasonable, objective, or legitimate purpose for this government policy.

6. Additional Barriers to Social Protection

6.1. Difficulties in accessing government facilities

Social Work Centers are often overcrowded, dark, cold, and dirty. People who have to wait in line for hours are often frustrated and nervous, and social workers seem under stress. Tensions are high; verbal, and sometimes physical, violence occurs.

Police officers and/or municipal guards dominate some centers in Romani neighborhoods. In Stolipinovo, Plovdiv, the center does not allow all applicants to enter the building at one time. Rather, they wait in line outside the gate, and a policeman admits them, one by one. Inside the building are another three municipal guards in police-like uniforms, one in each hall or room into which applicants enter.[250] Roma allege that social workers consider any attempt to explain a particular situation or to argue as a lack of respect or a threat. The police intervene and force applicants to leave.[251]

Employees of Social Work Centers have allegedly perpetrated verbal and physical violence against some Romani applicants, interviewees report. "The social workers are evil," one said. "When we wait on the line for aid they shout at us: 'Come on, move quickly, 'cause you smell bad!' Sometimes they beat us to stop jostling. I've never been hurt but other people have. If one tries to ask about something—why the support payment is late, or something else—they shout: 'Go away!'"[252]

Many reported police brutality against applicants, often against women. A twenty-three-year-old mother of eight from Nadezhda ghetto, Sliven, said, "They [employees of the Social Work Centers] always quarrel with us when we go to receive our benefits. They call policemen to beat us. They hit our legs, because we didn't keep our place on the line!"[253] In Silven, a fifty-two-year-old illiterate widower, father of three children and an amputee with a disability pension, said, "The support payments are always several months late. They didn't want to pay us until 1,000 people gathered in front of the mayor's office. When this happened, they managed to find the money in two hours. They said the money finally came from Sofia. They don't pay, 'cause they put the money in their own bank accounts to gather interest. When they keep the social assistance money for three months, they put a million in their pockets! And when we start talking about this they call the police. The policemen beat our women. They don't let us say a word!"[254] A thirty-three-year-old widow with six children from the same neighborhood reported, "They call the police when they give out the assistance. The policemen start beating people at the slightest pushing on the line. Once they hit a pregnant woman!"[255]

Several social workers, however, say that they feel safe only in the presence of the police. Some describe Roma as aggressive, impatient, uncivilized, and having no respect for the administration. These state officials argue that a police presence, fences around buildings, and prison-like metal bars in front of the windows are the only way to protect themselves against violence and robberies.[256]

The access of the Roma or representatives of the Roma to higher authorities in order to address these issues is also problematic. For example, Romani groups were repeatedly refused access to the mayor of Krasna Poliana, the district of Sofia in which the biggest Romani neighborhood, Fakulteta, is located. Even physical access to the mayor's office is barred: "All corridors . . . are sealed off with iron-bar doors that are opened only to officials and visitors with a preliminary appointment,"[257] which does not happen in other similar district offices.

Governmental officials engage in inappropriate discrimination if they block Romani beneficiaries from accessing government facilities at a greater rate than non-Romani beneficiaries. To the extent to which a particular person poses a safety problem, the government could and should provide additional security personnel so that the social workers and other administrators can do their jobs. However, officials must not be allowed to use the problems caused by a few to justify disparate and discriminatory treatment toward all Roma.

6.2. Delays in payment

Central budget subsidies and municipal revenues divide up the cost of social benefits on a fifty-fifty basis, with the exception of social aid for heating. Mayors and municipal councils have the discretionary power to decide on the distribution of funds from the national budget as well as the establishment of municipal priorities.[258] The payment of social benefits depends on the local council's policy as well as on the municipality's economic situation. Smaller cities with weak industry and commerce have problems covering all local needs from their limited resources.

According to Romani NGOs, special interests, corruption, and racial discrimination influence the allocation of social protection funds.[259] Local authorities reportedly tend to allocate less money for social protection immediately after winning the elections. Because the conventional wisdom is that the poor in general and Roma in particular are "left-wing voters," local councils dominated by the political right do not make payment of social support a priority. Cities with significant impoverished Romani or Turkish populations tend to allocate less money than is needed for the payment of social benefits.[260]

All of these practices result in considerable delays in payment or in nonpayment of social benefits, create problems for families relying on these benefits, increase social tensions, and sometimes lead to social unrest.

In 1998, in Lom, one of Bulgaria's poorest cities, the city delayed payment of social support for five months. Several Roma protested by initiating a hunger strike in front of city hall. For four days, the authorities did nothing. On the fifth day, seventeen people declared their intention to light themselves on fire if the authorities did not solve the situation. It took national authorities another four days to decide to talk with the protesters. They promised to set up a commission to investigate why the payments were delayed, to appoint a Romani representative to the Social Work Center to facilitate contacts between the community and the service, and to ensure that the municipality would create food pantries and jobs for low-income people. By December 1999, only the food pantry for the poor had materialized.[261] The government paid social support regularly for a couple of months and then delayed payments again.

In 1999, throughout the Montana region, the state delayed monthly support for six months.[262]

During the same year, seven hundred Romani families from Chirpan qualified for monthly support, but the local council did not allocate funds for six months in a row. Child allowances and maternity benefits were also not paid.[263]

According to international standards such as the ICESCR, even if a government has limited resources, it may not discriminate directly or indirectly because of race in the allocation of social benefits. A government may not discriminate on the basis of race when determining which groups of legally qualified persons will actually receive assistance when funds are limited. More research may be needed to establish that government officials single out the Romani community when deciding how to allocate funds and whether to pay out benefits in a timely manner.

6.3. Lack of knowledge about programs

Roma may lack knowledge about the existence of particular programs or whether they meet the qualifications for certain programs. Several interviewees, including Romani NGO workers, said that they did not know about the rent support program. Other NGO workers stated that many single Romani mothers are unaware of the special benefits available to single mothers, and they alleged that social workers do not tell the women that they qualify for these programs.

At this time, there is not enough evidence to indicate whether social workers intentionally do not inform Roma about these programs. It is possible that the workers themselves do not know of the programs or think that particular persons do not qualify. Researchers need to gather more data to determine whether social workers do not inform the non-Romani poor at the same rate. Social workers practice an illegal form of discrimination if they do not inform Roma about the programs, while informing other non-Romani groups. Furthermore, government officials are negligent if they do not know of the programs about which they are to advise clients.

6.3.1. Rent support

According to local NGOs, Roma rarely benefit from this program. In some cases, they are not eligible because they live in their own houses or in large mahalas, such as Fakulteta. In other cases, such as where they live in state-owned apartments, social workers do not inform them about the existence of rent support.

For example, approximately 20,000 Roma and Turks live in Stolipinovo, Plovdiv. More than half live in state-owned apartments, poverty is widespread, and unemployment ranges from 85 to 90 percent. According to official data, in 1999 only fifteen households received support for rent in the district, which includes both Stolipinovo and another area for a total of 58,000 inhabitants.

6.3.2. Single mothers

Romani NGOs report that single Romani mothers do not know about these benefits. They state that some social workers avoid explaining to Romani women the relevant legal provisions, although these workers allegedly are aware of the fact that the women concerned are "single mothers." For example, according to the local Roma Bureau in Stolipinovo, only seventy-four Romani women have registered as single mothers. A survey of a limited area of the district made by the Roma Bureau in 1999 revealed that 216 women were eligible for single mother benefits without knowing it.

6.4. Time limits on receipt of benefits

Bulgaria limits the length of time that a person can receive social support. Article 13 of Decree No. 243/1998 reads: "Able-bodied unemployed persons are entitled to monthly support for a period of no more than three years. The right to monthly support may be restored one year after it has been stopped." The clock appears to have started running in 1998 when the decree went into force.

Experts on the Roma predict that the decree will have a large and disparate impact on the Romani population, since a high percentage of the population is long-term unemployed. This measure, described as a "work incentive," will probably affect tens of thousands of long-term unemployed and low-income individuals and their families. In 1998, 359,605 persons registered with the unemployment office fit into the long-term unemployed category. Virtually all were applicants for monthly support or support for heating. The "work incentive" will deny support for one year to the tens if not hundreds of thousands who do not find a job by 2001.

Although seemingly neutral, this measure will have a clearly disparate impact on Romani families. As mentioned above, a disproportionate part of the Bulgarian Romani population lives in severe poverty, forced to rely on social benefits in order to survive. World Bank studies indicate that Roma have the highest rate of long-term unemployment in Bulgaria, almost three times more than any other at-risk category.[264] The opportunities offered by the labor market to uneducated or poorly educated Romani youth with no work experience are minimal; widespread racial discrimination in employment further diminishes their slim chances of finding jobs.

Empirical studies also suggest that the regulation will not fulfill its stated objective of encouraging unemployed persons to seek work. Research reveals that 28 percent of the unemployed are actively searching for jobs while only 15 percent of them are not actively looking for work. The job search effort does not appear to depend on the duration of unemployment, since the long-term unemployed showed neither increases nor decreases in job searching over time.[265] Finally, without underestimating the importance of avoiding dependency on the social welfare system, the monthly cash benefits can hardly be described as a "disincentive to work" when they are considerably below the average wage and even below the subsistence minimum.[266]

Under international standards, the time limitation regulation discriminates against the Roma because it has a disparate impact on the population. Some empirical evidence shows that the program does not achieve its stated objectives, thereby undermining a government claim that the restriction is reasonable and objective and serves a legitimate purpose under international law. This program does not respect the principle of proportionality, does not achieve a balance between the interest of the individual and the interest of the society, and places undue hardship on the individual.

Furthermore, the state has the responsibility to provide all persons whose income is below a determined level with minimum social support. Denying social protection to the needy just because, in a hostile labor environment, they are not able to find employment is not consistent with the principles of social justice. Restricting access to social assistance for the long-term unemployed, without simultaneously providing an effective mechanism to integrate them into the labor market, is to exclude them from the safety net in apparent violation of their constitutional right to social welfare as guaranteed by article 51(1) of the Bulgarian constitution.

6.5. Difficulties in establishing unemployment status

The Bulgarian state requires some beneficiaries for some types of support to demonstrate that they are unemployed. They meet this requirement by registering with the unemployment office.

In theory, it should be easy for persons to comply with this requirement; in practice, often it is not so straightforward. In fact, the manner in which the state administers the obligation discriminates against the Roma, who have family structures and mobility patterns that differ from other ethnic groups.

6.5.1. In-person declaration

Romani NGOs report that unemployed Romani women often do not have effective access to child allowances. The law requires both parents to prove each month that they are unemployed, but often the father of the child is not in the same place as the mother and is unable or unwilling to make the necessary declaration so that the mother can receive child support.

The law states that the government will pay child allowances to families in which both parents are unemployed. The administrative practice interprets this requirement to mean that both parents must sign, every month, a declaration that their joblessness continues. If one parent fails to sign the declaration, the other parent is not entitled to child allowances. The official explanation is that failure to sign the unemployment declaration is sufficient proof that the absent parent has a job.

The majority of absent parents in Bulgaria are male. Children usually remain in the mother's care. An unemployed woman receives child allowances only as long as the father of her children regularly signs the required document in the unemployment office. The "father" is the person whose name appears on the birth certificate of the child, and not the adoptive father or the stepfather. If the legal father goes away, leaves the town or the country, or, for personal reasons, refuses or fails to sign the declaration every month, the children remain without support. Both parents must make the declaration in person and in the presence of an employment officer. The law does not address situations in which the father cannot be physically present in the office, if he is out of town, in jail, or in the hospital, for example.

The structure of this requirement causes mothers, who most often have custody, difficulties in exercising parental responsibilities. Romani women state that social workers refuse to accept their explanations or to examine why the other parent is absent, even in legitimate cases. Furthermore, the mother has no legal mechanism to force the father to sign the unemployment declaration.

A significant number of Romani women do not receive child support because of this qualification. According to the chairperson of a local Romani foundation, almost half of the unemployed Romani women do not receive child allowances in Lom.[267] Roma from Plovdiv estimate that only one-third of Romani children benefit from state support.[268] The figures provided by local authorities support their assessment: in November 1999, only 500 out of the approximately 5,000 Romani and Turkish families in Istucen, which includes Stolipinovo, Plovdiv's largest Romani neighborhood, received child allowances.[269] This policy is not the only reason why so few families receive child allowances; however, it is certainly a significant factor.

This policy clearly has a negative impact on the Roma. However, advocates should gather more data to prove that it affects the Roma more severely than the non-Romani poor. The government may have a legitimate desire to prevent families from receiving social support from more than one municipal government, but there may be less restrictive ways for it to safeguard the country's coffers.

It is also worth noting that the policy may violate other human rights principles as well. The administrative practice may result in indirect gender discrimination, as the overwhelming majority of absent parents who fail to sign the declaration are male. It also may inappropriately decrease children's welfare in violation of the Convention on the Rights of the Child.

6.5.2 Age requirements

The state pays maternity benefits for unemployed persons. To receive the grants, a woman must register with the government as unemployed.

Although the minimum working age is eighteen, young people are allowed to work when they reach sixteen, if they do not perform tasks that endanger their normal development. Registration as unemployed should therefore start at sixteen. In practice, the minimum age to register as unemployed is eighteen.[270] As a result, young mothers who become pregnant before eighteen cannot receive maternity benefits.

The majority of Romani girls who live in a poor social and economic environment leave school at around fourteen, if not earlier. Virtually all are unemployed. Most become pregnant and have the first child before eighteen.[271] The condition sine qua non for them to receive maternity benefits is to register as unemployed, which, as explained above, they generally cannot do.

The practice has a disparate impact on Romani women because, again, the number of Romani women who have children before age eighteen is many times higher than the number of Bulgarian women who become mothers before this age. It may be reasonable for the government to require unemployed women to register with the state as unemployed, and employment status is an objective condition. However, there is no legitimate reason why the government cannot modify its policies to make it much easier for unemployed girls who do not attend school to register and receive benefits.

It is also worth noting that the policy and practice may also illegally discriminate against these women based on their age. One would think that very young mothers would have the same, if not greater, need for support during pregnancy than other mothers. It is unclear, therefore, how a policy and practice that has a discriminatory effect on them could be reasonable, objective or legitimate.

6.6. Difficulties in establishing single parent status

The Decree on Encouragement of Childbearing defines the "single mother" as a woman who does not receive court-awarded child support, does not live in the same household as the child's father, and is not legally married to another person.[272] The implementing regulations of the Social Assistance Law defines the "single parent" as a widowed, divorced, or unmarried person who is raising, on her own, a child or children under eighteen years old.[273]

However, in practice, Social Work Centers apply other standards: a woman is a "single mother" if the parents were never married in a civil ceremony and the father did not recognize the child.[274] Additionally, the mother has to prove she is not legally married to another man. As far as the condition of "raising a child on her own" is concerned, the mother has to prove that she does not live in the same household as the father of the children or with another man.[275] She has to sign, every month, a declaration to this effect.

Romani women interviewed state that social workers generally reject their applications for benefits as single mothers. They allege that social workers think that Roma do not marry legally to gain undeserved access to social welfare.[276] Consequently, they work with the assumption that most if not all Romani women live with the father of their children and are not single mothers.

For example, in Sofia's largest Romani district, Fakulteta, the Social Work Center used to require Romani women who claimed single mother status to bring a declaration from the police that they do not live in the same household with a man. Romani mothers were arbitrarily forced into the humiliating position of asking a non-Romani man (somebody outside of her family and, additionally, a policeman) to testify about their private life. The policeman was not, of course, under any legal obligation to perform the check or to issue the document. Romani Baht, a Romani NGO based in Fakulteta, documented individual cases and denounced the practice. The Ministry of Labor and Social Policy acknowledged the practice but claimed that it was an isolated incident, an abuse by an individual social worker from Krasna Poliana. Romani Baht discovered, however, that social workers were acting in accordance with an internal letter issued by the Ministry of Labor and Social Policy before 1989, which was never explicitly canceled. After four months of discussions between the ministry and the representatives of Romani Baht, the state finally abandoned the practice. Social Work Centers never imposed such a requirement on non-Romani applicants.

If the government has a policy that gives more or less benefits to a person based on that person's marital status, the state should take into consideration how it applies that policy. It should implement means of verifying marital status that are sensitive to the cultural norms of different groups, whether Roma or non-Roma, young or old, poor or rich. When members of a particular group do not participate in the program at the same rate as one would think based upon general statistical information, policy makers should investigate whether discrimination is occurring.

6.7. Poor relations between Roma and social workers

Many social workers regard the Roma with suspicion and sometimes fear. Some welfare officials assert that a number of Romani applicants lie about their income, savings, and real estate.[277] Many expressed hostility toward the Roma as a group. The author heard variations of several standard remarks in almost every interview, from those with office workers to those with the directors of regional Social Work Centers. "The country is too poor to afford continuing to pay for Roma," some said. "Bulgaria should support only children, disabled, and elderly, not all lazy adults," said others. "Discrimination in employment does not exist. Only individuals who do not want to work remain unemployed for years," a third group said. Other comments included: "Bulgaria should stop distributing money to the socially weak, permitting them to go home and watch TV all day" and "Roma do not need to be informed of their right to benefits, because they know too well how to take advantage of our social welfare system."

Most of those employed by social centers, and, to an even greater degree, the overwhelming majority of the centers' directors, have not received formal training as social workers. Their educational backgrounds have been in engineering, economics, or other non–social welfare subjects.[278] Only recently have centers started hiring young people with specialized university training.

For their part, many Roma regard most social workers with hostility. In general, the Romani community sees the absence of social workers of Romani background as one of the main problems of the welfare system. Romani NGOs claim that social workers have discriminatory attitudes, lack an understanding of Romani culture, and exercise discretionary power poorly when granting or refusing various social welfare benefits.[279] "Because of the fact that welfare officials are empowered to decide in which categories to classify applicants and, especially, who is entitled to occasional aid, their decisions are subject to constant protests and anger in the community," the World Bank noted recently.[280] Many Roma also state that they do not understand how to fill out the social welfare applications,[281] and that the social workers do not provide them with needed assistance.[282]

This mutual distrust permeates the relationships among most social workers and their Romani clients. It is not difficult to see how direct and indirect discriminatory treatment can arise from these attitudes and interactions. Nonetheless, when claims of discrimination are made, it is important that they are investigated thoroughly and impartially so that no official is wrongly punished or remains unpunished.

7. Existing Legal and Extra-legal Remedies

Roma and non-Roma do not have effective avenues for challenging determinations regarding receipt or level of social support. While an appeals process exists, the ultimate arbiter of the appeal may be the party that made the contested decision.

Applicants for assistance may appeal decisions of the head of the municipal Social Work Centers to the regional center. In turn, they may challenge the regional center's decision in court under the administrative procedure rules.[283]

The heads of local Social Work Centers (SWCs) make all decisions concerning social assistance. Although SWCs implement the policies of the Ministry of Labor and Social Policy, in practice the minister does not have control over the legality of the decisions made by the Social Work Centers.

The confusion governing the complaint mechanism leads to situations in which appeals are decided by the same authority that issued the contested act.[284] An ILO study describes the process in the following terms:

"Another problem with the decentralized system, or more precisely with its current legislative provisions, is the lack of an appropriate administrative procedure for appeals against decisions made by municipal social welfare centers. In the event of refusal, citizens usually address their appeals to the Ministry of Labor and Social Policy. However, although the minister is theoretically in a position to make a ruling, he is not able, in practice, to resolve an appeal because he does not have a higher administrative position than the head of the municipal welfare center. Appeals are therefore submitted to the mayor of a municipality even though the local administration does not have officials who are competent to rule on the cases in dispute. The administrative procedure simply results in the return of an appeal to the head of the welfare center—the center which made the original decision which prompted the appeal!"[285]

The Bulgarian law does not provide for legal aid in proceedings concerning social benefits. Judicial review is legally possible, but is not affordable for the poor.

Macedonia

1. The State's Obligations under International, Constitutional, and National Law

Macedonia is a party to all major human rights instruments, including the International Covenant on Civil and Political Rights (ICCPR),[286] the International Covenant on Economic, Social and Cultural Rights (ICESCR),[287] the International Convention on the Elimination of Racial Discrimination (ICERD) (recognizing under Article 14 the Committee's competence to consider group and individual complaints),[288] the Convention on the Elimination of All Forms of Discrimination against Women (CEDAW),[289] and the Convention on the Rights of the Child (CRC).[290] At the European level, Macedonia has ratified the European Convention for the Protection of Human Rights and Fundamental Freedoms (ECHR)[291] and the Framework Convention for the Protection of National Minorities.[292] The country has signed but not yet ratified the European Social Charter.[293]

The Macedonian Constitution states that lawfully ratified international treaties are part of domestic law.[294] The Constitution also establishes the principle of citizens' equality before the law.[295] The state has the obligation to organize social security schemes for its citizens and to ensure social protection in accordance with principles of social justice.[296] The right to social assistance for the disabled and citizens unable to work is guaranteed.[297]

2. Poverty and Unemployment in Macedonia

According to the 1994 census, the former Yugoslav Republic of Macedonia has 2.1 million inhabitants. The country has a large Albanian community (23 percent), as well as Turkish (4 percent), Romani (2.3 percent), Serbian (2 percent) and Vlach (0.4 percent) communities. Romani leaders claim that the country has significantly more Roma than the 47,400 persons who identified themselves as Roma for the census.[298]

In 1996, 20 percent of the country's population lived under the poverty line.[299] More than 32 percent of the labor force was unemployed. Out of this number, 44.7 percent were women and 80 percent were long-term unemployed.[300] In the same period, 80 percent of Roma were unemployed.[301] A UNICEF study revealed that 97.7 percent of Romani women were unemployed.[302]

3. National Strategies for Romani Integration and Social Support

The government of Macedonia does not have a specific strategy for Romani integration. The official body responsible for policy in the field of minorities is the Council for Inter-Ethnic Relations, a consultative body under parliamentary control. The Council consists of two Roma, two Slavic Macedonians, two ethnic Albanians, two Turks, two Vlachs, and two Serbs. The president is Macedonian. The Council does not have support staff or an office; members do not receive compensation. The budget is limited to expenses incurred in holding meetings.[303]

In the period 1992 to 1995, the European Community Humanitarian Office (ECHO) provided emergency aid to Macedonia in the form of food, primary health care, water, sanitation, education, and fuel oil.[304] Later, when Macedonia became eligible for traditional PHARE programs, it received financial support for "NGO capacity-building within the Romani community"—to provide information on social rights, to provide training in the legal protection of these rights, and to establish a Social Rights Information Center in Skopje.[305] The PHARE Lien Program supported a "Social and economic integration of marginalized Roma" project, aimed at improving conditions for the Roma in health, hygiene, and family planning through the development of employment opportunities.[306]

4. Social Protection Programs

The Macedonian social protection system includes temporary and permanent social assistance, means-tested child allowances for employed parents, and maternity benefits for previously employed mothers. It also includes many types of pensions, sickness benefits, and in-kind benefits for the elderly and the disabled.

4.1. Social assistance for low-income persons and families

The government provides six means-tested forms of cash transfer for low-income persons or families, including support for persons incapable of providing for themselves; one-time emergency support; salary compensation for part-time work for taking care of disabled children; and housing support. The most relevant for the long-term unemployed who are very poor are benefits for uninsured persons, called temporary support for those capable of working and permanent support for those incapable of working.

The 1998 Law on Social Assistance and government decision 23-715/1 from 16 March 1998 regulate the system. International lending organizations consider the social assistance system well targeted.[307] However, European groups have stated that the social protection system does not provide an adequate mechanism for protection against discrimination. The European Commission against Racism and Intolerance (ECRI) has recommended to the government to adopt specific antidiscrimination legislation in the social protection area.[308]

4.1.1. Temporary social support: Benefits for uninsured persons able to work

In 1999, the government provided social support only to persons and families whose income was less than 57 percent of the poverty line of 3,000 denars (U.S. $55.00) per month. In that year, the minimum basic income (MBI) was 1,700 denars per month for a person living alone, 2,200 denars per month for two-member families, 2,800 denars per month for three-member families; 3,600 denars per month for four-member families, and 4,200 denars per month for families with five or more members. The amount of social support is the difference between the real income and the established MBI.

Although the exact number of Roma who receive this type of social support could not be determined, it is clear that thousands benefit from this program. In 1999, 2,159 families qualified for temporary support in Shuto Orizari alone.[309]

4.1.2. Permanent social support: Benefits for uninsured persons incapable of work

The Macedonian government provides support to disabled adults, pregnant women,[310] single parents with children up to three years old, children up to age fifteen (or twenty-six if enrolled in higher education), and persons over the age of sixty-five. The benefit is based on average monthly net earnings over the last three months and the number of persons in the household. For example, in 1998, benefits were 1,900 denars for one-person households, 2,660 denars for two-person households, 3,420 denars for three-person households, and 3,800 denars for households with four or more persons.[311]

Surprisingly, relatively few Roma receive permanent social support. In Shuto Orizari, Skopje's largest Romani neighborhood, with a population, by official estimates, of more than 17,000,[312] only 121 persons receive permanent support; thirty-three of them are single mothers with children under three.[313]

4.2. Family allowances

The Constitution obliges the state to provide care and protection for the family without discrimination.[314] Two of the social assistance programs for protecting the welfare of the family are child allowances and maternity benefits.

4.2.1. Child allowances

The state provides means-tested child allowances for families with at least one employed member.[315] Eligibility is related to the average monthly net salary for the last three months.[316] The benefit is several hundred denars per month per child and is restricted to three children per family.[317] The program does not target poor children but children of employed parents.

4.2.2. Maternity benefits

Maternity benefits depend on the pregnant woman's employment status. The Health Insurance Fund pays employed mothers 100 percent of their earnings for nine months.[318] In contrast, unemployed mothers are only eligible for approximately 33 percent of their average monthly net earnings in the last three months. Unemployed mothers receive support for only one month before giving birth under the "support for the very poor" plan.[319]

5. Impact on the Roma of Eligibility Requirements and Recipient Responsibilities

Persons who receive social support must fit certain eligibility criteria and comply with additional responsibilities that government officials impose on them. While the rules and regulations set clear standards in some areas, administrators have a great deal of discretion in applying the directives in others.

As noted in previous sections of this report, some eligibility requirements for social protection have a disparate impact on the Roma. If there is evidence of disparate impact, government officials have the burden of showing that those policies are reasonable and objective and pursue a legitimate aim. More research should be conducted to gather comprehensive data and document illegitimate race-based discrimination. Direct discrimination by officials against Roma applying for social services is, of course, unjustifiable, indefensible—and illegal.

5.1. Means test

Applicants for social assistance must meet a minimum income test. As described above, social support is provided only to persons and families whose income is less than an established percentage of the poverty line, with a sliding scale dependent on family size.

Applicants are expected to make a truthful declaration about their household income. If the social worker who handles the case thinks that the applicant's declaration is untruthful, he or she may propose—and the director of the social center may decide—to cut the social support. The person concerned must return the overpayment and may not apply for a period of two years even if her/his situation deteriorates during this period.[320] Persons may appeal the administrative decision; however, the state is not required to pay benefits until the challenge is successful. An adverse decision can create enormous difficulties for those families that truly do not have any other source of income.[321]

Assumptions by social workers that Roma attempt to hide income and lack of understanding by those workers about Romani traditions can lead to inappropriate denial of benefits. In Shuto Orizari, Skopje, a Macedonian social worker cut the social assistance benefits of a Romani family when the family refused to admit the social worker inside the house, because she had refused to remove her shoes before entering. The social worker interpreted the denial of entry as an attempt to hide signs of additional income, and, based on this assumption, she recommended cancellation of the family's social support. The family sought the assistance of a social worker of Romani origin who was able to clarify the situation, by explaining to his colleague the importance of the traditional gesture of removing shoes before entering a home.[322] Poor application of the means test can have devastating consequences for families not as lucky as this one.

A number of respondents to a World Bank survey indicated that they "felt criteria for receiving or being denied assistance were arbitrary."[323] The same report describes a case in which a social worker cut off social assistance to a family because he found a new vehicle at the beneficiaries' home. During the appeals process, the claimant was able to prove that the vehicle was his brother's property, and the state restored the family's benefits.

The means test does not discriminate against Roma on its face, nor should its provisions discriminate against the Roma in practice. Advocates should investigate specific cases of direct discrimination and ensure that the state punishes the perpetrators. Researchers need to gather more information on general trends if they want to prove that Macedonian social work officials discriminate against Roma in a systematic manner.

5.2. Employment status

The child allowances and maternity benefits programs differentiate among persons based on employment status. The child allowances program is available to families with at least one employed member, and the maternity benefits program pays substantially more money to previously employed mothers.

This scheme adversely affects all unemployed families, Romani or non-Romani, which comprise one-third of the population of the country. It is more likely that Romani parents, who suffer the highest unemployment level in the country, are both unemployed. In fact, recent statistics show that the percentage of unemployed Romani women—97.7 percent[324]—is almost three times higher than the national unemployment rate of 36 percent for all women in Macedonia.[325]

When a prima facie case of discrimination appears to exist, as in this instance, the government must justify its discriminatory policies. It is difficult to think of legitimate, reasonable, or objective reasons why the government should treat employed and unemployed persons differently with regard to child allowances and maternity benefits, particularly since the policy has a disparate impact on the Roma. The government needs to change its policies in this regard so that it does not discriminate against the Roma.

5.3. Lack of identification documents

The Macedonian Constitution guarantees the right to social security to citizens only.[326] Macedonian law imposes strict requirements on those who seek to become citizens. They must have resided in the territory for ten years cumulatively,[327] have a permanent source of income, possess a place to live, and enjoy physical and mental health. They must also pay high administrative fees. The law effectively bars access to Macedonian citizenship and constitutional rights for a large number of Roma who live in Macedonia but are citizens of another former Yugoslav republic.[328] Minority groups and international observers have strongly criticized the law for its indirect discriminatory impact on Roma.[329]

The social support legislation requires applicants to have Macedonian citizenship. In single-parent families in which the parent does not have Macedonian citizenship, the parent and the children cannot receive social support. In two-parent families, the situation is more nuanced. If neither parent is a citizen, then they and their children cannot receive social benefits. If one parent is a Macedonian citizen, that parent and the children have access to benefits. The other parent receives benefits only if she or he has a valid residency permit.

Applicants for social support must also have valid documents indicating that they have complied with other particular legal requirements. For example, seekers of social support must register with the unemployment office, and prove indigence with a certificate from the tax office. They also must offer up a child's valid birth certificate in order to receive the child's benefits.

Lack of appropriate identification documents is a common problem. Social workers report that a month-long investigation in Shuto Orizari revealed that more than one hundred families had members who lacked valid identity cards or had one or more children without birth certificates.[330]

Children born in foreign countries often have problems acquiring the necessary documents. If foreign authorities did not issue the appropriate papers to a foreign-born Romani child, then the parents need specialized assistance from a social worker or lawyer to obtain a Macedonian birth certificate. Many Roma who came back from Germany reported to the European Roma Rights Center that after their return to Macedonia they had to pay exorbitant bribes to officials in various municipal offices to register their children.[331]

The lack of birth certificates also affects children born in Macedonia. The United Nations' Committee on the Rights of the Child noted with concern that "in spite of relevant legislation and an increasing number of births in hospitals, there are still children . . . who are not registered at birth and . . . a large proportion of unregistered births are among Romani children."[332] Recalling that official birth registration is a fundamental first step toward securing the rights of a child to a name and nationality, and to gaining access to social assistance, health, education, and other services, the Committee urged the Macedonian authorities "to make every effort to enforce birth registration requirements and to facilitate the registration process with regard to the children of parents, or other responsible persons, who may have particular difficulties in providing all available documentation."[333]

The dearth of appropriate identification documents appears to have a significant impact on members of the Romani community. Not having such documents seriously affects a person's ability to receive social benefits and impinges on other rights by placing a person's freedom in danger, jeopardizing his or her participation in community life, and barring access to employment and education.

6. Additional Barriers to Social Protection

6.1. Late payments

Romani NGOs allege that late payments of temporary support, permanent social support, and other forms of cash transfer are frequent, especially in small cities and rural Macedonia.[334] Their complaints are consistent with the World Bank findings that "benefit payments . . . are not adequately budgeted, resulting in delays of payment that compromise the poverty alleviation aspect of both programs."[335]

Delays in payments can have significant effects on Romani families. "We have to wait for two or three months without a dime and nobody is responsible for the delay," a Romani woman said. "But if we find work for three days, just enough to buy bread, the social workers cut our benefits."[336] Monitoring programs aimed at documenting the frequency, length, and social costs of these delays do not exist in Macedonia; consequently, in this area NGOs cannot provide more than anecdotal evidence.

Governments may not discriminate directly or indirectly because of race in the allocation of social benefits, even if the government has limited resources. Romani and non-Romani organizations need to gather more information in order to disprove local government claims of insufficient funds and lack of bias.

6.2. Time limits on benefits

Starting in 1998, the government introduced a system of work incentives by reducing payments after the first two years and limiting the duration of social assistance to four years. The level of social support is 100 percent during the first two years, 70 percent in the third year, and only 50 percent in the fourth. The government pays nothing for the next two years. Even if a person is so poor that he or she would qualify for social support for a fifth or a sixth year, the government pays him or her nothing. After two years without benefits, an eligible person can reapply, and a new four-year cycle of social support begins.[337] The government considered and rejected other forms of work incentives because of the complexity of calculating benefits.[338]

The existing system will have a clearly disparate impact on the Romani community, in which long-term unemployment reaches epidemic proportions. If the government applies the policy consistently, it will eliminate virtually all Romani families currently receiving social support from the rolls by 2002. They will fall into the most abject poverty.

The government may claim that the restriction is reasonable and objective, and for a legitimate purpose under international law. The government may say that such a policy forces recipients to find jobs and become productive and employed members of society. It may claim that the program encourages the unemployed to learn new skills so that they can find new paid positions.

Gathering data that disputes such claims would prove worthwhile. For example, documenting allegations of racial discrimination in employment,[339] proving that employers do not hire Roma because they are Roma, would show that it is difficult for Roma to find jobs, regardless of their motivation or skills. Demonstrating that the Roma already look for jobs in a serious manner would suggest that motivation is not the problem and that this program is unlikely to bring about the desired results yet it will have a significant disparate impact on the Roma.

6.3. Family size discrimination

For social support, the Macedonian government pays an additional amount for each member of the household, up to five members (e.g. two parents, three children). It pays an equal amount to a household of five as to a household of seven or eight.

This policy has a disparate impact on Roma, who usually live in households larger than five.[340] The program penalizes large families by requiring them to spread a fixed amount of social support over a greater number of persons. While it may be true that the cost of each additional child is marginally less than the one that preceded him or her, each additional child does cost more money.

The situation gets worse as the children grow and form their own families. According to the law, the new family is entitled to benefits only if they have a separate place to live,[341] which must include one room and eventually a kitchen and bath. Only then will the new family be considered a new household. Since young couples seldom have a separate place to live, they stay with their parents, with the girl usually moving into her husband's parents' house. The regulations characterize her as an additional member of the family, and she shares in their 4,200 denars per month. This situation continues until the young husband and wife are able to have their own house, which, for those living in severe poverty, might take very long or never happen.

If the family has space in the courtyard, however, and some bricks, wood, or even a carton, the parents will add an extra "room" for the newlyweds with space for a kitchen. The social worker is the only one who has the power to decide whether this arrangement meets the requirements for a new household. In the overwhelming majority of cases, social workers reportedly reject these requests as "false household claims," because they simply do not understand or do not want to take into consideration Romani overcrowding issues.[342] Authorities describe the phenomena as an attempt to obtain more benefits by "splitting" large families and falsely claiming that two separate households exist.[343]

These programs have a disparate impact on Macedonian Roma, who almost always have larger families and larger households than ethnic Macedonians. The government may claim that the purpose of such a policy is to discourage persons from having large families or from living in large households. It is doubtful whether such an objective is legitimate under international covenants—the policy obviously interferes with the private life of the family.

The United Nations' Committee on the Rights of the Child has described this policy as discriminatory. "The Committee is concerned that under the current arrangements with regard to the 'three child policy,' children from families with more than three children are at a disadvantage with regard to access to social service, financial and other assistance."[344] In light of Article 2 of the Convention on the Rights of the Child, the Committee recommended that the Republic of Macedonia "find alternative means to implement the three child policy, other than excluding the fourth child from social service benefits."[345]

The three-child policy discriminates against Roma and other ethnic groups that have more than three children on average. Macedonia must change its policies so that they do not violate international, regional, and domestic nondiscrimination standards.

7. Existing Legal and Extra-legal Remedies

Written refusals of social assistance explain that rejected applicants can appeal the decision to the Ministry of Labor. Claimants must file appeals within fifteen days. Romani groups report that the appeals procedure is lengthy, and families with no other source of income must often wait for months for an answer from the authorities. Applicants may appeal the ministerial decisions to the administrative court. However, without free legal assistance, this option is merely theoretical for the majority of Romani appellants, who have little education and live below the poverty line. Romani NGOs emphasize the urgent need for an effective legal aid system for civil cases, the creation of an independent complaint office, and introduction of expedited procedures for social support–related appeals.[346]

"Yesterday my wife had an accident and broke her ribs. The local hospital refused to admit her because she was not sent by a family doctor. They told us to go to Focsani [26 kilometers away]. We had no money for the bus so we started walking. After two kilometers she fainted because of the pain. I carried her in my arms the rest of the way."

ROMANI MAN IN MARASESTI, ROMANIA

Denial of Health Care

This section examines the ability of Roma to access adequate health care in Romania, Bulgaria, and Macedonia. It identifies policies and practices that discriminate against Roma directly or indirectly, and reports on cases in which public officials and health care personnel have treated Roma unfairly.

International law recognizes the "right to health." The Universal Declaration of Human Rights provides for the right of all to an adequate standard of living, including the right to adequate medical care.[1] The International Covenant on Economic, Social and Cultural Rights (ICESCR) establishes the "right of everyone to the enjoyment of the highest attainable standard of physical and mental health."[2] The Convention on the Rights of the Child (CRC) contains a similar provision and goes further in establishing a child's right to health care services and providing a nonexclusive list of measures states should take to ensure this right.[3] The Preamble of the World Health Organization Constitution calls the enjoyment of the highest attainable standards of health "one of the fundamental rights of every human being."

Antidiscrimination clauses are always present, integrated in the text of the relevant articles, described in the general comments of the committees that oversee reporting under the conventions, or provided by separate human rights instruments. The International Convention on the Elimination of All Forms of Racial Discrimination (ICERD) prohibits racial discrimination in "the enjoyment of the right to public health, medical care,"[4] while the Convention on the Elimination of All Forms of Discrimination Against Women (CEDAW) requires elimination of discrimination in "the right . . . to access to health care services, including those relating to family planning."[5] The Committee on Economic, Social and Cultural Rights has stated that "health facilities, goods and services must be accessible to all, especially the most vulnerable or marginalized sections of the population, in law and fact, without discrimination on any of the prohibited grounds."[6] The Revised European Social Charter also affirms freedom from discrimination.[7]

The constitutions of the three countries examined in this report establish universal health insurance as an entitlement for all their citizens. The Romanian Constitution recognizes the right of citizens to the protection of health and establishes the obligation of the state to ensure health and public hygiene.[8] The Bulgarian Constitution protects its citizens' "right to medical insurance guaranteeing them affordable medical care and the right to free medical care in accordance with conditions and procedures established by law."[9] The Macedonian Constitution guarantees the right to health care to all Macedonian citizens and provides for the citizens' right and duty to protect and promote their own health and the health of others.[10] These countries' constitutions also contain general antidiscrimination language.[11]

To assess the extent to which governments or private persons discriminate against Romani patients and interfere with their ability to obtain adequate medical care, the report:

- reviews the general status of Romani health in a particular country;
- highlights the relative cost of medical care and discusses health insurance schemes;
- describes stereotypical images of Romani patients in the media;
- identifies cases of direct discrimination against Romani patients during their treatment (or lack thereof) by doctors and other medical personnel;
- discusses how legal provisions related to the provision of health insurance and social support decrease the ability of Roma to receive the health care they need;
- outlines other barriers to Romani access to health care, such as lack of information and nonpayment of benefits;
- shows problems that Roma have in receiving emergency care;
- and discusses the general failure of the state to provide appropriate staffing and equipment and to locate facilities in Romani neighborhoods.

Romania

1. The State's Obligations under International, Constitutional, and National Law

Romania is a state party to the International Covenant on Civil and Political Rights (ICCPR), the International Covenant on Economic, Social and Cultural Rights (ICESCR), the Convention on the Rights of the Child (CRC), the Convention on the Elimination of All Forms of Racial Discrimination (ICERD), and the Revised European Social Charter. It has signed, but not ratified, the Convention on Human Rights and Biomedicine, which requires member states to ensure "equitable access to health care of appropriate quality."[12]

The Romanian Constitution recognizes a citizen's right to the protection of health and establishes the obligation of the state to ensure health and public hygiene.[13] A recently introduced system of social health insurance ensures the population's access to medical care services.

Romania does not yet have any specific health policy for Roma. The Ministry of Health, together with the representative of the Working Group of Roma Associations (GLAR), has established the basic "Elements of a Strategy on Improving the Health in Romani Communities."[14] Public Health District Offices have been asked to provide information related to the health situation of Romani communities in their territories but, for the time being, the data received is rather incomplete.[15] Through the Romani PHARE program, the Romanian government's Department for the Protection of National Minorities or DPMN (Departamentul Pentru Minoritati Nationale), in cooperation with experts on the Roma, MEDE European Consultancy Netherlands, and Minority Rights Group UK, is preparing a sectoral strategy that includes a health component. GLAR has recommended improved implementation of health care services for Roma through programs that expand diagnosis, prevention, and treatment efforts, provide better access to family doctors and health insurance, increase vaccination rates, enable more affordable medicine, train health mediators, and expand health education efforts.[16]

2. General Status of Romani Health in Romania

The health status of an individual Romani person depends, among other things, on his or her living conditions, lifestyle, socioeconomic status, and level of education. There are significant regional and group differences. However, nationally, demographers agree that Romani life expectancy is significantly lower than that of the majority population, and infant mortality is higher than in the population at large. Roma have one of the highest fertility rates in the region.[17]

Romani children and adults suffer from a wide range of health problems. Romani children have a higher rate of vitamin deficiencies, malnutrition, anemia, dystrophy, and rickets than their non-Romani peers.[18] Lack of safe drinking water, hygiene, and substandard living conditions often result in parasitoses and other infectious digestive diseases.[19] The Public Health District Office of Mures notes that the Romani community has the highest rate of TB, AIDS, hepatitis, and neuropsychological disorders of the various ethnic communities in the country.[20] The Public Health District Office of Ialomita has also identified significant numbers of cases of TB and AIDS.[21] The rate of infection is alarming and continues to grow.

Romania has the most AIDS-infected children in Europe; most of the approximately 8,700 children were infected through the use of unsterilized needles.[22] There are places in Romania where entire Romani communities are dramatically affected, yet medical and social assistance authorities fail to provide needed services to these striken areas. In Mizil, a small southern Romanian city, local doctors, speaking to television reporters, said that in the local Romani community they had thirty confirmed cases of HIV, and they believed that over 100, or more than half of the Romani children who lived in the Romani neighborhood, were HIV positive. Doctors recommend and perform HIV tests only when the symptoms are sufficiently clear to justify the expenditure. In one Romani family, father, mother, and child are all infected. They live on less than $14 a month. The neighbors avoid them. Community members do not allow the children to draw water from the common well or to play with the other children.[23]

3. Cost of Health Insurance and Medical Care

In 1998, Romania changed the health care system's financing from one based on taxes to a self-financing one based on contributions. The World Bank has supported this financial restructuring.[24] The 1997 Law on Social Health Insurance governs the new system based on the principle that all citizens, regardless of their income, have the right to adequate protection of health. [25]

The law seeks complete coverage of the population. The state's health insurance scheme is compulsory for all Romanian citizens who reside in the country, and almost all legal residents.[26] There are no provisions for refugees or asylum seekers. The law includes a nondiscrimination clause: "Insured persons and their family members have the right to receive medical care in a nondiscriminatory manner."[27]

The law requires employers to contribute 7 percent of wages to health insurance.[28] The law also requires self-employed persons to contribute 7 percent of their earnings to health insurance.[29] The state covers contributions for conscripts, employees during certain types of paid leave, prisoners, and persons in police custody awaiting trial.[30] Members of families benefiting from social support[31] are insured without paying a contribution as long as they receive social support.[32] This is the key provision that provides the very poor with access to health insurance. It is important to note that access to social support is the condition sine qua non for access to noncontributory health insurance.

Insured persons must pay a contribution to the health insurance fund.[33] The law defines several categories of people who are exempt from this payment.[34] Theoretically, health insurance is universal, but in practice, it is unlikely that the coverage will ever reach 100 percent. A percentage of the self-employed and nontaxpaying public, Roma and non-Roma alike, might choose, or their indigence might oblige them, not to contribute.

The key question is how many people lack access to health care because either they are not eligible for noncontributory health insurance or they do not have the money to pay the contribution. Furthermore, it is important to know whether the application of these neutral provisions has a disparate impact on Romani access to medical services.

It is difficult to quantify the number of Roma who lack access to noncontributory health insurance. There is a lack of raw data and uncertainty about the assumptions that would generate an estimate. All assumptions are highly controversial, from the number of Roma in Romania and the level of their poverty to the percentage of Romani beneficiaries of social support out of the total number of eligible persons.

However, qualitative evaluations are possible. Two different sets of factors concur to impede indigent Roma from exercising their health care rights. One set concerns access to social support, such as eligibility requirements, administrative practices, exclusion errors, discriminatory denials of benefits, abuses, and lack of information. The other set relates to problems that arise in the provision of health care services, such as doctors' reluctance to accept Romani patients, racial prejudices, hostility, lack of health personnel and facilities, and lack of interest on the part of patients.

4. Racial Prejudices toward Roma Who Receive Health Care

Romani patients are depicted in the media as dirty individuals who make noise, smoke and spit in hospital halls, and do not have the patience to wait.[35] They bring the entire family to the hospital, disturbing the peace of doctors and other patients.[36] They do not pay health insurance and take advantage of the "generosity" of the system at the expense of other Romanians. Occasionally they insult, threaten or even physically attack doctors,[37] demand the right to enter operating rooms, steal old ladies' handbags, and vandalize clinics.[38] They are the carriers of contagious diseases that threaten the health of the nation.

The image created by the press may influence doctors and their attitudes toward Romani patients. For example, a 1998 UNICEF study notes that Roma generally suffer from a socially degraded image and racial prejudice, particularly among the country's elite. This racial prejudice is "often insidiously manifested in the health care services and is not recognized as such,"[39] and health care institutions and medical staff practice a "discriminatory sociology" in the sense that they "do not welcome Roma."[40] Health professionals told UNICEF researchers that Roma are "difficult patients" with a "serious lack of intellectual understanding about prophylaxis, . . . medical logic and health in general," who "request too much medicine, visit the dispensaries too frequently, yet do not use the medication, refuse the vaccines, and are afraid of needles."[41] When questioned about the existence of prejudices and discrimination in the health care system, doctors answered by accusing Roma of not being users of health care in a "disciplined, polite, submissive, and cooperative way, something that is expected by health care personnel of . . . patients."[42] Racial prejudice also affects children's health. A survey of ten Romanian localities by Romani CRISS revealed that the majority of health personnel have negative attitudes and behavior toward Romani child patients.[43]

5. Direct Discrimination

5.1. Family doctors' refusal to accept Romani patients on their rosters

The family doctor is at the center of the health care system. He is the first one to be visited; he provides primary health care and refers the patient to specialists. Anyone who can afford it may, of course, choose to consult a different doctor, go directly to a specialist, or ask for more sophisticated tests; in these cases the insurance does not pay the costs. Indigents have no choice; their access to health care services depends directly on the existence of a family doctor willing to accept them on his roster of patients.

Procedurally, registering for a family doctor seems simple. All the client has to do is visit the doctor, ask to be registered, and present an insurance card. The patient's domicile is not relevant. Although it is recommended to have the family doctor as close as possible to one's home, everyone is free to choose a doctor anywhere, even in another city. Transportation is paid by the patient.

Theoretically, doctors have only limited rights to refuse to enroll a patient. Although the law on social health insurance does not explicitly address this issue, the professional code of ethics obliges doctors to attend to all patients equally, regardless of nationality, religion, or the doctor's personal feelings about a patient.[44] However, it also provides that "a doctor may refuse assistance for personal and professional reasons."[45] Assistance may be refused only at the very beginning. A doctor cannot unilaterally interrupt a treatment initiated by him. The doctor who refuses to attend to a patient has an obligation to make sure that the patient has access to other forms of medical care. "Personal reasons" cannot be based on prejudice or racism; physicians are under oath not to allow nationality, race, religion, party or social status influence the manner in which they perform their duties toward patients.[46] One of the "personal reasons" might be the doctor's obligation to provide quality health services by enrolling a limited number of patients, no more than he can properly take care of. The law stipulates that the family doctor may conclude a contract with the insurance company if he has a minimum of 1,500 patients and a maximum of 2,000. Under certain conditions, doctors are allowed—but not required—to have more than 2,000 patients. If a doctor does not want to receive a patient, it is sufficient for the doctor to tell the patient that there are no more places available on the patient roster. The refusal is verbal and needs no further justification.

Roma have significant difficulty securing positions on doctor's rosters. The 1998 UNICEF study was the first to document this well-known problem.[47] Two years later, in February 2000, a doctor from Bucharest declared to the press: "I know many doctors who refuse to enroll Gypsies, students, and indigents. They tell them that the lists are closed, that there are no places anymore. . . . If somebody well-off, such as the owner of a firm, wants to register, the lists are open." The Romanian Ministry of Health reports, on the basis of information received from the Public Health District Offices, that 30 percent of Romanian Roma—roughly more than half a million people—are not registered with a family doctor, because they do not have identity documents, doctors are reluctant to receive Romani patients, and some Romani patients are not interested in registering.[48]

The overwhelming majority of Roma interviewed stated that they want to register but doctors have rejected them. With no money to pay for private consultations and with no family doctor to refer them for treatment, the system is closed to them. They are not accepted by hospitals, cannot undergo medical tests, and cannot see a specialist. They are able to obtain emergency care only. These are not isolated cases; entire communities, especially in small cities or small rural settlements, are affected. As Romani CRISS reported to the UN Committee for the Elimination of Racial Discrimination, Romani health problems arise from low income and difficulties in accessing health care through health insurance schemes.[49]

Romani CRISS[50] reports that a doctor from Stefanesti—a commune situated near the border with the Republic of Moldova where 182 Romani families live—does not accept Roma on his list because he "prefers ideal patients, which Roma are not."[51] Ramses Foundation, Dej, states, "The majority of the Romani people in the district do not have a family doctor because at first they did not know what they have to do. Afterwards, when they understood that they have to ask a doctor to accept them, they were told that there are no more places on the lists for them."[52]

"In Marasesti there is no hope for us," said one Romani man. "Yesterday my wife had an accident and broke her ribs. The local hospital refused to admit her because she was not sent by a family doctor. They told us to go to Focsani [the nearest city, situated twenty-six kilometers from Marasesti]. We had no money for the bus, so we started walking. After two kilometers she fainted because of the pain. I carried her in my arms the rest of the way. In Focsani there is a good doctor. She always receives us and does not ask for money. We all go to her because nobody else looks at us."[53]

Nicolae Ficuta, the leader of the local branch of the Roma Party in Buhusi (which is in the Moldova region of Romania), reports that local doctors refused to enroll Roma on their patient rosters. V.M., a twenty-eight-year-old Romani mother of three, with a serious heart disease, told the author that she expressly asked three local doctors and all of them refused her. When she had a heart problem in 1999, she could not see a cardiologist because she had no family doctor to refer her to a specialist. She went directly to the hospital, but the medical staff of Buhusi Municipal Hospital refused to admit her, claiming that it was not an emergency case. Her relatives gave her sugar[54] and took her home without a doctor seeing her. When they complained and protested, one of the nurses allegedly yelled at them: "To hell with you Gypsies, we would be glad to see all of you dead."[55]

Many people interviewed by the author alleged denial of treatment on racial grounds. For example, indigent Roma from Geoagiu (Transylvania) complained that one local doctor refuses to examine Romani patients even if they have money to pay the fee. They are not even allowed to enter the dispensary when she is there. Once, when they tried to do so, she yelled: "Get out, Gypsies, you did not buy a doctor!" From that moment on nobody has dared to go to the clinic when she is on duty.[56] The inhabitants claim that nobody was ever interested in the health of these 650 people, not even public health authorities or those in charge of the protection of children.[57] "One of the village's doctors told me directly, 'I do not examine Gypsies,'" said Nicolae Bologa, a local Romani leader.[58]

Refusals by family doctors to accept Romani clients have a debilitating effect on Romani access to the health care system. Without a family doctor to refer them for treatment and no money to pay for nonsubsidized treatment, they cannot undergo necessary medical tests and cannot see a specialist. At best, they obtain emergency care only. These are not isolated cases; entire communities, especially in small cities or small rural settlements, are affected.

It is illegal for doctors to discriminate against patients based on their race. Instances in which doctors make derogatory comments about Roma and refuse to take them on as patients are evidence of discrimination. Also, more data is needed about doctors who work in or near Romani communities but who do not have any Romani patients. Advocates for the Roma should raise these matters with the authorities and should pursue them in court, if unable to resolve the issue through other means.

5.2. Refusal of health care institutions to treat Romani patients

In the autumn of 1999, health authorities from Iasi decided that public hospitals would not receive indigent Roma. The newspaper *Ziua* reported, on 7 September 1999, that directors of Iasi hospitals made this decision because "more and more Gypsies are hospitalized, especially with contagious diseases," "treatment costs are very high," and "Gypsies do not contribute to the health insurance fund."[59] Adrian Butuca, the president of the local Social and Health Insurance House, declared to the press: "The simplest way to get rid of them is to order hospital security to prohibit the entry of Gypsies."[60]

On 20 September 1999, in a letter to the DPMN, Liga PRO EUROPA[61] informed the department that preventing Roma access to hospitals is a discriminatory act and urged the DPMN, together with the Ministry of Health, to initiate an investigation of Iasi hospitals.[62] According to Dan Oprescu, head of the National Office for Roma within the DPMN, the investigation confirmed the allegations of the press. He addressed the matter in a meeting with the minister, who agreed with the results of the investigation and referred the case to the legal section of the DPMN for appropriate action.[63]

In October 1999, Iulius Rostas, a Romani employee of DPMN, informed PRO EUROPA that the department knows that the Social and Health Insurance House has ordered hospital guardians to prohibit the entry of Romani patients. Rostas reportedly added that, if able to prove the existence of the order, the DPMN will initiate legal action against the perpetrators.[64] However, to the best of the author's knowledge, no further steps had been taken as of August 2000.

A.S., an eighteen-year-old Romani woman from Buhusi, told the author that she went to the hospital in 1999 to give birth to her first child. She had no money to pay the doctor or the nurse. When the pain started, the doctor was called, but, although he was in the hospital, he refused to see her. The nurse in charge simply disappeared. The only one who was ready to help A.S. was the hospital's cleaning woman, a Romani herself. The child was born with the cleaning lady's help. The nurse showed up when everything was over, took the baby, and said: "Here we have another criminal."[65]

It is illegal for hospitals and their personnel to discriminate against patients based on their race. Instances in which hospitals adopt policies or practices that treat Roma differently from non-Roma should be documented, raised with the authorities, and pursued in the courts if no action is taken.

5.3. Romani patients subjected to verbal abuse and degrading treatment

Romani interviewees allege that some of the doctors who attend to Romani patients treat them in a degrading manner. Romani women from Modruzeni (Marasesti) claim that one of the local doctors does not allow Romani patients into his examination room, even if they pay for his services. His staff allegedly keeps them in the hall, at his direction. He refuses to touch Romani children or adults.[66] Another doctor permits them to enter the examination room but, before examining them, washes newborn children with cold water in the basin where she washes her hands and forces the mothers to take cold showers. "She never does this with non-Roma. She is doing this just to humiliate us. She knows very well that we wash ourselves before going to a doctor," a Romani woman from Modruzeni reported.[67]

Fear of humiliation and the belief that medical staff will not help them contribute to the indefinite postponement or refusal of some Roma to seek medical assistance. On 18 September 1999, P.A., another Romani woman, gave birth to a baby girl without medical assistance on the floor of an apartment in Buhusi. "I did not go to the hospital because I am afraid of them. They yell at us. They tell me that I am dirty and I smell. Of course, I smelled, during the pregnancy I ate from the garbage containers, because I was so hungry all the time. My husband left me for another woman. I had two children, and I was pregnant with the third. The social worker refused my request for food pantry assistance. My neighbor helped me to deliver the baby. Yesterday the other neighbors collected 1,000 lei each [approximately 5 cents each] to help me pay 10,000 lei for my daughter's birth certificate. The child is healthy. She is now one month old. I have no milk for her. Last night I gave her polenta with salt."[68]

The government has an obligation to investigate and prosecute those persons who discriminate against others on the basis of their race. Advocates for the Roma should continue to document these types of incidents, bring them to the attention of the authorities, and pursue them in court if no action is taken.

6. Legal Provisions That Have a Disparate Impact on Roma

Romanian social support and health laws have different definitions of family, with ramifications as to which persons receive government support. For the purposes of social support, the law defines "family" as parents and children, regardless of the existence of a civil marriage or the civil status of the child.[69] Therefore, couples who live in a common household are eligible for social support. Under the health insurance law, however, only the "wife" or "husband" of an insured person has the right to noncontributory health insurance.[70] The use of the terms "wife" and "husband" clearly implies the existence of civil marriage.

It is arguable that this provision, which discriminates against persons on the basis of marital status, has a disparate impact on the Roma. A large segment of Romani couples live in common-law marriages. A much higher percentage of Roma have this type of relationship than do Romanians. The government must explain why this provision is reasonable and legitimate under international law. The fact that the government does not employ this distinction for other similar social protection benefits makes it difficult for the government to argue administrative necessity.

7. Other Barriers to Accessing Health Care

7.1. Lack of information

Public health authorities must provide information in a timely and adequate manner about indigent claimants' access to health insurance. A significant number of poor Romani families, particularly in rural areas and in small cities, have not been informed that beneficiaries of social support are also eligible for noncontributory health insurance. Although they meet all legal requirements, they avoid using medical services, except in emergency situations, because they believe that they must pay for everything.

If public health authorities have not informed the Roma and have told other non-Romani groups, then they have engaged in impermissible discrimination based on race. If public health authorities have not informed any groups, then they are derelict in their duties and should be punished.

7.2. Local authorities' refusal to issue social support confirmation

According to the law, every insured person must receive a health insurance card.[71] In order to receive it, family members who receive social support must prove that they are eligible for insurance by presenting a written confirmation issued by city hall. Romani CRISS maintains that many local authorities refuse to issue these confirmations to Roma, blocking their access to medical care. Without the confirmation, family doctors will not enroll indigent or unemployed individuals. [72]

Public health authorities who issue confirmation cards to non-Roma but not to Roma are engaging in impermissible discrimination based on race. If they fail to issue cards to everyone who is entitled, they are not performing their duties and should be disciplined. Since a higher percentage of Roma receive social support, then the refusal to issue cards generally would have a disparate impact on the Roma, and government officials need to justify their inaction. Advocates for the Roma should continue to document these types of incidents and should work to resolve them with government authorities.

7.3. Unlawful practices that lead to loss of noncontributory health insurance

It has been reported that in some localities the social assistance offices ask eligible beneficiaries of social assistance to choose between social support payments and food from the food pantry.[73] People choose the food because they know that the social support payments almost never arrive. Social workers ask them to give up their right to social support formally by withdrawing their application or not making it, which they do without knowing that, in fact, they are also giving up their right to health insurance. Romani leaders claim that, although unlawful, the practice exists in several cities in the regions of Cluj[74] and Bacau.[75]

Forcing any person qualified for two independent benefits to choose between them is illegal on its face. Forcing only one racial group to make that choice is also unlawful racial discrimination.

7.4. Discretionary power of social workers and the loss of noncontributory health insurance

Access to medical insurance without payment of a contribution exists only during the period when the person concerned receives social support. Roma repeatedly complain, however, that they are cut off from social support by social workers without justification.[76] This discretionary withdrawal of social support results in the immediate loss of noncontributory health insurance.[77] The law does not provide for any transition period of coverage.

Systematic monitoring is necessary to determine how widespread these practices are and whether social workers treat the Roma differently from other similarly situated persons. If social workers do, then they are engaging in inappropriate discrimination.

8. Access to Emergency Services

All insured persons have the right to emergency medical services.[78] Notwithstanding the Romanian authorities' efforts to improve emergency care,[79] the poor quality of services and a lack of personnel, ambulances, and equipment often hinders the right. A multitude of additional obstacles make it difficult for Romani patients to access emergency services: settlements situated in remote locations, lack of private or public phones, the absence of street names and public lighting, lack of transportation, and nearly impassable roads. Furthermore, nongovernmental organizations claim that racial prejudice influences the manner in which Romani emergency cases are handled, with Romani patients being refused assistance or being cared for with considerable delay as compared to non-Romani patients.

Romani complaints of direct discrimination fall into four types. First, it is alleged that operators from emergency centers refuse to send an ambulance when they assume, based on the name of the patient, the area where he or she lives, or linguistic particularities, that the patient is a Romani man or woman. Operators systematically underestimate the seriousness of Romani calls for help. Second, it is claimed that operators do not send ambulances under the pretext that there are no cars or medical teams available. Third, it is said that operators give priority to calls from non-Romani neighborhoods, causing unreasonable delays. Fourth, it is alleged that doctors and nurses avoid, postpone, or refuse to attend to patients from remote Romani communities, especially during the night. This results in unnecessary delays and health hazards. Roma from Geoagiu, for example, report that doctors, nurses, and ambulances never enter the neighborhood at night. "During the night no doctor comes to this neighborhood. It does not matter how often we call them," one interviewee said.[80]

If true and unjustifiable, such practices would constitute direct discrimination. The frequency and seriousness of the complaints indicates that in-depth research and systematic reform is necessary.

9. Location of Health Care Facilities

Romani villages or settlements are sometimes located many kilometers away from the communes and almost never have their own health care facilities. For every health-related need they must spend hours on the road and make significant efforts to reach the clinics. Many of these rural roads are unpaved or have not been repaired in years. When it rains, they are full of mud, and, during the winter, snow and ice hinder travel. Walking is almost impossible even for young, healthy people. Parents are obliged to carry sick children in their arms for kilometers. For example, the distance from Balta Arsa (Botosani district) to the first health center is eight kilometers.[81] Roma from Gulea (Suceava) have to walk four kilometers to the clinic in Dolhasca.[82] The same distance separates the 1,450-person Romani community from the health clinic in Calvini (Buzau).[83] There are reports about Romani women from Stefanesti who cannot travel outside their village for a gynecological examination or a pregnancy test because the price of a bus ticket exceeds their financial means.[84]

Notwithstanding that distant clinics and bad roads are frequent in Romania, and similar situations exist for Romanian or Hungarian villages, Romani representatives assert that the Romani villages are disproportionately affected. The main cause of this disparity is the discriminatory manner in which national and local authorities allocate funds for the construction of health facilities. However, apart from the obvious lack of clinics and medical facilities in many Romani villages, researchers need to gather specific evidence to support the discrimination claim.

Bulgaria

1. The State's Obligations under International, Constitutional, and National Law

Bulgaria is a state party to the International Covenant on Civil and Political Rights (ICCPR), the International Covenant on Economic, Social and Cultural Rights (ICESCR), the Convention on the Rights of the Child (CRC), the Convention on the Elimination of All Forms of Racial Discrimination (ICERD), and the Revised European Social Charter. The Bulgarian Constitution protects its citizens' "right to medical insurance guaranteeing them affordable medical care and the right to free medical care in accordance with conditions and procedures established by law."[85]

The Framework Program for Equal Integration of Roma in Bulgarian Society, proposed by NGOs and adopted by the government,[86] emphasizes the elimination of discrimination against Roma in the political, social, and cultural life of the country. Elimination of discriminatory practices in the health care system is part of the plan. The Framework Program argues that a general strategy of improving Romani health will require intensification of health education programs, improvement of Romani housing, and greater Romani involvement. As of September 2000, neither the government nor the NGOs had put forth a detailed health strategy for the improvement of Romani health.

2. General Status of Romani Health in Bulgaria

Little quantitative data is available on the health status of Roma in Bulgaria. According to a 1998 survey, 44 percent of Romani households reported having a chronically ill member, and 20 percent reported having two or more ill members.[87] The government acknowledges that unfavorable living conditions, inadequate nutrition, and unsanitary conditions are among the main factors for the Romani population's relatively worse state of health.[88]

Doctors working in Romani neighborhoods identify several areas of concern. They note that cardiovascular conditions and kidney, liver, gastric, and intestinal diseases are especially widespread among Roma.[89] Poverty and poor nutrition deeply affect Romani health. Tuberculosis, associated with poor living conditions, is also a serious concern. In one Romani neighborhood in Lom, forty of seventy children examined tested positive for TB.[90] The last reported cases of poliomyelitis in Bulgaria were in Romani communities.[91] In the region of Sliven, approximately ninety Romani children have contracted polio, and half were disabled by the disease. No child from the majority population was affected.[92] In the same area, a diphtheria outbreak occurred among Roma in 1993.[93]

The immunization rate of Romani children seems to be significantly lower compared to the rate of non-Romani children. Recent studies have documented lapses in immunization coverage in Romani communities.[94]

There are indications that birthrates are increasing in the poorer subgroups of Roma.[95] At the same time, sociological research notes that abortion rates are higher for Romani women than for non-Romani women.[96]

3. Cost of Health Insurance and Medical Care

During the previous regime, Bulgaria was endowed with a generous share of health care personnel and physical facilities. However, by the mid-1990s, low productivity and widespread inefficiency permeated the health care delivery system; there was a continuous decline of all health care indicators and a rapid escalation of health care costs.[97] Medical care became increasingly inaccessible for vulnerable groups.[98]

The government, supported by international financial institutions, initiated the reform of the entire health system. The state used loans from the International Bank for Reconstruction and Development, the PHARE Program, and the Council of Europe Social Development Fund to ensure structural and financial reform, including the establishment of a National Health Insurance Fund (NHIF).[99]

Over the last several years, Parliament has adopted three key health care laws: the Health Insurance Act,[100] Health Care Institutions Act,[101] and the Act on Professional Associations of Medical Doctors and Dental Surgeons.[102] The Parliament also amended the 1973 Public Health Act.[103]

The introduction of the new health insurance system is a radical change for Bulgarian society, which, over the last fifty years, had become accustomed to free-of-charge medical assistance. The Health Insurance Act introduces two types of health insurance: a compulsory one, which guarantees a package of health-related services and is administrated by NHIF, and a voluntary one, which is optional and will be administrated by private joint-stock companies.[104]

The new system will be fully implemented in 2001. From 1 July 1999, Bulgarian citizens started paying a health contribution amounting to 6 percent of their income (3 percent paid by the employer and 3 percent paid by the employee).[105] The self-employed and workers under nonlabor agreements pay a contribution of 6 percent.[106] All insured parties pay for each medical visit: 1 percent of the country's minimum monthly wage for a visit to a doctor or a dentist and 2 percent for each day of hospital care (but not more than twenty days in hospital per year).[107] Minors, unemployed members of the family, persons under arrest, prisoners, and persons who receive social benefits are not required to pay.[108]

The law aims to ensure 100 percent health insurance coverage. All Bulgarian citizens, all legal residents, and all persons who have been granted refugee status or the right of asylum are subject to compulsory insurance by NHIF.[109] However, the universality of coverage remains theoretical. Operating with categories defined by the social welfare legislation, the law bars access to health care for a significant segment of the very poor in general and very poor Roma in particular.

According to the recent amendment of the Health Insurance Act,[110] the state insures certain categories of people who are or were somehow involved in defending the country or the public order (e.g. persons in temporary military service, war veterans, and war invalids), as well as asylum seekers, detainees, prisoners, institutionalized minors, and students up to the age of twenty-six who are without income.[111] As far as the poorest of the poor are concerned, the new regulations, even more restrictive than the previous ones,[112] are based on two principles: (1) access to noncontributory health insurance is permitted only to those who are eligible for monthly social support and their family members,[113] and (2) their contributions to the health insurance fund must be paid from municipal budgets.[114]

3.1. Exclusion from the "universal" health insurance system

As explained in detail in the section on barriers to social protection,[115] very few of the poor can meet the eligibility requirements for monthly social support.[116] Those who live in severe poverty but are ineligible under the social protection regulations, and who cannot afford to pay their contribution, do not have access to this so-called "universal" health insurance system. Romani Baht calls Bulgaria's health insurance system for indigent Roma a "contradictio in adjecto," because it requires indigents who want to qualify for insurance without paying a contribution to first prove that they already paid the contribution.[117]

The "noneligible" families do not appear in the social service system's records and do not register with the unemployment offices. They are administratively invisible. "Considering the fact that a significant number of unemployed are not registered at the labor offices, we can conclude that part of the poorest people will remain without health insurance," said Dr. P.T. at Sliven Regional Hospital. "After the end of the year, they won't be able to afford any kind of treatment, apart from emergency medical assistance. These people usually have many children, most of them sick." Dr. Zh. M., a Romani physician who has worked in one of Sliven's Romani ghettoes for nine years, told researchers: "The reform will lead to the mass withdrawal of Roma from health services. Ninety percent of people in the ghetto are unemployed, but only half of them are officially registered at the labor offices. The rest will not receive health insurance."[118] In Gorno Alexandrovo, 33 percent of the unemployed Roma are not registered as such, because they see no reason to spend money on transportation to Sliven every month to register with the unemployment office, when social support is not paid in their village anyway.[119]

Some Romani NGOs are trying to provide assistance.[120] Unfortunately, the need exceeds their capacity and available funds.

3.2. Forced donation system

Until the state implements the Health Insurance Act fully, health care is theoretically free—"theoretically" because the administration created a type of forced donation system. Doctors do not require patients to pay for health services, hospitalization, or medication, but medical professionals tell them how much they should pay "voluntarily." The delivery of babies is theoretically free, but mothers are required to bring pampers, syringes, talcum powder, and even rubber gloves for the doctor. In Sliven, there is a list of these items on the maternity wall. Some hospitals will not admit women who do not bring their own supplies.[121]

Health care for children is supposed to be free, but medical institutions require parents to pay for the medicines their hospitalized children need. If parents do not have enough money, hospitals and clinics allegedly deny Romani children medical care. Reports abound: Sliven Hospital allegedly refused to treat a child with pneumonia from Sotirya. A child with a serious kidney problem had a similar experience.[122] A father from Topolchane said that doctors refused to operate on his sick child because he could not pay for the treatment.[123] A mother from Nicola Kochev, Sliven, explained that her "child had a crisis. The doctor from the polyclinic said we had to take him to the hospital because he had appendicitis. At the hospital they said they would take the child if we bought syringes, bandages, and medicines—they wanted money. I told them I didn't have any. They said, 'Go find money and then bring the child back.'"[124]

To respond to the growing financial pressure on the poor and to the increasing exclusion of Roma from the health system, Romani Baht, a Romani foundation situated in Fakulteta, Sofia, in 1997 developed the "Life-Saving Vouchers Project." Besides establishing a close cooperative relationship with the hospital and ensuring good relations with the community, Romani Baht, together with the Foundation for Assisting Charity in Bulgaria, provided money for medical care in serious Romani cases. According to an agreement signed with the hospital, both NGOs had the right to request analyses, statements, and statistics on the number of registered cases, particular diseases, treatments, and results, as well as the right to monitor the treatment of patients. Between 15 May 1997 and 1 December 1998, medical personnel treated 101 Romani patients. The average cost per person was U.S. $350. These patients, who live on social support or unemployment benefits, have an income of less than U.S. $30 per month.[125]

4. Racial Prejudices toward Roma Who Receive Health Care

Discriminatory attitudes toward the Roma are an old problem in the Bulgarian health system. The Ministry of Public Health appears to have paid little attention to the Romani mahalas, except when some officials portray the Romani communities as centers of epidemics and threats to the rest of the population.[126] The media describes the Romani population as a potential source of contagious diseases,[127] carriers of tuberculosis,[128] syphilis, and AIDS.[129] The press quotes doctors who state that Roma take advantage of sick people in need of transfusions by selling infected blood.[130] The media describes Romani settlements threatened by typhus fever as places crawling with billions of lice.[131] Fakulteta, the biggest Romani neighborhood in Sofia, is presented as a potential health hazard for all Sofia residents.[132]

5. Direct Discrimination

5.1. Negative attitudes of medical personnel and hospitals' refusal of treatment

Under these circumstances, it is little wonder that issues of health and relations with health care personnel are particularly sensitive for the Roma. Hospitals can be difficult places, where Roma say they feel alienated and they are "treated like dogs."[133] Dr. Stefan Panayotov, who works in the Nadezhda ghetto, said, "Many health care providers are hostile, and consider Roma 'intruders' into the health system. Administrative staff in hospitals are often rude to Roma asking for medical consultations. When the doctor is himself Romani, he respects Romani patients, and he speaks to them normally. The patients feel much more confident and trust the doctor a lot more."[134] Romani interviewees indicated that they appreciate small, local health care centers where doctors treat them as "human beings."

Sociological research has revealed frustration and a deep mistrust on the part of Roma toward non-Romani health care personnel. "Many parents genuinely believe that non-Romani doctors and nurses hate their children and cast the evil eye on them. That's why one often sees Romani children in hospitals with a blue thread around their wrist and a blue sign on their forehead to protect them," said Ilona Tomova, one of the country's best known sociologists.[135] "I was surprised to hear them [Roma] openly speaking about their fear that doctors do everything possible 'to kill them,'" noted another sociologist. He described two cases from the village of Topolchane: A fifty-two-year-old man, frustrated because the pediatrician accepted Bulgarian patients while he and his daughter were waiting for someone to take care of his sick grandchild, reportedly said: "Racists! They want to kill our children! But we are the masters, we make more children and never die out." A man from Nadezhda, Silven, upset for being kept waiting a long time at a doctor's door, asked, "What should I do? I kept silent, because instead of medicine, she could give me poison!"[136]

It is illegal for doctors and medical facilities to discriminate against patients based on their race. It would be helpful to have further documentation of instances in which doctors make derogatory comments about Roma and refuse to take them on as patients, or treat them differently as compared to non-Romani patients. Advocates for the Roma should raise these matters with the authorities and pursue them in court, if they are unable to resolve the problem through other means.

5.2. Refusal to issue forensic certificates

Some doctors refuse or are reluctant to issue medical certificates, particularly when state actors have employed violence against the Roma. In 1992, police raided the Romani neighborhood in Pazarzhik, and doctors allegedly refused to document injuries to Roma.[137] In another incident, police stormed approximately fifteen houses in the village of Mechka, Pleven, and beat their inhabitants severely. The local doctor allegedly refused to refer the victims to the hospital in Pleven where they could have been examined and obtained forensic certificates. He stated that the police called him and forbade him to do so.[138] In a third incident, thirty-three-year-old Todor Panayotov Todorov from Nikola Kochev, Sliven, alleged that two policemen who were trying to force him to confess to a theft severely beat him. The Regional Police Department, where the beatings occurred, released him later that day. He went to the municipal hospital where doctors examined him and took an x-ray of his head. The hospital reportedly refused to issue a forensic certificate, stating that the forensic expert was off duty. A day later, Todorov obtained a medical certificate from the private hospital in Sliven. Todor filed a complaint with the Sliven Regional Police Department and with the Sliven Military Prosecutor's Office.[139]

It is illegal for doctors not to perform their duties, particularly when racial bias motivates their inaction. Instances in which doctors refuse to issue forensic certificates to Romani victims of racial violence should continue to be systematically and thoroughly documented.

5.3 Segregation of maternity wards

Some medical facilities allegedly segregate patients on the basis of race. The parenthood center in the Number 3 City Hospital in Sofia reportedly places Romani patients "isolated in separate rooms."[140] It has also been reported that medical personnel in the maternity ward in Sliven[141] put Romani women in the same room with other Roma, but almost never with non-Romani women.[142] Older Romani women say that this practice did not exist in Bulgaria under the communist regime.[143] It started around 1992, and by now is well established. "In the communist era, the accepted policy was assimilation, so Roma were mixed with other patients," a doctor from Sliven said. "Now, the generally accepted policy is segregation, and hospitals . . . put it into practice."[144]

At the maternity ward, hospital personnel reportedly assign rooms to expectant mothers based on the color of their skin. The appearance of poverty or wealth does not play an important role: “My wife is Romani, but she does not look at all like she is,” a Romani man said. “She is blond, with white skin and blue eyes, and she is very well educated. She definitely does not look rich. All her dark-skinned friends were sent to the Romani room, but when she went to the maternity ward to give birth to our child, she was sent to the ‘Bulgarian room.’”[145]

There is debate over whether the segregation practices arise from doctors, non-Romani patients, or even Romani patient preferences. Non-Romani women refuse to share the same space with Romani women, said Sliven physician Stefan Panayotov.[146] While some Romani women say that this segregation humiliates them, others say that they feel more comfortable and more secure being among Roma only.[147]

It is illegal for doctors to segregate patients on the basis of their race unless there is a reasonable and objective means of doing so for a legitimate purpose under human rights conventions. It is difficult to imagine such a means or purpose. Even if the facilities were separate but equal, they would run afoul of the international norms on race discrimination.

6. Legal Provisions That Have a Disparate Impact on the Roma

Under the health care law, the access of the very poor to affordable health care depends on their eligibility for monthly support. The mechanism of exclusion of many Romani applicants from monthly support, which results in their exclusion from noncontributory health insurance, is analyzed in the social protection section of this report.

7. Other Barriers to Accessing Health Care

7.1. Lack of information

According to doctors, a lack of information is one of the biggest problems Roma have in accessing the health care system in general and health insurance in particular.[148] The government failed to prepare information campaigns not only for the majority population, but also for the more vulnerable Romani communities. In Bulgaria’s Romani ghettoes and villages, people still do not know what they have to do to qualify for noncontributory health insurance. In a study, researchers reported on the Roma in Nadezhda: “Most of them had not heard about the health reform and didn’t know that they had to choose a personal doctor, nor did they know that unregistered unemployed would not be medically insured. In such cases, they lose the possibility of receiving free medical care, and they will have to pay expensive doctors’ honoraria, which they cannot afford. We tried to spread this information as far as possible, but nobody can predict what will be the result of this unorganized outreach campaign.”[149]

If public health authorities have not informed the Roma but have told other non-Romani groups, then they have engaged in impermissible discrimination based on race. If public health authorities have not informed any groups, then they are derelict in their duties and should be punished.

7.2. Nonpayment or delays in payment

For 2000, the national government required all municipalities to allocate the necessary funds for health insurance in their budgets.[150] Many of these municipalities, however, simply do not have sufficient resources to do so. In 1999, seven hundred Romani families from Chirpan qualified for monthly support, child allowances, and maternity benefits, but the local council did not allocate funds for six months in a row.[151] The state ceded responsibility by requiring the same local authorities—which were not able or willing to ensure funds for social welfare—to find additional resources to pay for health insurance for the very poor.

7.3. Vaccination

Bulgarian health authorities report that for the population at large, 3 percent to 7 percent of children have not received various vaccinations.[152] It has been reported that in some Romani neighborhoods the percentage of children who have not received vaccinations or revaccination against poliomyelitis and diphtheria is as high as 14 percent.[153]

Health officials do not appear to have collected data on the ethnicity of unprotected children. What is known, however, is that diseases that can be eradicated through vaccination are disproportionately present in Romani communities as compared to other ethnic groups. The last reported cases of poliomyelitis in Bulgaria occurred in Romani communities.[154] Approximately ninety Romani children contracted this disease in the regions of Sliven and Sotirya. A diphtheria outbreak occurred in the same area in 1993.[155]

Health care authorities do not deny that Romani children do not receive vaccinations at the same rate as non-Romani children, but they claim that the disparities are due to Romani women's cultural resistance to vaccination, combined with negligence and lack of information. Authorities blame the Romani community's "inadequate health culture and distrust of medical professionals" for the fact that Romani children are "more often ill than other children."[156]

Without minimizing the importance of cultural factors, Romani NGOs maintain that discrimination also plays a role in the deterioration of children's health. Practices such as failing to address lack of information, unjustified fears, and misunderstandings, as well as blaming illiterate women for not responding to written invitations to bring children in for vaccinations and aggressive attempts to impose vaccination by force rather than by convincing people, are all identified as discriminatory.[157]

Both the health care system and the educational system do not respond well to Romani needs. Romani children do not go to kindergarten; they leave school early, and the state authorities do not follow up with vaccinations. Changes of domicile and lack of formal residence documents also impede vaccination follow-up.[158] Romani women fear being sterilized by vaccination.[159] Confused and lacking innovative ideas, some health care professionals "periodically discuss proposals to impose fines or cut off social support in order to force parents to bring their children to be vaccinated."[160]

Health authorities and advocates for the Roma need to work together to ensure that Romani children and adults receive the vaccines that they need. All parties need to join forces to educate Roma about the health benefits of vaccination and to root out any discrimination against the Roma in these programs.

7.4. Doctors' refusal to recommend treatment for disabled Romani children

According to the Foundation Ethnic Minorities Health Problems, an NGO led by doctors who work intensively with institutionalized children, Romani children comprise between 30 percent and 50 percent of all children placed in homes for disabled children,[161] a disproportionately high number when one considers that Roma account for less than 10 percent of the total population in Bulgaria.

One theory is that social workers act out of prejudice and intentionally institutionalize Romani children at a greater rate than non-Romani children. Although some Roma believe this to be the case, there is no empirical data yet to support such an allegation.

A second explanation is that Romani children suffer from some diseases at a higher rate than the rest of the population. In fact, three diseases do strike the Romani community with greater frequency than the non-Romani community.[162] "Lom disease" starts with an abnormal gait before the age of ten and continues with upper-limb weakness, deafness, and skeletal deformity.[163] In Congenital Cataracts Facial Dysmorphism Neuropathy (CCFDN),[164] congenital cataracts and microcorneas appear in infancy, followed by upper- and lower-limb disability, short stature, facial dysmorphism, and hypogonadism. The third disease is muscular dystrophy.[165]

According to advocates for the Roma, the government and the doctors who benefit from its payments have made very few, if any, contributions to the treatment of these conditions. For example, patients with CCFDN do not receive surgery at regional hospitals. They should get referrals for operations at specialized hospitals, but they allegedly do not receive them because, at the local level, Bulgarian doctors maintain that surgery is not effective. Experts in the field have a different opinion. According to Dr. Ivailo Tournev, a neurologist at the University Hospital in Sofia, foot surgery, proper therapy, and rehabilitation programs might help Romani children walk for many more years than they do now. However, at 400 leva plus the cost of the hospital stay, the operations are too expensive for most Roma.[166] Theoretically, the University Hospital may treat chronically ill people free of charge. For this, the general practitioner must send the patient to the district hospital where the specialist and the director must agree to send him or her to the University Hospital. Some doctors are incompetent and do not know that they should recommend surgery. However, it is alleged that many of them do not recommend the standard treatment because the patients are Roma. No CCFDN patient received an operation until 1998 when University Hospital doctors formed a foundation, started identifying Romani cases, and personally shepherded Romani patients through the administrative process.[167]

Advocates also decry the lack of government support for disabled children. Although the legislative framework exists, the government allegedly has not organized sufficient social assistance for them. Some families with no financial resources institutionalize their children with disabilities. Normal children or children with slight mental retardation are wrongly referred to homes where children have severe handicaps, thus drastically reducing their chances of development. Social workers place Romani children with somatic diseases in institutions for mentally retarded children. There are even cases of young people placed in institutions for chronically ill old people. [168]

More research is necessary to determine whether the government intentionally does not provide medical assistance or social support to the families of disabled Roma because they are Roma. It would be inappropriate and illegal discrimination for the government to shift funds away from researching or treating particular diseases because a particular ethnic minority group suffers more from the condition than others.

8. Access to Emergency Services

Laws require hospitals to provide emergency health care round-the-clock to all persons who suffer from life-threatening conditions, "regardless of citizenship, place of residence and health insurance."[169] Pregnant women are included among those to whom medical personnel should provide emergency care.[170] Every hospital or clinic is required to give emergency care and to record emergency calls, diagnoses, and care provided.[171] Emergency centers must submit a summary of usage to the Ministry of Health every month and keep records for three years.[172]

Romani Baht reports that, much too often, ambulance services do not answer emergency calls from Fakulteta, Sofia. "The least offending pretexts" are lack of gasoline, available vehicles, or doctors.[173] Romani NGO workers state that medical and emergency personnel consider Romani neighborhoods "dangerous" and Romani patients aggressive.[174] Ambulance drivers reportedly blame delays on the bad roads in Romani neighborhoods, which, admittedly, are often poorly lit, unpaved, and full of holes, water, and mud. A forty-four-year-old woman from "The Jungle," a part of the Nikola Kocev district in Sliven, told researchers: "My mother had a stroke at night. It was a very cold winter. We called emergency services but they sent neither an ambulance nor a doctor to examine her. In the morning, when we called again, they said they were coming. The ambulance came by noon. They don't want to hear about the Jungle. They said it was because of the slippery and steep road that they couldn't come earlier. One should stay on the phone until it gets hot from ringing to attract their attention."[175]

Human rights organizations in Lom also report that, when ambulances agree to come, they tend to arrive in Romani neighborhoods after a delay of two to three hours. The distance from Humata, which is one of the mahalas in Lom, to the maternity ward is ten kilometers. There is no public transportation between Humata and the rest of Lom; Humata has no public phones by which a person could summon a vehicle. One frequently sees men bringing their wives, who have gone into labor, to the hospital on the back of a horse.[176]

It appears that there are problems of direct and indirect discrimination in the provision of emergency services. Direct discrimination occurs when negative attitudes toward the Roma lead individual health personnel not to provide services in a timely manner. Indirect discrimination affects the Roma through the location of emergency facilities and the difficulties Roma face in accessing them. The government has an obligation to address both forms of discrimination through appropriate planning, investigation, and punishment.

9. Location, Staffing, and Equipping of Health Care Facilities

Small, medium, and large Romani areas do not have access to the needed amount of health care services, according to advocates for the Roma. Most small Romani neighborhoods do not have health care facilities. In large Romani mahalas, such as Fakulteta in Sofia or Stolipinovo in Plovdiv, the clinics are underequipped, understaffed, and unable to respond properly to community needs.

For the Fakulteta mahala, the main health care facility should be clinic number 10, which serves the whole municipality of Krasna Poliana. All Roma should receive medical attention at this clinic, but, in fact, mainly non-Roma use it. With the intention of facilitating both Romani and non-Romani access to health care, the Bulgarian health authorities built a Fakulteta branch of the clinic in the middle of the mahala. This met with the approval of the non-Roma from Krasna Poliana who no longer need to wait in line and to share "their" clinic with Roma.

For Roma, however, the "branch" is only a source of never-ending problems. It is little more than a sanitary set of rooms in the same building as the police station. There are four examination rooms and three doctors, a pediatrician, a gynecologist, and an internist, who take turns staffing the facility. On any given day, the clinic has no more than one doctor and one nurse. The place is continuously overcrowded. People who need primary care wait together with crying babies and pregnant women for the same doctor to see them. Many patients need to be referred for tests or to be sent to the hospital. Patients have access to specialized health care only if sent by a primary health care doctor—in other words, if they have a document issued by the "branch" doctor. In urgent cases, doctors, even when actually present, cannot provide much assistance, because they lack equipment for emergencies and have little or no medication.[177] Fakulteta's population is 25,000 to 30,000 and growing rapidly.[178] A handful of doctors in an ill-equipped clinic for such a population is not nearly enough.

Topolchane has only a medical assistant,[179] who does not have the authority to refer patients to specialized care in hospitals. However, the medical assistant still sends difficult cases to a specialist. Patients go to the hospital where they are denied care—or they are asked for payment because they do not have a proper recommendation. "My child cut his mouth, and I took him to the hospital in Sliven," one person reported. "There they said we should pay because we didn't have a doctor's note."[180]

Another interviewee described a similar situation in Gorno Alexandrovo. "In the village, there is no doctor, only an assistant. He does not have the right to send people directly to the hospital, so patients have to go first to the village of Blatez, five kilometers further," she reported. "There is no transportation and people have to walk. In Blatez, if the doctor is there and has time for them, they receive a recommendation for a specialist in Sliven. They have to go another thirty kilometers. Provided that they have money for the bus, by the time they enter the hospital, the workday is over and all the specialists have left. The system is so rigid, so complicated that it is almost impossible, even for the insured, to obtain the free medical care they are entitled to."[181]

Notwithstanding that distant dispensaries and bad roads are frequent in Bulgaria, and similar situations exist for other villages, Romani representatives assert that the Romani or Romani-dominated villages are disproportionately affected. The main cause of this disparity is the discriminatory manner in which national and local authorities allocate funds for construction of health facilities. However, apart from the obvious lack of clinics or medical facilities in many Romani villages, researchers need to gather more evidence to support the discrimination claim.

Macedonia

1. The State's Obligations under International, Constitutional, and National Law

Macedonia is a party to all relevant international treaties for the protection of health rights and prevention of discrimination: the International Covenant on Civil and Political Rights (ICCPR),[182] the International Covenant on Economic, Social and Cultural Rights (ICESCR),[183] the International Convention on the Elimination of All Forms of Racial Discrimination (ICERD) (recognizing under Article 14 the committee's competence to consider group and individual complaints),[184] the Convention on the Elimination of All Forms of Discrimination against Women (CEDAW), [185] and the Convention on the Rights of the Child (CRC).[186] At the regional level, the country has signed but not yet ratified the European Social Charter.[187] Ratified international treaties are part of domestic law.[188]

The Macedonian Constitution guarantees the right to health care to all Macedonian citizens and provides for the citizen's right and duty to protect and promote their own health and the health of others.[189] It also establishes the principle of equality of all citizens before the law.[190] Antidiscrimination legislation in the field of health care is still missing.[191]

2. General Status of Romani Health in Macedonia

Very little information on the health of the Roma is available. Romani life expectancy is significantly lower[192] than the average Macedonian level of 72.9 years for women and 68.6 years for men.[193] The Romani birthrate increased slightly from 4.9 percent in 1990 to 5.02 percent in 1995.[194] The highest infant mortality rate in Macedonia[195] is found among the Roma,[196] a rate twice as high as the national average.[197]

Romani children do not receive the same level of preventive care, and their health is worse than the health of the general population. Over the past decades, immunization programs have covered between 92 percent and 98 percent of the children in Macedonia, with a decline in the level of coverage after 1992 due to transportation problems that led to a shortage of vaccines.[198] Data from the Romani community indicates that immunization programs have been less effective at reaching Romani children. In a recent UNICEF survey, 15.3 percent of Romani women said that their children did not receive any vaccine up to the age of two, and 39.3 percent said that they had never had a vaccination card.[199] There is an extremely high number of diarrhea cases among Romani children,[200] who also suffer from high exposure to respiratory illnesses.[201]

3. Cost of Health Insurance and Medical Care

The health insurance system has a long history in Macedonia. Unlike in Bulgaria or in Romania, where health insurance is a new concept, Macedonians have had health insurance for more than fifty years.

When Macedonia became independent, the government established a centralized Macedonian health care system. The Health Insurance Law,[202] adopted in March 2000, established six major categories of people whom the national health insurance system covers: (1) employees; (2) self-employed persons; (3) pensioners; (4) beneficiaries of permanent financial assistance; (5) individuals temporarily unemployed while receiving unemployment benefits and unemployed individuals registered with the Employment Bureau, if they have no other basis for insurance; and (6) other groups, including war veterans, conscripts, detainees, prisoners, and individuals in monastic orders.[203] Macedonian citizens who are not included in any of the above-mentioned categories for various reasons may obtain health insurance by paying the contribution themselves.[204] All groups are entitled to receive basic health services as defined by law.[205]

Health insurance is compulsory for all Macedonian citizens. Spouses, children born in or out of the wedlock, stepchildren, adopted children, and children in the foster care of the insured are provided with health insurance.[206]

The law describes two types of health insurance: (i) compulsory, for which all employers, self-employed people, and state institutions responsible for certain categories of people are required to pay;[207] and (ii) voluntary, for which already insured individuals[208] may decide to pay in order to receive health services not covered by the compulsory health insurance.[209] The Health Insurance Law established the new Macedonian Health Insurance Fund.[210]

The health care sector consists of three levels: primary, secondary, and tertiary. Primary health care (PHC), the basis of the overall health system, provides basic health care on the municipal level. The patients can access the secondary and tertiary levels only through referrals by general practitioners and specialists of general medicine employed at the PHC level. In everyday practice, patients can access health care services covered by health insurance only via the "selected general practitioner"[211] who assesses what is necessary for further treatment of his or her patient. The general practitioner "may refuse to accept the insured patient who shows mistrust or fails to comply with the physician's professional advice."[212]

The contribution to the Health Insurance Fund is paid by employers,[213] by the insured person when self-employed or belonging to a special category,[214] by the Pension and Disability Fund,[215] or by the relevant state administration organs.[216] The Employment Agency pays the contribution for temporarily unemployed persons who receive unemployment benefits and for the unemployed who do not receive unemployment benefits but are registered with the Employment Bureau.[217] If the contribution is not paid regularly or the payments are delayed for more than sixty days, the rights encompassed by the compulsory health insurance (except emergency health care services) are suspended and reestablished on the day of payment of all overdue obligations.[218]

The insured and his family members pay a percentage—up to 20 percent—of the cost of health care services and drugs.[219] In contrast with the previous legislation,[220] children of the insured are now also obliged to pay for participation in the plan.[221] The indigent[222] and certain age groups pay a reduced copayment, according to the regulations issued by the Health Insurance Fund and approved by the Minister of Health.[223] Certain groups are exempt from the copayment: beneficiaries of continuous financial social assistance; persons accommodated in social protection institutions or with other family; mentally disabled persons in psychiatric hospitals; mentally disabled persons without parental care; insured persons who during one calendar year have paid for participation in the costs for specialist-consultative and hospital care services, in an amount higher than 70 percent of the previous year's average monthly net salary in Macedonia. Insured persons do not pay a copayment for medical examinations by the selected general practitioner and for emergency health care.[224]

The health insurance system covered nearly 100 percent of all Macedonians at the beginning of the 1990s. Coverage dropped sharply in 1995 to 67.6 percent, but gradually increased in the next two years to 80.5 percent in 1996 and 83 percent in 1997.[225] Information on the ethnicity of those who were not covered is not available.

Interviews with Romani leaders and Romani families in Skopje and other Macedonian cities reveal that a significant percentage of Romani families do not have access to health insurance.[226] The percentage of Roma without health insurance varies from community to community and ranges from approximately 30 percent in Shuto Orizari, Skopje's largest Romani neighborhood and home to the bulk of Macedonia's Roma,[227] to 90 percent in Stip,[228] to 100 percent in small settlements outside of Skopje.[229] Unlike previous regulations,[230] under the new Health Insurance Law children of uninsured parents do not have access to noncontributory health insurance.[231]

The Health Insurance Law, regulations, and actual practices create barriers to health care for low-income adults and their children, who cannot pay the health insurance contribution. First, the law refuses access to health care to persons who have not acquired Macedonian citizenship. Second, health insurance rights are provided for the family members of the insured, which can discriminate against those who have a traditional but not a civil marriage. Third, some administrators refuse access to those individuals—and their children—who, although Macedonian citizens, do not possess a primary school diploma. The report reviews these barriers, which have a disparate impact on the Roma, in detail in sections 5 and 6 below.

4. Medical Personnel's Perceptions of Romani Patients

All medical personnel interviewed in Macedonia seem to be convinced that their health care system is free of racial discrimination. They did not contest, however, that some Romani patients might provoke hostility or defensive reactions. One doctor summarized the most common beliefs and complaints of the medical staff about Romani patients: "They come from poor neighborhoods and are dirty, . . . ask for the most expensive medical tests, . . . [and] put pressure on doctors to obtain what they want. They use the hospitals just to have free housing and three meals a day. . . . When really sick, they don't stay long enough to finish their treatment. . . . Romani mothers run away, abandoning their children in hospitals."[232]

Roma state that doctors and nurses do not regard their health as important, and that medical professionals minimize their complaints, refuse to perform in-depth medical check-ups, and do not recommend specialized medical care. Roma also complain about not receiving enough medical information.

5. Direct Discrimination

The state and its employees may not engage in activities that have the purpose or effect of discriminating against racial minorities. The state may not hire private parties to engage in conduct that would be illegal for the state or its agents. Since Macedonian hospitals and doctors receive the bulk of their funds from the state through mandatory health insurance, they are either effectively state employees or state agents, and, as such, may not undertake actions that have the purpose or effect of discriminating against racial groups.

5.1. Access to health care services during pregnancy and delivery

The legislation in force until March 2000 guaranteed free medical care for uninsured women during pregnancy and delivery and exempted insured women from the 10 percent or 20 percent copayment.[233] However, some health care facilities required uninsured Romani women to pay the full costs related to the birth of their children, and those who were insured had to pay copayments. Virtually all Romani women interviewed in Skopje and other cities in November 1999 said that hospitals made them pay for gynecological consultations, treatments, and costs related to birth, including hospitalization.

These illegally imposed costs were significant, particularly for persons who were eligible for social support. A normal birth with no complications costs around 9,300 denars (approximately U.S. $170). An insured person was made to pay a 10 or 20 percent copayment of 93 denars or 186 denars.

Pressures to pay led to appalling outcomes, according to interviewees. On occasion, hospitals allegedly did not treat people seeking urgent care. Other times, health care institutions effectively held a patient or her child hostage until they paid for treatment.

In October 1999, a seventeen-year-old Romani woman gave birth in the hospital without assistance from a doctor. She had no health insurance and no money; the person in charge of admissions to the maternity ward refused to admit her and refused to call the doctor. After two hours of crying and begging in the hall, a nurse felt sorry for her and came to help. It was already too late; the woman gave birth to the child in front of the reception desk.[234]

Also in 1999, a Romani woman from Radanski Pat, Stip, who was born in Serbia and did not have Macedonian citizenship, gave birth to a child. She had to pay 3,410 denars but had only 3,100. The administrative staff told her that she could go home to obtain the rest of the money, but, until she paid everything, the child would remain in the hospital. Her grandmother borrowed money from relatives and took the mother and child out of the hospital.[235] Her neighbors report that the case is not unique; many of them were obliged to leave their newborns in the hospital, sometimes for days, until they were able to pay all the costs.[236]

These practices resulted in many women giving birth at home, where they did not have the technology or equipment necessary in case of a difficult birth. In addition, children born at home were not registered. The United Nations' Committee on the Rights of the Child noted with concern that Romani children make up a large proportion of unregistered births and drew the Macedonian government's attention to the fact that official birth registration is a fundamental first step toward securing a child's access to health care and other services.[237] The frequency of complaints indicated that health care personnel did not provide free care to pregnant women—as the law required them to do.

The new Health Insurance Law has legitimated the practice, further limiting indigent pregnant women's access to health care services. Those who are insured are obliged to pay copayments of up to 20 percent, while those who are not insured and cannot pay the health insurance contribution themselves have no access at all to health care services.

This new law may have a disparate impact on Romani women who are disproportionately affected by unemployment,[238] lack of primary education,[239] lack of citizenship, and poverty. Furthermore, the harassment of uninsured pregnant women and the denial of medical care to these women might become more frequent now that the law does not offer them even minimal protection.

Monitoring programs need to be established to determine the extent to which the new legal provisions and practices affect women in general and Romani women in particular. If researchers confirm disparate impact, then advocates for the Roma should raise these matters with the authorities and, if necessary, the courts. The state will argue that it has a reasonable and legitimate right to shift the cost of health care to individuals. Advocates will then need to show that the government's claims are a subterfuge. It is unclear how courts and other observers would judge the relative claims; international standards state that although governments may not cut all benefits to those in need during times of transition, governments do have the right to change social policies.

5.2. A different quality of services for Romani patients

Romani interviewees said that hospitals and doctors do not provide services to Romani patients that they do provide to non-Romani patients. It is illegal for hospitals and their personnel to discriminate among patients based on their race when providing them with services.

Romani women from Prilep state that pediatricians go into Macedonian houses to take care of children but never enter a Romani house. Mothers must carry sick children to the hospital. They allege that, in recent years, not one pediatrician has visited their Romani neighborhood. In Gostivar, Roma say that it is difficult to secure hospitalization, even if they have insurance: "They tell us that there are no beds available. But if Albanians ask, there are always free beds for them. And if we ask why, they tell us that the Albanians made reservations."[240]

Researchers should gather more evidence in order to understand how widespread these and other discriminatory phenomena are. It is unlikely that the government could offer any legitimate, objective, or reasonable justification for medical policies or practices that treat Roma differently from non-Roma.

6. Legal Provisions That Have a Disparate Impact on the Roma

Persons who wish to receive health insurance must comply with a number of discrete qualifications, many of which have a disparate impact on the Roma. At best, these requirements do not take into consideration Romani culture and the structure of Romani life. At worst, the government may intentionally implement policies and procedures that blatantly discriminate against the Roma.

6.1. Citizenship requirement

According to Macedonia's constitution and health care law and regulations, the country provides comprehensive health care protection primarily for its own citizens, with a few exceptions. The health care system insures foreigners or stateless persons if they are employed, educated, or trained in the Republic's territory.[241]

As discussed previously, Macedonian law sets a high standard for determination of citizenship. It requires ten years cumulative residency,[242] a permanent source of income, possession of living facilities, sound physical and mental health, and payment of high administrative fees.

Minority groups and international observers have criticized the law for its indirect discriminatory impact on Roma.[243] The European Roma Rights Center (ERRC) thoroughly examined these requirements to explain why large numbers of Roma possessing citizenship in other former Yugoslav republics never acquired Macedonian citizenship.[244] The omission in the law also rendered many Roma stateless.[245] According to the 1994 census, a total of 18,851 persons, out of whom 4,356 were Roma, lacked any citizenship.[246] Field research conducted by the ERRC in 1997 indicated that thousands of Roma were still de facto or de jure stateless.[247] The European Commission against Racism and Intolerance (ECRI) stressed that "the requirements related to living facilities and the administrative fee could also contribute to render acquisition of citizenship more difficult for certain parts of the population, notably ethnic Albanians and Roma/Gypsies." Furthermore, it noted that the criterion related to health might potentially lend itself to arbitrary and discriminatory application.[248]

Interviews with Romani women in Macedonia indicated that they are the ones most affected by the citizenship law. It appears that the majority of cases involve Romani women who were born in other regions of the former Yugoslavia, married Macedonian Romani men in traditional—but not civil—ceremonies, and came to live in Macedonia with the families of their husbands.

Under some international treaties, such as the European Social Charter, it is not inherently illegal for the Macedonian government to distinguish between citizens and noncitizens when allocating health care benefits. Nonetheless, the government may not discriminate, directly or indirectly, among racial groups in the allocation of citizenship. More research on the effect of the citizenship requirement on the Macedonian Romani population in general and Romani women in particular would be helpful.

6.2. Education requirement

If they have no other basis for health insurance, individuals who are unemployed may receive health insurance, provided that they register with the Employment Bureau.[249] To register as unemployed, applicants must prove that they finished a minimum of eight years of education. Based on this registration, individuals receive an unemployment card, which allows them to apply for health insurance. For married couples, each spouse must prove separately that he or she finished primary school in order to obtain an unemployment card.

Although it appears to be widely used,[250] the "education requirement" does not exist in Macedonian unemployment or health insurance law. The law on unemployment defines the "unemployed" but does not impose any explicit condition about education.[251] According to the unemployment law, the Ministry of Labor and Social Policy was required to establish the exact conditions for unemployment registration, but the responsible authority—the National Employment Agency—claims that the ministry never promulgated implementation rules.

The National Employment Agency nevertheless defends the education requirement, as its deputy director made clear in the following statement:

"To register as unemployed, the law establishes only two conditions to qualify: age under 50 and ability to work. The education requirement does not exist in the law. From a constitutional perspective, the requirement is justified because Article 44 of the Constitution provides that primary education is compulsory; in fact, the requirement should be included in the law. The standard form used for unemployment registration contains a question concerning primary education, but no more than that. Each person has to bring to the office proof (a diploma) that he or she graduated from primary school, because the level of education is written on each person's unemployment card. If the person does not have any education at all, a dash will appear on the unemployment card. Perhaps the Employment Bureaus still use the old Yugoslav Unemployment Registration Law."[252]

When asked about the education requirement, an official from the Ministry of Health answered: "This is a generally accepted practice of the unemployment offices, but there is no trace of it in the law. It is probably established through internal regulations."[253]

This problem appears to be widespread. Most of the 30 percent of the inhabitants of Shuto Orizari who do not have health insurance did not graduate primary school and cannot secure health insurance certificates.[254] Of the 90 percent of Romani families in Stip without health insurance, 80 percent do not fulfill the education requirement.[255] The percentages are similarly bleak in smaller Romani settlements such as Kvantasi, a small Romani settlement ten kilometers east of Skopje; Lisice, a small Romani area near Skopje; and Batinci, twenty-five kilometers southwest of Skopje.[256]

The manner in which officials apply the education requirement also affects young people who lived in Germany for several years with their parents and then returned to Macedonia. Although they finished primary school in Germany, it is reported that the Ministry of Education does not recognize their diplomas. When they turn eighteen, they may not obtain health insurance. For example, Senaj Osmanov's wife, who was born in Germany, graduated from high school there, which is equivalent to ten years of education, but her diploma is not recognized. Since she does not have health insurance, she paid 11,655 denars for the delivery of her baby in Stip City Hospital in 1999.[257]

Regardless of the education requirement's lack of legal status, it is obvious that officials apply it in practice. Researchers need to gather more data to establish whether the provision and its implementation have a disparate impact on the Roma, as anecdotal evidence suggests. Romani NGOs do not have specific data gathering or monitoring programs.[258] While the government may argue that the legitimate purpose of the policy is to encourage uneducated persons to seek and receive their primary school diplomas, it will have difficulties demonstrating that this is a reasonable practice when it has at its disposal educational incentives to reach the same objective.

6.3. Discrimination against large families

Until adoption of the new Health Insurance Law, in March 2000, the health care law regulated the health insurance field. Article 14 of that law provided that all family members of the insured enjoyed the same health insurance rights. Article 29, however, introduced a difference in treatment, establishing that families larger then five (as a rule, two parents and three children) had to pay for additional compulsory insurance. This was the so-called "three child policy" that was also applied in the social welfare sphere, which the UN Committee on the Rights of the Child strongly criticized as discriminatory.[259]

The regulation was aimed at cutting the costs associated with the health care of large families. Until its adoption, for the purpose of health insurance, "family" meant relatives sharing the same household, not only parents and children but also grandparents and other close relatives. In 1991, the government modified the definition of "family" to include only parents and children, and further limited it to five members, which was closer to the size of the average Macedonian family. The legal principle was that compulsory health insurance would cover only the normal Macedonian family while any "extra" child was a personal option that "additional health insurance" must cover.

In practical terms, this meant that the insured paid a fixed contribution, which was a certain percentage from his or her income, for a family of up to five members (two parents, three children). For the fourth child, the parents were obliged to pay 2 percent more, for the fifth child another 2 percent, and so on. If they did not pay, the "additional" children did not have access to health insurance. The law provided that Employment Bureaus cover the contribution for unemployed persons from their own budgets.[260] The contribution was fixed: 540 denars whether the insured-to-be was single or had a wife and two or three children.[261] The Employment Bureaus paid the fixed contribution and, because the law did not explicitly state who must pay the additional compulsory insurance, decided that the parents must pay it.[262]

This practice not only affected uninsured Romani children, but also had unpredictable consequences for the insured ones: "When I go to the office, the social worker asks: 'How many children do you have?' And I say: 'Six.' He says: 'If you have six, you have to pay so many hundreds of denars for the insurance.' I say: 'I do not have the money.' He says: 'If you do not pay, your whole family will remain without insurance.' I say: 'But I don't have money.' He says: 'Then you declare that you have only three children, and the office pays the insurance for three of them.' I declare that I have three, and he asks me the names. I have to choose. How can I choose? And what am I supposed to say when I go home? 'Child number 2, child number 4, child number 5, you have insurance, but the rest of you better stay fit?' When a child without insurance is sick, I go with him to the doctor with the papers of another one who is insured. Might be a brother, or a cousin, or the child of the neighbor if he has the same age and more or less the same weight. The doctor writes in the file, gives him pills, and everybody is happy. Except that after a few months, you cannot trust these files anymore, because they contain the medical histories of five different kids."[263]

NGO workers in Gostivar said that the local authorities never explained that families could pay additional contributions to cover all their children. Officials told Roma simply that according to the law only three children could be insured.[264] All over Macedonia, Roma, particularly Romani women, criticized the law. Some of them believed that the officials did not intend to discriminate against them: "I do not think that the government had anything against us, Romani people. I think that the 'three children' requirement was specially invented for Albanians, to encourage them to have fewer children. But the Albanians have money and they can pay 2 percent, so the law works only against Roma. Our children remain without health care."[265]

The new Health Insurance Law adopted in 2000 addresses all family members and eliminates additional compulsory insurance. On its face, the law provides that the health insurance of an insured person covers all his or her children under the age of eighteen.[266] However, thousands of Romani families have registered as having only three children, when in fact they have more than three. The elimination of the consequences of the discriminatory practices of the past will require additional measures. The administration has the task to correct the files and to ensure Romani children de facto access to health insurance while health professionals have the task of reviewing and clarifying children's medical files. Human rights advocates need to monitor the new system.

6.4. Civil marriage

The health insurance rights of spouses rely on the civil institution of marriage. Health insurance rights are provided for the family members of the insured: the spouse, the children born in or out of wedlock, stepchildren, adopted children, and foster children.[267] The direct consequence is that, in Romani families married only in a traditional ceremony, even if one of the parents has coverage, the other one, usually the mother, remains uninsured.

The problem seems to be implementation. The general practice of the Health Insurance Fund requires a marriage certificate, but Macedonian civil and family law provide for extended definitions of the family that do not necessarily require a civil marriage. For example, a notarial declaration may replace the marriage certificate. If the problem is that the health law does not sufficiently accept a notarial declaration of a traditional union, then it can be amended. If the difficulty is that officials do not recognize a notarial declaration for the purposes of health insurance, then those persons need to receive appropriate training and supervision.

The civil marriage requirement has a disparate impact on the Roma because many Romani couples live in traditional unions, rather than civil unions, and a higher percentage of Roma, at a younger age, have this type of relationship than do Macedonians. The burden shifts to the government to explain why such a policy is reasonable and legitimate under international law. The fact that the government does not use this distinction for other similar social protection benefits makes it difficult for the government to argue administrative necessity.

7. Other Barriers to Accessing Health Care

7.1. Lack of information

As do their counterparts in Romania and Bulgaria, Roma living in Macedonia lack information about available treatments and health care programs. They depend on social workers for details about health care facilities and insurance options. Their ability to obtain health care often depends on the correct or incorrect assessments of health care workers as to their employment status, educational level, and marital arrangements. Social workers who treat Roma more poorly than other similarly situated persons are engaging in inappropriate discrimination and should be disciplined, and the discriminatory treatment should be eliminated.

8. Access to Emergency Services

Medical care in case of emergency, including transportation when necessary, is provided only to insured persons.[268] In emergencies, the patient does not need to provide the health insurance card or a doctor's recommendation immediately.[269] The law assesses fines to health care organizations and workers who fail to provide emergency medical help.[270]

Throughout Macedonia, patients—regardless of their ethnic background—complain about ambulance delays. Indeed, emergency services seem to be in bad shape: Ambulances and equipment are lacking, and the system suffers from a chronic absence of financial resources and managerial skills.

In this context, delays in providing emergency care to Romani patients might result from lack of resources or efficiency rather than intentional discrimination. However, Romani NGOs suggest that racial prejudice against Roma also plays a role in the failure of the system to provide them with emergency care.

Advocates for the Roma allege that emergency services personnel fail to recognize and treat emergency cases when the patient is a Romani man or woman. "In

November 1998, in Gostivar, a three-year-old Romani girl fell from a first-floor terrace and suffered internal bleeding," Memedali Rahmani, president of "Mesecina" Gostivar, said. "The parents had no health insurance and no money. At the local hospital, the doctor refused to examine the child saying that the case was not serious enough to qualify as an emergency. The child died the same day."[271]

Romani NGOs state that there are systematic delays in responding to emergency calls from Romani neighborhoods. In Skopje, although ambulances serve Shuto Orizari, they usually arrive two or three hours late. In Gostivar, there are two Romani neighborhoods, Fazanerija and Bajnica, which cars cannot reach when it rains or snows. Ambulances never go there. Sick people have to walk kilometers on muddy roads, or relatives carry them to the hospitals.[272]

Health care professionals refuse to provide emergency services to certain Romani families. For example, people from Batinci, a Romani settlement twenty-five kilometers from Skopje, report that every time they call the ambulance company, the operators answer that they have no right to emergency services because they have no insurance.[273]

For the time being, only anecdotal evidence supports these claims. To assess the existence of racial discrimination within the Macedonian emergency care system and its extent, there is an urgent need for focused programs and monitoring at the local level.

9. Location of Health Care Facilities

Unlike Romania and Bulgaria, Macedonia does not have specific problems related to the location of health care facilities. The country is small and the network of health care institutions is relatively well developed. Although the number of facilities is high, the country could improve the quality of care delivered at those centers, particularly in Romani neighborhoods where facilities are underequipped, understaffed, and poorly maintained.

"We're excluded as if we were lepers.
We've been left here to die."

ROMANI RESIDENT, WALLED COMMUNITY
OF SHEKER, PLOVDIV

Lack of Adequate Housing

The issue of housing is particularly difficult throughout the transition countries. An increasing number of people, both Roma and non-Roma, are at risk of exclusion from housing. The key risk factors arise from the impact of privatization, housing restitution processes, changes in the legal status of the land on which many houses are built, decreasing employment opportunities for unskilled workers, and changes in social protection policies.

The right to adequate housing and freedom from discrimination in the exercise of it are well-established and recognized under international and regional human rights law. The Universal Declaration of Human Rights provides for the right for all to an adequate standard of living, including the right to adequate housing.[1] The International Covenant on Economic, Social and Cultural Rights states that everyone has the right to an adequate standard of living for himself and his family, including to adequate food, clothing, and housing and to the continuous improvement of living conditions.[2] The International Convention on the Elimination of All Forms of Racial Discrimination prohibits racial discrimination in the enjoyment of the right to housing.[3] The Convention on the Elimination of All Forms of Discrimination against Women provides for the right of rural women to adequate housing.[4] The Convention on the Rights of the

Child establishes the positive obligation of state parties to provide children in need with material assistance and support programs, particularly with regard to nutrition, clothing, and housing.[5] The Revised European Social Charter contains several provisions that speak to the right to adequate housing and freedom from discrimination.[6]

The national constitutions in all three countries under review incorporate the international human rights instruments that recognize the right to adequate housing and the prohibition of discrimination in the enjoyment of that right.[7] Although the constitutions guarantee the legal right to housing, the exercise of this right is often a privilege unavailable to the very poor in general and to Roma in particular.

Only in Romania is there specific legislation to combat racial discrimination and other forms of intolerance, with components covering housing-specific matters.[8] In Bulgaria and Macedonia, the civil and administrative laws do not ensure effective and equal protection of housing rights. The case law in all three countries is virtually nonexistent.[9]

In addressing Romani housing conditions and implementation of the right to adequate housing, policymakers and researchers must consider several elements:

- There is a clear difference between the living standards of Romani families who are highly integrated into the national majority and those families who are not. "Integrated" families share equally with the rest of the population the economic problems of the country or the comforts of personal wealth. While acknowledging the existence of this category of persons, this report does not examine their particular situation. Rather, the report focuses on the poorest segments of the Romani population and their housing problems.
- Generalizations about Roma need to be avoided. Clear distinctions must be drawn between various groups of Roma when assessing their housing needs and their living conditions.
- Housing issues are intimately connected to the historical context, the circumstances in which various Romani groups were obliged to settle, the fall of the communist regime, and the events of the last decade. Part of the problem, especially in rural areas, lies in the century-long exclusion of Roma from land ownership.
- There are significant differences between urban and rural areas. While recognizing the importance and seriousness of housing problems in the city, it must be emphasized that, at least in Romania and Bulgaria, the housing problem is not only an urban problem, but also an equally important rural one.

To assess the extent to which governments discriminate against the Roma or fail to address the inadequate housing available to the Roma, the report:

- mentions the national strategic plans for improving housing conditions for the Roma;
- outlines the types of housing conditions for Roma in a given country;
- reviews issues involved in property ownership, such as illegal occupancies and land restitution programs;
- examines particular communities that suffer from segregation, such as those which are separated from other areas by walls or which were displaced en masse;
- details differential treatment in the provision of basic municipal services, such as electricity, transportation, garbage collection, and running water;
- and describes police and private harassment of Roma in their homes and apartments.

Romania

1. The State's Obligations under International, Constitutional, and National Law

Romania is a party to all United Nations conventions relevant to the right to housing: the International Covenant on Civil and Political Rights (ICCPR),[10] the International Convenant on Economic, Social and Cultural Rights (ICESCR),[11] the Convention on the Rights of the Child (CRC),[12] the Convention on the Elimination of All Forms of Discrimination Against Women (CEDAW),[13] and the International Convention on the Elimination of All Forms of Racial Discrimination (ICERD)[14]. At the European level, Romania has ratified the European Convention for the Protection of Human Rights and Fundamental Freedoms (ECHR),[15] the Revised European Social Charter,[16] and the Framework Convention for the Protection of National Minorities.[17]

The Romanian state has pledged to fulfill the obligations deriving from the treaties to which it is a party.[18] Lawfully ratified treaties are part of the national law.[19] Constitutional provisions concerning citizens' rights and liberties must be interpreted and enforced in conformity with the Universal Declaration of Human Rights, with the covenants and other treaties to which Romania is a party.[20] When any inconsistencies exist between the covenants and treaties on fundamental human rights and internal laws, the international regulations take precedence.[21]

The Romanian Constitution binds the state to ensure a decent standard of living for its citizens through measures of economic development and social protection.[22] The right to a decent standard of living is interpreted as meaning the right to "reasonable living conditions" and their continuous improvement, the right to food and clothing, and the right to "satisfactory housing."[23]

The Housing Act regulates the housing sphere.[24] It includes lease and eviction rules,[25] as well as guidelines for the distribution of social[26] and emergency housing.[27] Further regulations establish fiscal incentives for investing in housing construction.[28]

In August 2000, the government adopted an Ordinance on Preventing and Punishing all Forms of Discrimination.[29] The ordinance[30] provides that the exercise of the right to housing is based on the principle of equality among citizens without privilege or discrimination. Regulations and orders issued by natural or legal persons, as well as active or passive behavior that unjustifiably favors or disadvantages a person, a group of persons, or a community, trigger contraventional liability.[31] The refusal to sell or rent a plot of land or building for housing purposes, to grant a bank credit, or to conclude any other kind of contract with a person or group of persons on account of their appurtenance to a race, ethnic group, a social or a disfavored category constitutes an offense.[32]

2. National Housing Strategies for Roma

Romania does not yet have any specific housing policy for the Roma. The Romanian Government Program 1998–2000 explicitly calls for developing a national strategy to improve the situation of the Roma. At present, the PHARE Program is supporting the development of the strategy.[33]

In the housing field, local Romani organizations have emphasized the elimination of ghettoes and the construction and repair of infrastructure within Romani communities.[34] In a document submitted to the Inter-Ministerial Subcommission in September 2000, the Romani expert group GLAR highlighted the need for nondiscriminatory access to public services, clarification of the legal status of Romani houses and land, the construction of social housing, and the rehabilitation of existing housing.[35]

In general, the government denies claims that racial discrimination interferes with the enjoyment of the right to housing. Rather, its representatives state that budgetary constraints do not permit the development of medium- and long-term housing projects, which admittedly hampers exercise of the right.[36]

3. Romani Settlements in Romania

Many Roma live among the majority population, sharing with them the comforts or difficulties of city and village housing. However, most Roma live in segregated areas, in slums and ghettoes, in abandoned buildings or near garbage dumps. Occasionally a couple of Romanian or Hungarian families share with the Roma the unimaginable desolation of these places, but this does not change the overwhelmingly ethnic character of the exclusion and ghettoization.

Roma live in several different types of settlements, the first of which is called a "mahala," a naturally developed area with a compact Romani population. As a rule, mahalas, or at least parts of them, are included in urban plans. The quality of building is acceptable but the infrastructure has been neglected for years or simply does not exist.[37] In Romania, the mahalas are smaller, more heterogeneous, and more integrated into the fabric of the city than the huge mahalas in Bulgaria and Macedonia.

Roma also dwell in small urban ghettoes in apartment buildings abandoned by state enterprises and municipalities. These living arrangements exist in virtually all Romanian cities and have begun to appear with much greater frequency in recent years. Homeless families seeking temporary shelter quickly take over these buildings.

Roma also reside in slums, comprised of shacks and hovels, often built without authorization on municipal or private land on the outskirts of the city. Many families ended up living in slums after the communist authorities demolished their houses to build industrial parks. These slums, with populations ranging from a few hundred to more than a thousand, exist in cities and towns throughout Romania. Everyone living in a slum is poor. Water sources are scarce. In communities without electricity, residents have improvised connections from nearby lines. The unpaved roads are full of holes.

All the slums are located in the immediate vicinity of non-Romani apartment buildings and neighborhoods, which have water, electricity, streetlights, and paved roads. The differences between the two communities are visible and shocking. The slums have existed for dozens of years. Many residents said that they are tired of protesting against the inhuman conditions.[38] As a rule, municipalities justify the lack of infrastructure within the slums by claiming that Romani dwellings are outside the city's jurisdiction, or that the residents do not have legal possession of the land, or that there is a lack of organization within the community, or, most simply, that the local budget has no money.[39]

Poverty, overcrowding, and lack of infrastructure dominate Romani neighborhoods. In Romania, the average number of people per room is 1.29, while the average number of Romani people in one room is 3.03.[40] In 1993, more than 10 percent of Romani families surveyed were living with more than five persons in one room.[41] Cases in which more than ten persons share the same room are not unusual. There are reports of incredible overcrowding—up to twenty-one people living in one room.[42] During visits to Romani neighborhoods, the author observed run-down buildings with seven or eight people living in a studio apartment of approximately 17.5 square meters.[43] Data from 1998 indicate that Romani houses were, on average, 20 percent smaller than Romanian houses, although Romani families are significantly larger.[44] A little more than 10 percent of the Romani houses did not have electricity in 1992, while approximately 4 percent of the majority population lacked this necessity.[45]

The government appears unwilling to care for many of the dwellings that it owns or controls directly or indirectly. In Cluj, the Roma Federation asked the city government to transfer ownership of the "NATO" block of apartments (so called because the buildings look bombed out) to the federation, but city hall chose to pass the apartments on to the Ministry of Defense.[46] The police eventually acquired the property; neither they nor the previous owners made any improvements to the apartments.[47] In Orastie, the Construction Trust transferred ownership of building number 7 on Muresului Street to the Municipal Administration Enterprise. Residents say they have asked officials at city hall repeatedly to repair the substandard one-room apartments, to help keep them clean, and to install water and electricity, but municipal officials never responded.[48] Those who live in the Rovinari district of Targu Mures state that the government is waiting to remove Romani residents before improving buildings 24 and 26, which have no water, no sewage system, no electricity, no heating, and no gas. The buildings sit next to a stinking heap of garbage.[49]

Approximately 45 percent of Roma live in rural areas. The country has 2,686 communes with 13,000 villages, for an average of four or five villages in each commune.[50]

Villages entirely inhabited by Roma, or where Roma are the majority, are scattered throughout Romania; they are usually very small and form a commune together with three or four majority villages. Regardless of the percentage of Roma within the commune population, they are rarely represented in local councils. At best, there is one Romani representative, who has difficulty influencing the decision-making process or directing a proportional part of the funds for the improvement of infrastructure to his own community. The underrepresentation persists even in places where Roma are not poorer compared to the rest of the inhabitants.

The entire infrastructure in rural areas is underdeveloped: Only 19.4 percent of communes and villages have water systems[51] and only 2.8 percent have sewage systems.[52] Only half of the Romanian communes have direct access to paved national roads.[53] As for phone service, 43 percent of the communes have telephone lines for all constituent villages, while in 20 percent of the communes less than half of the villages have telephone lines.[54]

In general, widespread rural poverty, and not discriminatory policies or practices, is the main reason for the lack of water or sewage systems, the bad roads, and the absence of telephone lines. In certain cases, however, direct or indirect discrimination may cause poor living conditions for Roma. For example, if all but Romani neighborhoods have access to certain services, or if local councils refuse to allocate financial resources to address Romani needs even though sufficient funding exists, then one can reasonably assert that discrimination is the determining factor.

The government does not dispute the fact that Romani living conditions are worse than conditions for the majority of the population, and that special measures should be taken to guarantee them "decent and civilized living standards." It maintains, however, that affirmative action "in favor of Roma or Gypsy families would be unfair and constitute unjust treatment of the families of Romanians or other races living in poverty."[55] It should be noted that this position is inconsistent with the recently passed antidiscrimination law, which condones affirmative action programs.[56] The reality is that, with the exception of the area of education, the Romanian government accepts affirmative action in theory, but thinks it is unfair in practice.

4. Property Ownership

4.1. Legality of settlement

Illegally built structures and the illegal occupation of land and buildings occur all over Romania in Romani and non-Romani neighborhoods alike. A large number of Romani families do not own the land on which their houses are built and do not have building authorizations or proper property contracts for their houses. The lack of legal status makes them particularly vulnerable to forced evictions and demolitions. Many others do not have the right to live in the buildings in which they dwell. They may not have a formal lease, they may have overstayed a lease, or they may have moved in as squatters. The continuous impoverishment and forced eviction of Romani families result in further ghettoization of the Romani population.

Although there is no comprehensive quantitative information about the dimension of this phenomenon, its regional features, or the number of persons affected, there are many anecdotal accounts that illustrate the difficult situations in which many Roma find themselves. Forced evictions are common. For example, in spring 1999, police and army troops evicted the approximately forty Romani families who illegally occupied "Hotel Nato II" at 4 Taberei Street in the Manastur district of Cluj.[57] The threat of eviction looms large for those who may not have formal arrangements securing their housing. Those who live in the Rovinari district of Targu Mures state that the government is merely biding its time before evicting Romani residents: "When the municipality finds buyers for the apartments, it will evict all of us, repair the buildings, and give them to Romanians."[58]

In at least one case, Romani activists were able to work with local officials to forestall the eviction of dozens of Romani families. The "NATO" building in Buhusi had belonged to a college. In 1998, when the college did not have any more students, it abandoned the building, and Romani families moved in. Many of the families are young couples without a place to stay in their parents' overcrowded houses. Others moved to the building after their houses burned, and they received no assistance to repair them.[59] There is only one Romanian family in the building, and the unemployment rate is 100 percent. Every now and then men find work in agriculture where they earn 20,000 lei (under U.S. $1.00) and a plate of boiled potatoes for eight hours of work.[60] There is no running water, and residents carry water in buckets from a nearby well. Two outhouses sit in front of the building. There is no electricity and no heating. According to residents, no representative of the local authorities ever came to learn about their fate or the fate of the dozens of children living in the building. However, the president of the Roma Party's Buhusi branch signed an agreement with the college to protect these families from eviction, if they do not damage the building and keep it clean.[61] Indeed, the place is impressively unsoiled: Residents have cleaned and locked all unused studios, they collect the garbage carefully in a special place behind the building, they trim the grass in the front of the building, and they prune the trees. The local Romani leader visits the place almost daily trying to solve individual problems for each family.[62] Unfortunately, local authorities reject nine out of ten requests for assistance.[63]

In rural areas, local authorities accept or tolerate the majority of Romani communities, yet a significant number of the Romani families live in houses built without authorization on land that does not belong to them.[64] Under Romanian civil law, courts may resolve the legality of these holdings on a case-by-case basis. However, legal action does not seem like an effective solution to the problem considering the huge number of actual and potential cases, the legal complexity of the issues, the clients' lack of legal education, the lack of inexpensive legal assistance, and the human and financial resources required.

4.2. Land privatization and restitution

Historically, very few Romani families owned any land in Romania. During the communist regime, a large segment of the Romani labor force in the rural areas, together with the majority population, was employed in agricultural cooperatives. After 1989, the large state farms disappeared, and the farmers began to regain their property rights to the land under the Land Law.[65] The return of state-owned land was a rather slow and complicated process. During the first years, the restitution procedures were affected by irregularities: the mayors who were responsible for land redistribution often sabotaged the restitution process, and land was often assigned to people other than its owners.[66] By the end of 2000, the government had privatized approximately 80 percent of the land.[67]

The Land Law stipulated that those who did not bring land to the agricultural cooperatives or brought very small plots, as well as those who were not members of the cooperatives but had worked there for three years, were entitled to land, provided there was enough.[68] Case studies of settlements indicate that Roma, who could have benefited from this legal provision, gained very little because there never seemed to be enough land to go around.[69] Whenever remaining land was parceled out to those who had not been previous owners, Roma were always last on the list of recipients.[70] In a document recently submitted to the Romanian authorities, the Romani group GLAR emphasized the need to consider the distribution of agricultural land to Romani families as one of the priorities of the government strategy for improving conditions for the Roma.[71]

5. Profiles of Segregated Communities

Residential segregation is the rule rather than the exception throughout Romanian villages and urban areas. In the rural areas, residential segregation is partly the result of initial settlement patterns and of a natural tendency of a group to "protect itself by staying together."[72] However, the main responsibility for the segregated status quo lies with the state, which, for decades, has conducted forced settlements, displacements, resettlements, demolitions, and, in the last ten years, systematic evictions of Roma from their central state-owned apartments. The few housing projects recently financed or supported by local authorities also foster racial segregation. Public authorities, echoed by public opinion, conveniently blame Roma for "opting" for the margin, for preferring to live together, and for promoting their own social exclusion.

The Romanian authorities do not recognize the existence of racial segregation. In a report submitted in 1999 to the United Nations Committee on the Elimination of Racial Discrimination, the government maintained that Romania has not had to deal with any racial segregation practices and therefore "has not taken any action to prevent or eliminate" them.[73] In reply, the Committee requested the Romanian authorities to take into consideration the scope of Article 3 of the Convention as clarified by General Recommendation XIX.[74] The recommendation draws the attention of the state parties to the fact that, although the reference to apartheid may have been directed to South Africa, Article 3 of the Convention prohibits racial segregation in all countries.[75] The recommendation further points out that residential patterns in many cities are influenced by group differences in income, which are sometimes combined with differences of race, color, descent, and national or ethnic origin so that inhabitants can be stigmatized and individuals suffer a form of discrimination in which racial grounds are mixed with other grounds.[76]

5.1. Forcibly displaced communities

Alba Iulia is a Transylanian city of 72,744 inhabitants, of which 93 percent are Romanians, 3 percent Hungarians, 2 percent Roma, and 1 percent Germans and Jews. In the 1970s, in Alba Iulia, as in many other Romanian cities, "Tsigania" (The Gypsy Land), was situated at the edge of the city. The government demolished the Romani houses to make way for factories and dormitory-style housing for their workers. The owners of large, well-built houses received some financial compensation, while the rest received nothing. Some families found work in the factories and lived in the newly built dormitories. Some went to work for a company in the next city and found housing there. The majority, however, moved to an empty field a few hundred meters away and started building "Lumea Noua" (The New World).[77]

After 1989, Romani families living in apartment buildings in the center of Alba Iulia gradually lost their jobs. Because they could not pay their rent or bills, they were evicted or they gave up their leases and found places to live with their relatives in the Lumea Noua slum or in illegally improvised dwellings in that area. The New World, without legal status or infrastructure, grew ever more crowded and hopelessly poor.

5.2. Communities in converted pigsties and garages

In Deva, Hunedoara, Romani families used to live scattered in state-owned apartments all over the city. The loss of employment has resulted in impoverishment, inability to pay rent, and systematic evictions.[78] Homeless, some of the evictees gathered in an abandoned building at the edge of the city. In May 1998, the company that owned the building obtained a court order and forced more than a hundred people, including children, out onto the streets.[79] Some of these families and other homeless Roma from the city gathered in front of city hall asking the municipality for help. After a two-month demonstration, the mayor offered the protestors and their families some pigsties on the outskirts of the city.

Before moving in, the families cleaned the pigsties, filled the channels for pigs' waste with cement, and connected the pigsties to the water pipe running under the building. In October 1999, the structures still lacked toilets and a sewage system, but there was a common bathroom and several toilets in the middle of the courtyard built by a German Catholic organization. Stoves provided heating. The place was relatively clean and free of garbage. A resident said that the municipality does not provide garbage collection, but some of the inhabitants are employees of the local garbage collection company and every now and then they bring their trucks into the neighborhood.[80]

Residents also reported that they were not required to pay rent, but they had to improvise their own infrastructure and services, without any assistance from city hall in money, materials, or equipment. Leasing contracts do not exist, and residences do not have addresses. When residents have to fill out forms, they write in the space for the address: "to the pigs" (la porci).[81]

In 1998, in the Izvoarele District of Bacau, the local government reportedly converted twelve garages into houses for Romani families. The place, which is far away from the non-Romani area, is across the railroad tracks, near the garbage dump. There is water and electricity, but no telephone lines. The closest bus station is two kilometers away. Local Romani leaders participated in the project's development. They accepted substandard construction because the families concerned were living on the streets after being evicted from their previous apartments.[82]

5.3. Walled-off communities

Geoagiu, Hunedoara, is a Transylvanian commune near the city of Deva. Most houses in the commune are large, recently painted, and repaired; roads are carefully maintained. The municipality recently renovated the city hall, an old building in the middle of a park.

The Romani community is located almost in the middle of the commune, on the border of the Geoagiu River. The only way to reach it is by walking over a small bridge. Out of the 164 families, 108 are eligible for social support, which means that they live in extreme poverty.[83] Approximately a quarter of the Roma live in brick houses, in the "good" part of the neighborhood, with electricity, gas, and wells in almost every courtyard.

A 1.60 meter high, 80 meter long concrete wall built in 1988–1989 hides the truly poor part of the community from the eyes of passersby.[84] According to the local Romani leader Nicolae Bologa, the Hunedoara regional council discussed the problem of the Geoagiu wall in 1991. The councilors rejected Bologa's request to demolish the wall, arguing that the Romani houses are "too ugly" to be seen from the street and that the wall would stay there until all the houses were repaired. Eight years later, in the autumn of 1999, the wall was still there.

Approximately fifty families live behind the wall in hopeless misery. In one place, eleven children sleep on the floor in a ten-square-meter room. Three of them have tuberculosis. In another house, parts of the broken roof hang fifty centimeters above the bed, threatening the lives of those who try to rest. There is no water system; dozens of adults and children drink from an old well full of sand and worms. Children do not go to school, because they have no clothes.

6. Access to Municipal Services

6.1. Electricity

Lack of electricity and high rates for electricity are never-ending sources of concern for Romania's poor, including the Roma. Some Romani settlements are totally deprived of electricity, either because the houses are illegal or the electricity company and local authorities failed to provide electricity to the area. In the Alba Iulia "Lumea Noua" Industrial Zone, a power line passes directly through the slum. Residents allege that the electric company refuses to connect their homes because the buildings were constructed without authorization.[85] They dare not tap into the power line without authorization for fear of criminal prosecution.[86]

In some mahalas and ghettoes where power supplies exist, the electricity is cut off for months because people do not have money to pay the bills. Residents must improvise. For example, in the "NATO" block in Cluj, at 21 Albac Street in the Gheorghieni District, authorities reportedly cut off the electricity and methane gas supplies in 1994 and never turned them back on. The two hundred people living in one of the two seventy-room buildings heat the apartments by burning wood, while petrol lamps and candles supply artificial light. Some families had lived in this building for ten years.[87] In the Rovinari District in Targu Mures, the men who had lost jobs in the area were compelled to leave to earn a living in Ceausescu's palace in Bucharest or at the Danube Black Sea Canal when the economy began to decline.[88] Women and children remained home with little or no money to pay the bills. Gradually, because the bills were not paid, the utility departments cut off the electricity, heating, and water. The families improvised stoves and heated the apartments with wood. The buildings started to fall apart, and, by 1998, they looked as if a fire had swept through them.

Somewhat surprisingly, according to a 1998 report, 98.5 percent of rural households have electricity.[89] Taking this into consideration, a significant overrepresentation of Roma within the population without electricity may be an indication of discriminatory practices or proof of the disparate impact of otherwise neutral policies. For the time being, there are no available statistics or studies concerning the legal status of housing and the ethnic background of those without electricity. However, sociological research indicated in 1992 that 11.3 percent of Roma did not have access to electricity, almost three times higher than the overall rate of 3.9 percent without electricity in that year.[90]

6.2. Transportation

The inhabitants of the Romani neighborhoods rely on public transportation to travel to work, to reach medical or legal services, to go shopping, and to attend educational institutions. The Romani settlements tend to lie on the outskirts of a city or even outside the city limits, beyond the industrial zone. As a rule, these areas have very little or no social or commercial infrastructure. Almost no Roma own private vehicles or can afford private taxis. Under these circumstances, a well-organized transportation system is the condition sine qua non not only for accessing other public services but for leading a normal life.

However, normal municipal transportation networks do not reach many Romani settlements. Buses stop at the edge of Romani neighborhoods. Where public transportation does operate, the quality of the services is visibly lower than for the rest of the network. There are fewer buses, the buses are older and in need of repair, transportation officials draw the routes carelessly, and the hours of operation do not meet community needs. These conditions can reduce the mobility of the Roma, imposing unjustified limitations on freedom of movement.

Location of Romani settlements and lack of infrastructure investment can cause problems as well. For example, in Valea Rece in the southern part of the city of Targu Mures, 1,000 persons live in 150 houses, built on two streets on the side of a hill. The steep incline of the hill does not permit access to vehicles, including ambulances, taxis, and other forms of public transportation.[91]

6.3. Garbage collection

The cleanliness of Romani neighborhoods varies widely. The mahalas in the city centers can be as clean as the non-Romani neighborhood around them, whereas the overpopulated ghettoes on the outskirts of the city usually have huge sanitation problems. Those neighborhoods located near industrial centers are often particularly filthy.

For example, in the "Lumea Noua" Industrial Zone, there is no organized garbage collection. Although the nearby factory has dumpsters out front, it allegedly forbids residents from using them. When the smell and the amount of garbage become unbearable, the people haul it in wheelbarrows to a dump five kilometers away.[92]

6.4. Water

According to the 1992 census, 53.7 percent of the houses in Romania were connected to a water system (88.2 percent in urban areas and 14.3 percent in rural areas)[93] while, according to sociological studies, only 43 percent of Romani households were connected.[94] The 1998 household survey indicates an even bigger difference: 46 percent of the total population and only 24 percent of Roma had access to water. Such differences are disturbing; however, they can barely describe the disastrous situation of some Romani communities, where people are forced to drink infested water, to share one source of water among dozens of families, or to make considerable efforts to reach water.

Many water sources are contaminated. In Glina,[95] the high concentration of nitrates has already led to the poisoning of several Romani children.[96] In Rasinari, 1,000 people drink infected water from an old water basin.[97] In Pata Rat, Cluj, hundreds of people were drinking water from an underground industrial pipe[98] until an international NGO built a new pump in 1995.[99] However, in October 1999, the pump was not functioning, and residents had reverted to drawing water from former sources.[100] In Ciocarliei street (Medias), where around 2,500 Roma live, the only source of water available to residents is contaminated. When asked to expand the water system into the Romani area, the local council responded that there was no money. However, in the same period, the council approved an expenditure of 420 million lei (approximately U.S. $28,000) to improve the local sports arena.[101]

The primary or only source of water for Romani communities is often not located in those communities. In Calvini, where approximately 1,450 Roma live in a separate neighborhood,[102] the water sources are situated more than 500 meters away.[103] There is only one source of water for around 1,000 residents of the Valea Rece neighborhood in Targu Mures while the majority neighborhood across the road has running water.[104] In buildings 7 and 8 in Orastie, people carry water from a pump in the neighboring cemetery, some two hundred meters from their apartments. They pay a 10,000 lei contribution per month per family. Residents consider lack of water the most important problem of the community. Interviewees said they would pay the cost of reconnecting the buildings to the water system, which is only ten meters away.[105] In Alba Iulia, the water pipe that serves the Romanian neighborhood ends fifty meters from the start of the Romani area. Two or three families have wells in their yards, but they do not allow others to use them. The two hundred remaining residents share one well of smelly, sandy, red-worm-filled water.[106]

Lack of running water typically leads to inappropriate sanitation. Libertatii Street in Buhusi is a typical small Romani mahala in a small Romanian provincial town; there is no sewage system and no water, so the entire neighborhood uses two toilets improvised on one of the streets.[107] In the NATO block in Cluj, there is no functioning toilet in either building for the 200 residents; those who live there use vacant rooms as toilets.[108] In buildings 7 and 8 in Orastie, people occupy only eight to ten apartments; the rest have no windows or doors and are used as toilets. The smell is unbearable.[109]

In the NATO building in Buhusi, there is no running water. People carry water with buckets from a nearby well. The studios never had bathrooms. Each floor shared a toilet and a shower. Because there is no water in the building, the toilets are now locked. Residents have built two outhouses in front of the building.[110]

7. Unjustified Intrusions into Romani Houses and Destruction of Property

As a state party of the European Convention on Human Rights,[111] Romania has pledged to fulfill in good faith its obligations[112] and to observe the right to respect for one's home, as protected by Article 8, and property rights, as safeguarded by Article 1 of the First Protocol.[113] The Romanian Constitution guarantees the inviolability of the domicile[114] and protects private property.[115]

Romania has acquired notoriety for its pogroms against Romani communities, the frequency and severity of the attacks on Romani houses and families, and violent police raids. During the last ten years, there have been approximately thirty pogroms during which non-Roma killed Roma and forced several hundred Roma to flee.[116] Romani houses have been burned to ashes, Romani property destroyed, and entire families chased away from villages. In most of these incidents, the authorities failed to protect Romani lives and property. The conduct of the police in such incidents has never been fully and impartially investigated.[117] Although the events took place years ago, Roma still suffer the consequences today. Hundreds of Romani victims of community violence fled to the outskirts of Bucharest[118] and live in abandoned buildings, in absolute poverty, without domicile or access to social protection. They face constant threats of evictions and homelessness.

The earliest episodes took place in the first days following the fall of the communist regime: In Virghis, Covasna County, villagers killed two Roma and destroyed two houses on 24 December 1989. In Turulung, Satu Mare County, one child disappeared and thirty-six houses were burned on 11 January 1990. In Reghin, Mures County, locals set five houses on fire on 29 January 1990. In Lunga, Covasna County, the non-Romani population killed four Roma and set six houses on fire on 5 February 1990.[119] On 13-15 June 1990, groups of miners brought in by the authorities in special trains to break up antigovernment demonstrations in the capital, together with officials from the militia, rampaged through Romani houses in Bucharest, allegedly destroying apartments and other dwellings, beating many Roma, some to the point of unconsciousness, and raping Romani women.[120] An angry mob of locals set thirty-four Romani houses on fire on 10 July 1990 in Cuza Voda, Constanta County. Others burned thirty-six Romani houses in the same county, in Mihail Kogalniceanu village, on 9 October 1990.

The official reaction to such "social conflicts" was that they were "emotionally understandable."[121] The non-Romani majority interpreted these remarks as tacit consent for malicious attacks against the Roma.

Consequently, incidents between Roma and non-Roma triggered destruction of Romani settlements and denial of access to villages. In Bolintin Deal, Giurgiu County, villagers set twenty-two houses on fire and damaged another two during the night of 7-8 April 1991. All Romani inhabitants were forced to flee. One month later, when thirty-four of the expelled Roma attempted to reoccupy one of their houses, 2,000 non-Roma again gathered and burnt the house and two others belonging to Roma down to the ground.[122] On 17 May 1991, 3,000 villagers in the town of Ogrezeni, Giurgiu County, gathered and destroyed seven houses belonging to Roma. Villagers in the neighboring village of Bolintin Vale burned Roma out of thirteen houses on 18 May. In Gaiseni, also in Giurgiu County, villagers set three houses on fire and destroyed a further six on 5 June. On 11 August 1990, following a period of increased hostility between Romani and non-Romani residents of Casinul Nou, and amid accusations that local Roma had engaged in theft, approximately four hundred predominantly ethnic Hungarian villagers chased out the entire Romani population and burned or otherwise destroyed their houses and property. During the rampage, many Roma faced the very real threat of being lynched. One hundred fifty people were left homeless. The perpetrators have never been tried.[123]

Even when authorities were aware that such events were about to take place, they rarely acted to prevent them. Furthermore, after such attacks, little was done to make amends and to help Roma who had lost their property. For example, in June 1991, in Plaiesii de Sus, following an incident between Romani and non-Romani neighbors, a crowd of villagers beat to death two Romani men. Shortly after, a public notice appeared on the outskirts of the Romani settlement, informing the inhabitants that their houses would be set on fire. The authorities were informed but did nothing, except to advise the Romani families to leave their houses for their own safety. The next day, as planned, an organized group of non-Romani villagers cut the electrical wires leading to the Romani settlement, knocked down the telephone pole connecting the village with the neighboring city of Miercurea Ciuc, and then set all of the twenty-eight Romani houses on fire, completely destroying the houses as well as personal and household possessions. The Romani families with numerous children were forced to live in nearby stables in sub-human conditions, with no heating and no running water. A year after the pogrom the Romani houses were rebuilt by the ethnic Hungarian villagers who had set them on fire. None of the Roma ever received compensation for the destruction of their personal and household possessions. The victims' request that the competent prosecuting authorities undertake the necessary steps to identify the perpetrators and secure their conviction was rejected, on the grounds that the offense at issue had been committed "due to serious provocative acts of the victims" and that the large number of people involved made impossible the identification of the perpetrators. On 21 January 1999, having examined the merits of the case, the Prosecution Department of the Romanian Supreme Court confirmed the rejection of the victims' request.[124]

On 12 March 2000, on behalf of several victims, the European Roma Rights Center filed applications for Casinul Nou and for Plaiesii de Sus with the European Court of Human Rights in Strasbourg. The applicants allege violation of Article 3 of the ECHR for failure to carry out a prompt, impartial, and effective investigation and to provide redress for the community violence they have been subjected to and deprivation of the right to a fair and public hearing within a reasonable period of time under Article 6, paragraph 1 of the ECHR. The applicants also alleged that the conduct of the Romanian authorities violated their right to respect for their home and private and family life[125] as well as their right to peaceful enjoyment of possessions.[126] Furthermore, they complained of being denied an effective remedy for the ill treatment they had suffered and the destruction of their possessions.[127] Finally, they alleged that the violations of rights were due in substantial part to their Romani ethnicity.[128]

Public authorities have stated an unwillingness to bring to justice those who have committed these attacks. For example, in a pogrom organized in September 1993 in the village of Hadareni, Mures County,[129] two Romani men were lynched and one was burned to death, thirteen Romani houses and annexes were burnt entirely, and another five houses damaged.[130] For several years, no one was brought to justice, either for the killing of the three Roma, or for the destruction of the houses in Hadareni.[131] The chief prosecutor is reported to have stated publicly that there was enough evidence to indict more than a dozen persons, but that local political leaders were making it impossible for him to bring charges.[132] Formal charges were finally brought in 1997.[133] In 1998, the trial court handed down prison sentences ranging from one-and-a-half to seven years. The Court of Appeals handed down a second, more lenient verdict on 15 January 1999.[134]

By the mid-90s, mob violence against Roma decreased, and police raids replaced the pogroms. The police attacks intimidated and frightened whole groups of Roma, including women, children, and old people.[135] Excessive use of force has characterized these raids, which have an unclear legal status.[136] There were raids, for instance, in Acis and Mihaieni, Satu Mare County, on 25 August 1995; Colentina, Bucharest, several times during the summer of 1996; Pata Rat, Cluj County, on 23 June 1995;[137] Bontida, Cluj County, on 25 February 1995 and 23 February 1996;[138] Balteni, Dimbovita County, on several occasions in 1996. People were beaten, and some were forced onto lorries and brought to police stations to do cleaning work. The police even invited TV teams to some of the raids, so millions could see commandos as they wielded axes to break into houses without any prior warning; half-naked Roma trying to put on their trousers; and Roma thrown on the floor to be handcuffed."[139] In another incident, at around 3:30 a.m. on 29 June 1998, the Calarasi County police carried out a massive raid involving between 60 to 120 police officers in Sarulesti, approximately fifty kilometers southeast of Bucharest. According to the victims, the police officers broke into their homes without warrants or their consent and beat them—including women and children—without giving any explanation for their actions. During the raid, a thirty-one-year-old Romani man was shot, suffering serious injuries in the spine and leg.[140]

In 2000, abusive police raids continued. A large number of police officers from the special forces reportedly raided a Romani neighborhood in Sector 3 of Bucharest, on 15 May 2000, searching Romani houses without warrants. When one inhabitant asked to see an arrest warrant, the police reportedly responded that they did not need any, "as this was a routine operation."[141] Human rights organizations note that the raid was the third of a series of such actions that police carried out in the same neighborhood, following a raid in November 1999 and another one at the beginning of 2000.[142]

Police officers conduct monthly raids in the NATO block in Cluj and write fines to anyone not properly registered at their address, which is to say, just about every adult.[143] People say that they would rather starve than not pay the fine and risk going to prison.[144] The situation in buildings 7 and 8 in Orastie, where twenty-five to thirty Romani families live, is identical. Residents claim that the police make frequent raids and impose fines on people for living at an unregistered address.[145] In the Alba Iulia "Lumea Noua" Industrial Zone, residents report that the police make regular raids, often before 6 a.m., pounding loudly on the doors of randomly chosen residents, who are then taken to the police station and fined for not having registered formally at the address where they live.[146]

Bulgaria

1. The State's Obligations under International, Constitutional, and National Law

Under Article 11, paragraph 1 of the International Convenant on Economic, Social and Cultural Rights (ICESCR),[147] Bulgaria has an obligation to ensure the right to adequate housing and continuous improvement of housing conditions. As a state party to the International Convention on the Elimination of All Forms of Racial Discrimination (ICERD),[148] Bulgaria must ensure the exercise of the right to housing in a nondiscriminatory manner.[149] Bulgaria has also ratified the Revised European Social Charter.[150] All the rights set forth in lawfully ratified international human rights instruments can be invoked before domestic courts. These instruments are part of the domestic law and take precedence over national norms that stipulate otherwise.[151]

The Bulgarian Constitution does not include a right to housing or to an adequate standard of living. There is no legal definition of the right under domestic law.[152] Some elements of the right, such as security of tenure and prohibition of eviction if homelessness results, are established under the Law on Obligations and Contracts and the Civil Procedure Code and are, in practice, judicially enforceable.[153] The European Commission against Racism and Intolerance (ECRI) has noted that Bulgaria does not have a specific body of civil and administrative legislation concerning discrimination in the field of housing and has recommended the introduction of comprehensive antidiscrimination provisions.[154] Bulgaria does not have any system of data collection to record the incidence of discrimination in housing or in any other field of life.[155]

2. National Housing Strategies for Roma

On 22 April 1999, the Bulgarian Council of Ministers approved the Framework Program for Equal Integration of Roma in Bulgarian Society.[156] The document calls for the adoption of specific antidiscrimination clauses in territorial development laws,[157] the encouragement of acquisition of land by Roma with little or no property,[158] and the legalization of illegally built houses and simplification of administrative procedures.[159] The European Commission praised the adoption of the Framework Program as a significant step toward the integration of Roma into Bulgarian society. [160]

However, almost two years after its adoption, little had been achieved. The government declared that budgetary constraints impeded its implementation.[161] Leaders of the Romani movement argued that the failure to undertake any measure, even in the areas that do not require financial resources, demonstrates the state's lack of political will.[162]

3. Romani Settlements in Bulgaria

As elsewhere in the region, the communist regime in Bulgaria subjected the Roma to forced assimilation policies. These policies reached a culmination in 1958 when the authorities forced the last remaining nomadic families to settle down.[163] Some of the Roma settled near villages and remained in rural areas to work in agriculture together with the majority population. Others stayed at the margins of the cities, thereby creating large mahalas. In time, more families moved to the cities, looking for employment. Their arrival continuously increased the size of the mahalas. Under the communist regime, big companies that employed Romani workers gave them, as well as Bulgarian and Turkish workers, small apartments in buildings near the industrial zones.[164]

During the 1990s, people employed and housed by big companies lost their jobs. They also gradually lost their houses and their residence permits, and found themselves forced by necessity to move in with their relatives into already overcrowded houses. This triggered the creation of a large number of "potential homeless"[165] and "illegal" residents. Today, in the cities, highly urbanized[166] Roma live in large mahalas, such as Fakulteta and Hristo Botev in Sofia and Nikola Kochev in Sliven, in smaller street districts, in multistoried and multifamily prefabricated housing complexes, such as Stolipinovo in Plovdiv, or in appalling conditions in ghettoes, such as Nadezhda in Sliven. In rural areas, Roma live on the outskirts of villages.[167] The dissolution of cooperative farms after 1990 left many without work, and land restitution legislation excluded them from land ownership.

Although statistical data based on ethnicity are scarce, studies reveal that in the houses of the Roma, as compared to the general population, approximately twice as many people live in roughly the same amount of space. The average Romani household consists of 6.9 persons, while the average household in the nation has 2.6 persons.[168] The available living space per capita for the Roma is 7.1 square meters while the figure for the country as a whole is 16.9 square meters.[169] For the average West European country, the average floor space per capita is about 40 square meters.[170]

It is worth noting that there are substantial differences among Romani mahalas and even different parts of the same mahala. For example, in the Nikola Kochev mahala in Sliven, each person has around 11.6 square meters of floor space while in its poorest part, called "The Jungle,"[171] only 6.7 square meters.[172] In Nadezhda ghetto, Sliven, the figures are even smaller, each person having approximately 6.0 square meters of floor.[173] Reported figures for rural areas, such as the village of Topolchane, are as low as 5.2 square meters of floor area per person.[174]

Romani dwellings have less access to hot water, running water, central heating, and appropriate sewage systems. Fourteen percent of Romani homes have hot water, whereas 82.4 percent of non-Romani houses in towns and 37.7 percent in villages have hot water through either a central heating system or a boiler. According to data from the 1992 census, only 2.6 percent of Romani houses have water, sewage, and central heating while 21.8 percent of Bulgarian homes have all three.[175] Leaving aside central heating, which can be a luxury even for Bulgarians of all backgrounds, only 34.7 percent of Romani homes have water and sewage as opposed to 66.1 percent of non-Romani homes.[176]

All over Bulgaria, as in Romania and Macedonia, it is relatively simple to establish, by statistical evidence, prima facie cases of the disparate impact of facially neutral housing policies on Roma. Unfortunately, existing housing regulations do not include any clear-cut provisions related to adequacy or fairness of housing, or a fair housing act.

4. Property Ownership

4.1. Legality of settlement

Illegal structures exist all over Bulgaria in Romani and non-Romani neighborhoods alike. Problems are particularly acute in the urban Romani settlements of Fakulteta in Sofia, Stolipinovo in Plovdiv, Nadezhda in Sliven, and Novi Put in Vidin.[177] Buildings are mainly ramshackle. Infrastructure is reduced to primitive electrification, partial water supplies, and inadequate streets. Construction standards are generally ignored.[178] A large number of Romani families do not own the land on which their houses are built and do not have building authorizations or proper property contracts for their houses. The lack of legal status makes them particularly vulnerable to forced evictions and demolitions.[179]

When titleholders reassert their rights to the land, the resulting demolitions and forced evictions have a significant effect on the poorest members of society, many of whom are Roma. The poor are the least able to contest the methods of displacement, due to their lack of knowledge of and access to legal remedies. The poor must then locate other suitable accommodations, which may not be readily available.

It has been reported that in the mid-1990s, the mayor of Plovdiv issued an ordinance to destroy illegally built houses in Stolipinovo. The protests of Romani NGOs led the mayor to suspend implementation of the ordinance.[180] However, the legal basis remains, and similar ordinances may be adopted anywhere in Bulgaria, at any moment.

The Human Rights Project reports that in November 1999, residents of Meden Rudnik in Burgas petitioned the mayor to demolish a part of the city's Romani neighborhood and to expel the inhabitants. In February 2000, they renewed the appeal. The Bulgarian authorities had not reacted as of August 2000, but they also had not sanctioned the petitioners in any way.[181]

The Framework Program for Equal Integration of Roma places emphasis on the urgent need to legalize Romani housing.[182] Legalization on a case-by-case basis, however, is almost impossible, taking into consideration the huge number of buildings and the lack of respect for construction standards.[183] Furthermore, high administrative fees and complicated procedures bar access to the courts for the indigent with a low level of education, which is the majority of people who live in the ghettoes.[184]

New legislation is considered the only option that might effectively address the huge number of illegal homes.[185]

4.2. Land restitution issues

Romani families living in rural areas usually own the houses in which they live[186] and possess ownership documents for the land on which these houses sit. With very few exceptions they never possessed agricultural land, or had only very small plots.[187] At the beginning of the 1990s, the large collective farms where many Roma used to work were dismantled, and landless Roma remained without jobs.

Noting that Roma are discriminated against in the land distribution process, the Committee on Economic, Social and Cultural Rights asked for an explanation from the Bulgarian government. In its reply, the government acknowledges that 93 percent of Roma in Bulgaria have been left out of the restitution process, but it argues that Roma, "due to their traditional way of life," never had land. The Agricultural Land Restitution Act regulates restitution of property rights to the former owners (or their heirs) of land that the state seized for use by cooperatives and does not restore rights for those people who never had them. After the restitution process is completed, the government said, those who never owned property will have the opportunity to request land from the municipality, provided that there is any left.[189]

For the time being, the restitution process is not over. The municipalities do not know how many Romani or non-Romani families will request land, how much land will be available, and whether the land remaining will be suitable for agricultural purposes.[190] Nongovernmental organizations fear that local authorities will simply deny Romani claims for land, or Romani families will receive only the lowest quality plots.

Roma Bureau, an NGO that assists Romani families in obtaining temporary leases of agricultural land, insists that Roma desire to own land, contrary to the frequent claim that they are not interested in farming. In the regions of Plovdiv, Sliven, and Lom, Roma lease and work the land. Although they do not have a tradition of farming, Roma have worked for dozens of years with the Bulgarians and learned many of the skills needed to farm.[191]

The current practice of land restitution has worked against some Roma who have successfully toiled on the land and want to own farms. For the moment, Roma can lease land only for a one-year period, because the municipalities must be prepared to return the land to the real owners when they restore owners' property rights. Quite often a Romani family will clear and prepare the land in the first year, and in the second year, when they are ready to harvest their first crop, the land is taken away from them.[192]

The Committee on Racial Discrimination has stated its concern about the Bulgarian government's policies and practices. "Concern is also expressed . . . that rural Roma are discouraged from claiming land to which they are entitled under the law disbanding agricultural collectives."[193]

The Framework Program for Equal Integration of Roma emphasizes that the state should simplify and encourage the acquisition of state and municipal land by Roma with little or no property. However, the government has not yet developed a detailed strategy for accomplishing this objective.[194]

5. Profiles of Segregated Communities

Most Roma in Bulgaria live in segregated areas of the inner city with little or no infrastructure, sometimes literally surrounded by massive walls or high sheet metal fences.[195] These walls isolate the Roma from their ethnic Bulgarian neighbors and access to community spaces.

Walls surround the big Sheker mahala in Plovdiv, where approximately 10,000 Roma live, so as "not to disturb people driving on the [nearby] highway."[196] The walls around the Romani ghetto in Kazunlak create a similar prison-yard-like image.[197] A two-meter-high cement wall built in the 1960s separates Romani houses in the Nadezhda neighborhood of Sliven from the rest of the world. The wall supposedly protects Romani children against accidents by separating the mahala from the railroad. However, this does not explain why the wall continues around the back of the area, where there are no trains, only an empty field in which children could play safely. Behind the walls, in their ghettoes, Romani residents feel that the majority wants to get rid of them: "We're excluded as if we were lepers; we've been left here to die."[198]

The press writes that the majority "wants segregation and Gypsy ghettoes."[199] Some local initiatives seem to go in this direction, sustaining and deepening the existing distance between Roma and non-Roma. In a report submitted to the Committee on the Elimination of Racial Discrimination, the authorities described how Bulgarians are moving out of Romani neighborhoods:

"Hunger, poverty and lack of job opportunities have compelled many Roma to reassess their traditional values and norms of behavior. Stealing and cheating are on the increase and have already become steady means of survival. The crime rate, according to data provided by the Ministry of the Interior, is significant: 37 percent of all crimes in the country have been perpetrated by Roma. The number of homeless Roma as well as prostitution involving minors are increasing. This generates, though completely unjustifiably, a negative attitude towards the Roma. Again, according to the Interior Ministry's data, there is a growing tendency among Bulgarians to move out of Romani neighborhoods and settlements because of being subjected to systematic thefts, threats, and persistent fear of physical assaults and threats of having their property ransacked and destroyed. Roma have attacked uniformed policemen and military servicemen. It is obvious that the Bulgarian society finds it difficult to overcome prejudices against Roma."[200]

An article published in the Hungarian newspaper *Nepszabadsag* notes that the Plovdiv municipality has launched a program to help Bulgarians move away from Stolipinovo. The head of the local police, after declaring himself as being "definitely against the ghettoes," explains that it "is the Roma themselves who do not like to live scattered apart," while Bulgarians "annoyed" by Romani culture and lifestyle "want to move away." Romani organizations have a different explanation. According to Anton Karagiozov, from the Foundation for Regional Development "Roma" Plovdiv, Bulgarians do not move away because of the Roma, but because conditions in the district are impossible.[201]

6. Access to Municipal Services

6.1. Electricity

Electricity is a critical resource for all people who live in Bulgaria. Most of the country's households depend on electricity to power the heaters that keep living quarters warm during the colder months, since few houses or apartments have central gas, oil, or other nonelectric heating methods.

Lack of electricity and the high price of electricity concern the Bulgarian poor, including the Roma.[202] Given the difficult situation in which the poor find themselves, some have attempted to reduce the cost of electricity by modifying the electrometers.

Many Romani settlements are totally deprived of electricity, either because the houses are illegally built, they do not have clear legal status, or the electric company and local authorities failed to provide the area with electricity. In some mahalas and ghettoes where power supplies exist, the electricity is cut off for months because people do not have money to pay the bills.[203]

To prevent electricity theft, local utility companies have invested significant resources in installing special meters in Romani neighborhoods—but only in Romani neighborhoods. Utility workers relocated electrometers, the small boxes traditionally placed in houses on the outer wall near the entrance, to the electricity and telephone poles on the street. Almost all Romani houses received a new electrometer, locked inside a huge silver-metal box and attached to the pole two to five meters above the level of the street. Such a system makes it impossible for persons to modify the meters to reduce the fees.

In December 1999, the author observed Nicola Kochev and Nadezhda, two Romani neighborhoods in Sliven, where such "prevention" programs were developed. Both areas look like surrealist antirobbery experiments. With the huge shining silver boxes in front of the houses and dozens of cables hanging down, the appearance of these Romani streets is dramatically different from the look of a non-Romani neighborhood. The inhabitants say that they feel as if the companies are treating them like criminals.

"This is a public humiliation campaign against the Roma, not an electricity-saving campaign," a resident of Nicola Kochev said. "I have lived here for 30 years. I've always had a good job, and I still have it. My electrometer was placed on the outside wall of my house, near the entrance door. I never stole electricity. I paid my bills on time. One day the electric company came and, without even notifying me or asking my permission, placed this huge box in front of my windows. Anybody passing on the street would think: 'This is a thief's house. He was caught stealing electricity.' After a lifetime of work, I am treated like a criminal just because I am a Romani man. I feel deeply humiliated. I feel bitter and furious. I look around, see hundreds of silver boxes filling up the neighborhood, and I feel powerless. The whole Bulgarian society is against us."[204]

Identical situations reportedly exist in other areas, such as in the Romani neighborhoods in Vidin and in Kusharnik and Ogosta (Montana). Vesselin Lakov, project coordinator of the Human Rights Project in Montana, said: "Last year, the electric company introduced streetlights. At the same time, the company placed electrometers on the posts five meters above the ground, in front of each Romani house." As in Sliven, the electrometers are in locked, highly visible, silver boxes. As in Sliven, they exist only in the Romani community. The Human Rights Project protested against this differentiated treatment. The director of the local electric company answered that electrometers are located in the streets only in Romani neighborhoods "to prevent Gypsies from stealing electricity."[205] In Lom, utility workers have already installed electrometers in the four mahalas in which Roma live, and nowhere else in the city.[206]

Montana local authorities explained that the municipality paid for new electrometers as a favor to the poor who do not have money to cover the costs. However, they have difficulties explaining why the electric company installed the meters for poor and not-so-poor Roma alike, and why they bestowed the favor upon Romani communities only."[207]

Some municipal authorities genuinely believe that any measure against Roma is, or might be, justified. The secretary of Iztocen, Plovdiv,[208] criticized the failure of a collection campaign organized by the electric company. "In the city's main Romani area, there are more electrometers than anywhere else in the city," he said. "Last year the electric company employed a security firm, which sent guards to frighten the Roma into paying—but unfortunately the action was not a success."[209]

Some advocates for the Roma believe that the authorities are wrong to presume theft because of low consumption of electricity in Romani areas. Instead, they argue that the people in these communities simply use very little electricity because they are very poor.

Ironically, building and installing the boxes was probably very expensive. And reading the meters from vehicles equipped to reach the boxes is probably costly and time consuming.

6.2. Transportation

The inhabitants of the Romani neighborhoods rely on public transportation to travel to work, to reach medical or legal services, to go shopping, and to attend educational institutions. The Romani communities on the outskirts of a city, as a rule, have very little or no social or commercial infrastructure. Almost no Roma own private vehicles or can afford private taxis, leaving them at the mercy of the municipal transportation system.

However, normal municipal transportation networks do not reach many Romani settlements. Bus lines stop at the edge of Romani neighborhoods. The buses on these lines are fewer, older, and more in need of repair. Transportation officials draw the routes poorly, and the hours of operation do not meet community needs. All of these conditions impose unjustified limitations on the freedom of movement of the Roma.

6.2.1. Allocation of bus lines in Romani neighborhoods

It appears that transportation companies do not allocate the same number of buses and bus lines to Romani communities as they do to the neighborhoods of other ethnic groups. The Romani communities generally have less frequent service and less coverage than comparable neighborhoods.

In Fakulteta, there are only two bus lines for the 25,000 to 30,000 people living there. Only one bus serves each line, and each bus runs up and down the main street only, ignoring dozens of other streets.[210] Although the city of Dimitrovgrad has excellent infrastructure, only a single bus serves the Romani neighborhood, passing once every three hours.[211]

6.2.2. Effective curfew on Romani residents without transportation

In at least one Bulgarian town, the termination of public transportation in the early evening effectively imposes a curfew on the Romani residents. Kusharnik is a Romani neighborhood of 2,500 people located approximately two kilometers from the center of Montana. Anyone who wants to reach it by walking needs to cross the industrial zone. At night, that portion of the road, almost one kilometer, is completely dark. The area is empty. Almost no people, particularly no women, walk there after sunset because of safety concerns.

Residents seldom leave the neighborhood at night. Only a handful of families have cars. The only bus serving the Romani community stops operating at 7:00 p.m. Those without private transportation who are not back home by that hour remain in the city. "It's almost like a curfew imposed on the Roma," a human rights activist from

Montana, said. "The public bus in Kusharnik stops running at 7 p.m. In the city's center, public buses run until 8 p.m., but after 8 p.m. private bus companies cover the city until almost midnight. No private company wants to serve Kusharnik."[212]

More research is necessary to determine how widespread these practices are and whether these actions fit the legal definition of discrimination. Nonetheless, what is clear is that the Roma suffer more from the termination of public transportation services in the early evening than do other groups.

6.2.3. Allocation of poor quality public transportation vehicles to Romani neighborhoods

In general, the buses that serve Romani neighborhoods are in terrible condition and can barely travel the poor roads. Most buses for other parts of the city are not in such bad shape. In Sofia, it is a miracle that the two buses that serve Fakulteta are still in circulation. The doors are broken. The stairs have seen better days. The ceilings are full of holes. On rainy days, people on the bus get soaked. On cold days they freeze. In contrast, many of the buses serving the nearby ethnic Bulgarian communities are brand new.

Although the allocation of particular buses to particular lines in particular neighborhoods may not rise to the level of a gross human rights violation, members of the Romani community cannot help but question why the buses serving Romani neighborhoods are of such inferior quality. Some believe that the public transportation companies provide the Roma with substandard services because bus company managers believe that the Roma are inferior. More research is necessary to determine whether the bus companies are engaging in an illegal practice.

6.3. Garbage collection

Sanitary conditions in the back areas of Romani ghettoes are desperate. In the poorest streets, the garbage stays on the roads and in the courtyards for days. Rubbish tipcarts, where they exist, are breeding grounds for rats and insects, which transmit diseases.[213] Skin diseases are common. Some slum areas in Sofia "are polluted and stink, as there is no garbage collection or other community services."[214]

Understaffed and underequipped municipal enterprises are responsibile for garbage collection. Many of these enterprises fired Romani men as paid employees and "rehired" them—or their wives—to clean the streets for free as part of the work requirement for recipients of social protection benefits.[215] The financial situation of many of these companies is admittedly difficult, but lack of funds cannot explain or justify inequalities in providing services to Romani neighborhoods.

Romani neighborhoods fare less well in the provision of sanitation services than other similarly situated neighborhoods in at least three ways. First, the number of garbage trucks allocated to serve Romani areas is lower than the number of trucks used in non-Romani districts. Second, the trucks collect garbage less frequently in Romani neighborhoods than in other districts. In Nadezhda, Sliven, workers collect street garbage once every two weeks, while in the rest of the city they collect it once a week. Third, instead of entering the mahala and collecting the garbage from every street, the trucks take only the garbage deposited at the entrance of the Romani area, such as in Lom.[216] This practice becomes a public health problem when not all residents are diligent in moving their garbage to the entrance.

These practices appear to have a disparate impact on the Romani community. Given the public health considerations and inability of the Romani community to pay for private garbage removal services, one would think that the government would place more, rather than less, emphasis on the services to the Romani neighborhoods. It is unclear how a reduction or elimination of services to these particular neighborhoods would be a reasonable, objective, or legitimate policy, given its impact on the Romani people.

7. Unjustified Intrusions into Romani Houses and Destruction of Property

Of special concern in Bulgaria are the frequent instances of intrusion of authorities into Romani houses, in violation of the sanctity of the home, as protected by Article 8 of the European Convention[217] and the Bulgarian Constitution,[218] and in breach of property rights as safeguarded by Article 1 of the First Protocol[219] to ECHR and constitutional norms.[220] Reports about such instances abound.

On 10 July 1998, approximately eighty police officers raided the Romani neighborhood of Mechka, near Pleven, allegedly in search of stolen goods. At least fifteen houses were destroyed.[221] The police broke down doors and smashed windows, beat men, women, and children indiscriminately, while insulting the villagers with ethnic slurs. Those beaten reported that the police showed no warrants (with one exception, approximately thirty minutes before the real raid began) and gave no explanation for their actions.[222]

Roma also suffer from attacks by racist groups, local mobs, and private security guards. They are often beaten, their houses are raided, and their property destroyed. It has been reported that the Bulgarian authorities often fail to take measures to prevent these types of incidents or to prosecute the perpetrators. These failures may constitute a violation under Article 8 of the European Convention.[223]

It has been reported that in early March 1998 the peasants from Hadji Dimitrovo, near Yambol, organized a pogrom against the local Romani community following an altercation between two Romani girls and two non-Romani males. At least thirteen houses were raided, inhabitants were beaten, and furniture was broken.[224] No arrests were made in the case in 1998.[225]

Vicious attacks on Romani houses clearly aimed at forcing Romani families to leave the villages have also been reported. The best-known example is the attack against a twenty-family Romani community in Dolno Belotintsi. Bulgarian villagers, infuriated by a murder committed by a young Romani man, broke into Romani homes and destroyed windows, furniture, and other household belongings. Villagers armed with guns reportedly mistreated Romani women and children. The attacks continued for two days. The villagers, led by their mayor, sent a letter to Bulgaria's president demanding that the government expel the Roma and reinstate the death penalty.[226]

In April 2000, the mayor of the village of Mechka in Pleven led a drive to expel Roma from the village as retaliation for their alleged crimes. The Bulgarians attempted to demolish all Romani houses and denied Roma access to local public service facilities.[227]

Macedonia

1. The State's Obligations under International, Constitutional, and National Law

Macedonia is a party to all relevant international treaties for the protection of housing rights and prevention of discrimination: the International Covenant on Civil and Political Rights (ICCPR),[228] the International Covenant on Economic, Social and Cultural Rights (ICESCR),[229] the International Convention on the Elimination of All Forms of Racial Discrimination (ICERD) (recognizing under Article 14 the Committee's competence to consider group and individual complaints),[230] the Convention on the Elimination of All Forms of Discrimination against Women (CEDAW),[231] and the Convention on the Rights of the Child (CRC).[232] At the regional level, the country has signed but not yet ratified the European Social Charter.[233] The right to housing and the right to an adequate standard of living do not appear as such in the Macedonian Constitution, but ratified international treaties are part of domestic law.[234] Citizens' equality before the law is constitutionally protected.[235]

2. National Housing Strategies for Roma

In the autumn of 1999, the Council of Europe Social Development Fund granted Macedonia a U.S. $20 million loan for construction of social housing.[236] The authorities will sell apartments under favorable financial conditions to young couples in need. Theoretically, those in charge will allocate some apartments to very poor families. The government has stated that Roma will benefit from this initiative.

In general, the efforts to design a national housing policy toward the Roma are more limited in Macedonia than in Romania or Bulgaria. NGOs have begun to discuss options for improving housing, but have not issued a detailed strategy for doing so. The government has a housing policy, but very little of it addresses Romani issues.

3. Romani Settlements in Macedonia

The overwhelming majority of Roma in Macedonia live in residentially segregated areas.[237] According to official data, 95.3 percent (47,408) of the Macedonian Roma live in the cities and only 4.7 percent (2,185) in rural areas.[238] Most dwell in large mahalas, in slums or unplanned settlements that lack asphalt roads and connections to water, electricity or sewage disposal.[239]

The oldest mahalas are in the city's center, usually near the river, if there is one. More recently, Romani-dominated areas tend to be located on the margins of the cities, the newest ones a bit further out, in places that are difficult to access. In many cities, there are small areas, usually located near industrial zones or between apartment blocks, where ten to fifteen families live together in indescribable misery. They survive from social support and by selling what they find in garbage containers.

Almost 85 percent of the country's Roma live in Shuto Orizari, the first Romani mahala that has obtained the status of a municipality.[240] Its residents describe the area as the largest Roma-only neighborhood in the world, and, as the first one run by Roma themselves, it is rapidly becoming a symbolic place.

Shuto Orizari was created in 1963 after the disastrous earthquake that almost destroyed Skopje, including the old Romani settlement of Topaana at the center of the city. The municipality of Skopje offered Roma who lost their houses some substandard housing built on an empty field several kilometers from the outskirts of the city. The initial plan was to accommodate around 7,000 people. There was water, electricity, a bus station, paved streets, and public lighting. The population grew quickly, with more Roma and some Albanians coming from other parts of the country. New houses were built, with or without authorization permits.[241]

According to the 1994 census, 14,301 people live in Shuto Orizari,[242] but nongovernmental organizations estimate that the number of inhabitants is between 30,000 and 50,000, of which 90 percent are of Romani origin.[243] The area has a Romani mayor, and Roma dominate the local council. Shuto Orizari is six kilometers from the center of Skopje but within the city limits. The central government has allocated between 2 and 4 million denars (approximately U.S. $70,000) for the municipality's budget in the past few years. The Ministry of Finance approved 3.5 million denars for the reconstruction of roads and sewage systems in the area.

Although Shuto Orizari is the size of a small city, it has only modest amounts of municipal, educational, social, and cultural infrastructure. The area has two schools and one NGO-organized kindergarten, but no high school. There is only one law office and no notary. The municipality's only cinema needs major repairs and does not function; there is no theater.[244] For thirty years, Skopje's local authorities did nothing to provide light for the neighborhood streets. Now the situation is a little better, with many streets having some light, even though only half the streetlights have bulbs.[245] The mayor estimates that 40 percent of the streets are still dark at night.[246] The water supply and drainage system have not been repaired for thirty years.[247]

However, not all Roma live in difficult housing conditions. Some families became comparatively rich by working several years abroad, usually in Germany, and they built or purchased large houses when they moved back to Macedonia. German organizations also funded respectable living arrangements for Romani families forcibly removed from Germany and returned to Macedonia several years ago.[248]

The rest of the country's urban Roma live in a variety of settlements, typified by those in Gostivar, a city of approximately 120,000 inhabitants with 4,000 to 5,000

Romani residents.[249] Roma reside in relatively small numbers in neighborhoods throughout the city. While a few families live in mixed neighborhoods, the majority live in segregated Romani areas.[250] The unemployment rate in the Romani community is as high as 95 percent. The majority survives by selling products on the streets. As in Shuto Orizari, some Roma worked abroad and returned to build large houses in Romani neighborhoods.[251] In general, however, housing conditions are poor. Bajnica-Grudajci, a relatively new Romani neighborhood of 100 to 120 houses just outside the city lines, is approximately five hundred meters from the city garbage dump. Many houses have no water or electricity. Of those homes that do have electricity, owners improvise the service by taking electricity from a home in which professionals installed the service. [252]

In rural areas, Roma live in Macedonian villages; their presence in Albanian or Albanian-dominated villages is rather rare. Their housing conditions are similar to those of the rest of the village; they usually have electricity and individual pumps with safe drinking water. There are, however, several cases of settlements situated near garbage dumps, such as in Kvantasi, and of communities forcibly evicted years ago and forced to settle between villages in ghettoes created by the authorities, such as in Batinci. Villages entirely inhabited by Roma or where Roma represent the overwhelming majority do not seem to exist.

4. Property Ownership and Legality of Settlements

Many people who live in Macedonia have accommodations that they or prior owners built without governmental authorization, on land that they do not necessarily own. If the legally recognized owners of the property turn up to assert their rights, the state can force those living there to relocate. Insecurity of tenure affects tens of thousands of ethnic Macedonians, Albanians, and Roma. It has been estimated that up to three-quarters of all structures existing in Macedonia have illegally built components, meaning that municipal authorities did not give formal permission to build or to add to existing structures.[253]

The lack of legal rights to occupied property appears to have a greater effect on the Romani community than others. First, there are many large Romani neighborhoods in which the majority of houses do not have authorization. Second, there are extremely poor Romani settlements where no houses have authorization. Finally, there are many settlements in which people live in shacks, such as in Kvantasi near Skopje or Fazanerija in Gostivar. Their inhabitants do not need legalization, but decent social housing.

The law contains a three-step process through which the state agrees to recognize the legal rights of those who occupy unauthorized dwellings. First, the urban plan must include the building, settlement, and entire neighborhood. The law provides that urban plans more than five years old are considered nonexistent; competent authorities have the legal obligation to regularly review urban plans, and, if necessary, to pay for new plans from the city budget. The law also permits changing the plan before the five-year period elapses. Second, an expert who understands urban development regulations must make measurements and check whether the construction is sound. A building may be included in the urban plan even if it is not built according to accepted safety or esthetic codes. Third, the Ministry of Urban Development must give permission for the building, even ex post facto.

The size and nature of unauthorized Romani settlements pose serious challenges to the existing legalization process. First, it would take years, if not decades, to gather and process the data for each dwelling. Trying to legalize Romani ownership on a case-by-case basis would be hopeless and unreasonable. Second, even if inhabitants could meet all the other legal requirements, they cannot afford the legalization fees.[254] Experts charge legalization fees of approximately U.S. $625 for a house of one hundred square meters.[255] Third, the existing legalization process depends on the willingness of government officials to draw up new urban plans. In practice, when asked to authorize infrastructure projects in Romani neighborhoods, some local authorities require payments for services that are ordinarily free of charge.[256]

Researchers need to gather more data to determine whether government officers intentionally make it difficult for Roma to secure legal title to the land they occupy. Insecurity of tenure prevents some Roma from accessing social services and allows some governments to justify not providing municipal infrastructure. It would be illegal for government officials to treat Romani neighborhoods differently because a particular ethnic group—the Roma—lives there. What is clear at present is that this problem is significant, and it affects a greater percentage of the Roma than the population at large.

5. Profiles of Segregated Communities

5.1. Forcibly displaced communities

Batinci[257] is a Romani community of four hundred people, situated between two villages, twenty-five kilometers southwest of Skopje. The people of this community once lived on the outskirts of the nearby Macedonian village, Dracevo. To make room for a health clinic, the communist authorities evicted the Roma and demolished their homes without offering them any kind of material compensation.[258] The municipality moved them to Batinci, a place on the side of a hill, literally in the middle of nowhere. Unlike their demolished homes, the new houses did not have water, electricity, or gas. To "legalize" the arrangement, the authorities registered the new "address" on their identity cards as a "temporary residence." Twenty years later, the "temporary," incomplete nature of their homes in Batinci persists. The houses are overcrowded; the average number of persons per room is eight, but there are rooms in which eighteen people sleep.[259]

The only source of available water for all of Batinci's inhabitants is a pump at the bottom of the hill. During the winter, when mothers wash children inside houses, all bathing must occur on the same day, so as not to waste too much wood for fires. On bath days, mothers carry tens of liters of water up a muddy, often icy hill. Women state that carrying buckets of water up the hill exhausts them.[260] The International Rescue Committee, in cooperation with the Roma Center, has planned a project to install several more water pumps.[261]

Residents have an improvised electrical system in Batinci. The community does not have any garbage containers, and the municipal service does not send trucks to collect the garbage. Residents throw garbage into an open space at the bottom of the hill, in between some makeshift toilets. Every now and then, people pay the drivers of passing bulldozers to push the garbage into the river.[262] The community has no telephone lines. The closest private and public lines are approximately three kilometers away. In emergency cases, it is practically impossible for an ambulance to respond in time. With the exception of several families from Kosovo, who do not have Macedonian citizenship, almost all the others qualify for social support.[263]

5.2. Community located near garbage dumps

Kvantasi is a Romani community located ten kilometers east of Skopje. Administratively it belongs to the Skopje municipality of Gazi Baba. It is a one-street settlement consisting of eighty people (fifty of whom are children under the age of fourteen) living in fifteen houses. A tiny stream, highly polluted by a nearby chemical plant, separates the houses from a garbage dump, fifteen meters away. A row of large Macedonian houses obscures the dump and the Romani community from the highway.[264]

The community started more than twenty years ago. Shortly thereafter, the city began to use an abandoned sand pit as a garbage dump; the facility remained in use until October 1999 when the city made a haphazard attempt to clean up the site, pushing some of the garbage into the pit and then covering it with a thin layer of soil. Kvantasi inhabitants survive by searching for empty bottles and scrap metal and selling them in the city. Of the thirty adults living in the community, twenty do not have Macedonian citizenship. Nobody has social protection or health insurance. Not one of the school-aged children is in school.[265] Residents have improvised unauthorized houses from pieces of scrap metal and wood, plastic, and cardboard. While the nearby Macedonians have indoor plumbing and clean, filtered water, the settlement shares one source of highly polluted, yellow water.[266]

6. Access to Municipal Services

6.1. Electricity

The majority of urban households rely on electricity not only for light but also for heating.[267] As everywhere else in the region, access to electric power often straddles the borders of legality. In Romani settlements, municipal power lines exist only on the main streets or along the border separating the Romani area from Macedonian or Albanian neighborhoods. To access electricity, Roma either connect their houses to a neighbor's house that has electric service or they run a line from their house to the main power cable.

A home with a legal, professionally installed electric line has an electrometer and is responsible for the bill, but everyone who takes electricity from the line pays his or her part. For example, Agim, a Romani man from the Eastern Macedonian town of Vinica, applied for an electricity connection, but his request was rejected because his house was built without a permit. He has electricity from a cable he has attached to the house of his neighbor with whom he shares the bill.[268] Obviously, nonpayments or late payments can be continuous sources of tensions, quarrels, and brawls. Moreover, this is not a safe system. The dangers of fire or electrocution are always present.

The other option is to connect a line directly to the house from the main source. This method carries a high risk of electrocution because it is necessary to work, without special protective equipment, directly on the power line. The electricity is free but the risks, both legal and mortal, are high.

In at least two cities, utility companies have not provided power to Romani communities while making electric service available for other ethnic groups. In Kumanovo, in the neighborhood of Bavce, electric cables skirt the Romani settlement while linking ethnic Macedonian areas to each other.[269] In Gostivar, Fazanerija, the power line follows all Macedonian streets but avoids the area where Romani houses are located. City officials allegedly ignored repeated requests for an electric line.[270] The area occupied by Roma, maybe seven hundred meters, was the only part of the neighborhood without electricity until Mesecina, the local Romani organization, paid to install a power line for all Romani houses. However, the electric company refused to install an electrometer and now each family pays a flat rate, which, according to Mesecina, is higher than the maximum consumption possible.[271]

The practice of running power lines around the neighborhood of one, and only one, ethnic group obviously has a disparate impact on that group. The government must offer a reasonable, objective, and legitimate purpose in order to justify such a practice under international human rights standards. The state might argue that it does not want to provide electricity because some members of the group might steal the power. Yet it is highly doubtful that the state has the right to deny essential services to the majority of members of an ethnic group, just because some members of that group steal those services.

6.2. Transportation and roads

In the slums, ghettoes, and settlements on the outskirts of cities, the roads are almost never paved, full of potholes, and impassable when it rains or snows. All over Macedonia, "the roads lead up as far as the Romani communities and then stop."[272] The lack of acceptable roads impedes the access of ambulances, taxis, cars, and public transportation to Romani areas, such as Bavce (Kumanovo). There are streetlights in big mahalas such as Shuto Orizari or on the main streets of other large Romani areas, but almost never on side streets.

Generally, the level of services provided by public transportation and emergency vehicles is systematically much lower in Romani areas on the outskirts of cities than in non-Romani residential areas. Some services do not exist at all. Often, bus lines stop where Macedonian or Albanian areas end and Romani neighborhoods begin. Few Roma have cars, and taxis often refuse to take passengers too far into the mahalas.

Although the poor road conditions and lack of public transportation may not rise to the level of a gross human rights violation, members of the Romani community have every reason to question why Romani neighborhoods have such an inferior transportation infrastructure.

6.3. Garbage collection

Although few neighborhoods in Macedonia are clean,[273] one does not need to be particularly attentive to observe that many Romani neighborhoods are much dirtier than other communities. Almost all Romani neighborhoods have no garbage cans or dumpsters and have more garbage in the streets. Many Romani neighborhoods contain or are located near "official" garbage dumps, or illegal waste disposal sites where private enterprises leave trash without paying, as in Shuto Orizari, or dumps improvised by the inhabitants who have no other choice.[274] "The entire place is a garbage dump [and there are] dead animals everywhere," said Steve Kosokoff, a retired professor who interviewed refugees in Macedonia for the War Crimes Tribunal, after visiting a Romani suburb of Skopje. He "remembers seeing one pile of refuse in which bedraggled trees had snagged many plastic bags that fluttered in the breeze like flags."[275] It is obvious to the naked eye that rivers and streams are not as clean in Romani areas as elsewhere.

Poor communities, many of which are Romani, suffer from a reduction in the government subsidies that supported essential municipal services, such as garbage removal. Before 1989, the government did not require the so-called "social cases"—people with serious financial difficulties—to pay taxes for garbage collection or water. Garbage collection, water, and electric companies did not sustain losses, because local budgets paid their expenses.

Today, the collection and disposal of communal waste is the responsibility of public enterprises that cover major municipal centers. In the capital city of Skopje, for example, the local council elects the public enterprise's director. The city subsidizes part of the enterprise's budget, while citizens' contributions cover the remaining costs. A commission created in 1998 with the participation of one representative from each municipality, including Shuto Orizari, controls the quality of services, including garbage collection. A lack of enforcement powers has undermined the commission's work; for example, it may sanction irregularities in the functioning of the enterprise only with a token fine.[276]

Since the fall of the old regime, the poor no longer receive tax breaks for sanitation services, and many find it difficult to justify spending the little money they have on garbage collection taxes. Municipalities inhabited by a predominantly poor population, such as Shuto Orizari, cannot afford to cover the cost of the unpaid taxes either. As a result, Comunalna Higiena in Skopje takes a financial loss and considers itself entitled to provide less service in the Romani neighborhood under the theory that the municipality should provide services according to the amount of taxes that each residential area pays.

The mayor says that Comunalna Higiena, the local garbage collection company, does not clean Shuto Orizari as frequently or as thoroughly as non-Romani areas, that there are no garbage cans, and that German Caritas' money—not city money—paid for the few dumpsters that do exist. He affirms that Comunalna Higiena allocates only four employees and one truck to work in Shuto Orizari, while other municipalities of comparable size get twenty employees and four trucks.[277]

Shuto Orizari is not the only Romani community that has these problems. In Prilep, a municipality inhabited by approximately 100,000 people, with about 14,000 Roma, the local garbage collection enterprise does not clean Romani neighborhoods such as Dabnicki Zavoj with the same frequency as the rest of the city. In the city, workers empty garbage containers twice a week, while in the Romani area the garbage trucks come only once a week or once every ten days.[278] The entire Romani neighborhood sits upriver while further downriver is a Macedonian neighborhood of modern apartment buildings. A bridge separates the two neighborhoods. The river, which is cleaned once every four years, during elections, is usually full of trash and dead animals. Instead of mandating regular cleaning of the river, city hall in 1998 installed an iron fence under the bridge. The fence keeps most of the trash on the Romani side, while leaving the Macedonian area relatively clean.[279] With every heavy rain, the trash and filth becomes stuck against the fence; dirty floodwater invades the Romani neighborhoods, spreading dirt on the roads and in people's gardens. Families living near the bridge must clean everything, otherwise the smell would make their lives impossible.[280] In summer, the river is so dirty that the entire community stinks.[281] The residents allege that city hall never responded to their frequent requests to have the river cleaned.[282]

The differential provision of sanitation services appears to have a disparate impact on the Romani community. Although local governments may not have much money to provide for these services, they should provide them to those neighborhoods that need them most. It is unclear how a reduction or elimination of sanitation services to these particular neighborhoods would be a reasonable, objective, or legitimate policy, given its impact on the Romani people.

6.4. Water

Access to safe water is essential for good personal hygiene, wholesome meals, and public health. It is necessary for persons to have access to sufficient amounts of water through a water system in the city or neighborhood, connections between the water system and individual houses, and water in the pipes. It is also essential for persons to have water of sufficient quality; in other words, water that is safe for consumption and cleaning.

The national agency responsible for environmental matters is the Ministry of Environment, which has established a National Environmental Action Plan (NEAP). At the local level, the key institution for providing services and promoting community affairs are the municipal councils. Each city hall organizes and subsidizes its own "Water and Sewage Company," which are public utility enterprises. The municipal councils appoint the directors and control the operations. A recent administrative reform increased the number of municipalities from 33 to 121. Those that existed before the reform preserved their companies, but the new ones started almost from scratch and created their own enterprises.

Due to the systematic neglect of many local authorities and to the chaotic manner in which Romani neighborhoods grow in urban areas, Romani regions generally have less developed water systems as compared to those in non-Romani neighborhoods. In the countryside, many local councils do not allocate money from their budgets to improve access to water in Romani communities. In the majority of cases, they will accept nongovernmental offers to install pipes or to dig wells with foreign funds.[283]

6.4.1. Availability of clean water in urban areas

Romani urban areas generally have access to water, but the water is of poor quality and sometimes not sufficient for normal use. In the past, officials have subordinated Romani needs for safe drinking water to the interests of businesses and other residential communities.

Romani communities are often downstream from polluting factories. According to Romani sources, a tannery in Kumanovo dumps all of its toxic waste into the river upstream from Sredorek.[284] Until a year ago, the Romani families in Sredorek drank water from the river. The majority suffered from hepatitis or kidney stones.[285] National and local authorities did not take any measures to provide safe drinking water to the mahala, although it was known that the waste water treatment system at the leather processing facility was "obsolete" and in need of rehabilitation[286] and that a couple of thousand people, including children, were drinking from the river's polluted waters. In 1998, local Romani organizations raised funds from abroad and connected the Romani houses to the city water system.[287] This is no compensation, however, for the Romani inhabitants whose health has been affected by the authorities' neglect for so many years.

In the Romani community of Jivkova Karpa-Bavce (Kumanovo), sewage from nearby Macedonian houses runs down the hill through a pipe and spills out onto the road and into Romani courtyards. The houses in the community, which has approximately 250 families, do not have their own sewage systems. The entire area around Bavce has safe drinking water, with the exception of Romani houses.[288]

Romani settlements near garbage dumps generally have the worst quality water. For example, a tiny stream, highly polluted by a nearby chemical plant, separates the houses of Kvantasi from a garbage dump, fifteen meters away. As described earlier, the city made a half-hearted attempt to clean up the site by covering the garbage with a thin layer of soil. Nearby Macedonian houses have indoor plumbing and clean, filtered water, but the Romani settlement of some eighty members shares one source of highly polluted, yellow water. A Romani NGO is helping the community dig a well.

Access to water is also a serious problem in Bajnica, a Romani neighborhood at the edge of Gostivar, where the organization Mesecina reports that dozens of families share water from a single well.[289] In the city center, on Baraki street, the Romani inhabitants complain that they are the only ones in the entire neighborhood not connected to the city water system. Each family has a pump in the courtyard, but the water is so dirty that they use it only for washing.[290] To have safe drinking water they must beg for water from their Albanian or Macedonian neighbors.[291] Romani NGOs allege that local authorities refused to meet with community leaders to discuss finding a solution to the problem.[292]

Some municipalities may be willing to improve the quantity and quality of water in Romani settlements, but officials indicate that they cannot do so until city plans incorporate Romani neighborhoods. Due to the development of Romani areas, it is common for city plans to omit these areas. In Kumanovo, the local administration is ready to include Romani neighborhoods in the new urban plan if Romani NGOs raise funds to draw up the plans.[293] The existence of the updated plans is a necessary condition for improving infrastructure.[294] Until then, many of the 6,000 Romani inhabitants in the 110,000-strong city will not have sufficient water or safe drinking water.[295]

Numerous Romani and foreign NGOs are trying to solve the practical aspects of access to water. The Water and Sanitation Program of the International Rescue Committee (IRC) works in twelve communities.[296] A UNDP–Macedonian government project seeks to improve Shuto Orizari's water supply problems.[297]

The absence of safe disposal systems for human waste, more accentuated in Romani neighborhoods than elsewhere in Macedonia, is a serious threat to the health of the community.[298] Only 63.7 percent of Romani homes are connected to a public sewage system. Out of the remaining 36.3 percent, 58.7 percent use private latrines, 5.5 percent public latrines, and 35.8 percent various other unsanitary methods.[299]

Discrimination abounds in the provision of sufficient clean water. The practice of running sewage systems around the neighborhood of one, and only one, ethnic group obviously has a disparate impact on that group. It is doubtful that government can offer a reasonable, objective, and legitimate purpose in order to justify such a practice under international human rights standards. Furthermore, the unwillingness of government officials to update urban plans to incorporate Romani areas may constitute impermissible race-based discrimination. Since mostly Romani neighborhoods do not appear on these maps, mostly Roma, and not Macedonians, suffer from these problems.

Recommendations

1. General Recommendations for Improving the Access of Roma to Public Services

- Adopt comprehensive antidiscrimination legislation following the principles established by the EU Race Directive. Prohibit both direct and indirect discrimination. Adopt specific measures to prevent or compensate for disadvantages linked to racial or ethnic origin.
- Establish judicial and administrative procedures to implement antidiscrimination legislation and authorize associations, organizations, and other legal entities to engage in seeking legal remedies on the behalf of the victims they represent. Designate a body capable of providing independent assistance to victims of discrimination in pursuing their complaints.
- Ensure detailed legal analysis of existing laws, decrees, and regulations in the field of social protection, health care, and housing. Eliminate all discriminatory provisions, as well as provisions that have a disparate impact on the Romani community, from existing legislation.
- Encourage high level officials to take public positions against discrimination and to communicate to all government employees and agents that direct and indirect discrimination is not tolerated and will be punished.

- Create specialized bodies for the monitoring of social rights at the national and regional level. Ensure a large participation of Roma in the monitoring process. Encourage data-gathering activities and transparent decision-making processes. There is a need for qualitative assessment studies, as well as for the gathering of ethnically sensitive data, in order to illuminate the existence and real extent of discriminatory practices.
- Support the elaboration of detailed, meaningful national strategies for improving the access of Roma to social welfare, health care, and adequate housing. Some of the issues related to access to social protection, health care, and adequate housing can be solved at the local level. Real solutions to structural problems, however, require legislative reforms and financial commitments at the national level. In this context, effective access of Roma to public services can be achieved only through a combination of national strategies and actions at the local level. The national strategies should be elaborated by multidisciplinary teams of experts with the active participation of Roma and based on integrated, culturally appropriate approaches.
- Eliminate requirements that prevent Roma from acquiring citizenship in the countries where they live. Solve the crisis of statelessness as soon as possible. Provide low-income persons with appropriate identification documents quickly and for no fee. Allow people to establish their de facto residency as their legal residency.

2. Specific Recommendations for Improving Access to Social Protection

- Review all social assistance legislation and eliminate provisions that have a disparate impact on certain groups. Provide children with equal access to social benefits, regardless of family size. Eliminate requirements, such as the travel, corporate ownership, and housing sale tests, which have a disparate impact on the Roma. Develop alternative methods of assessing wealth and income.
- Ensure payment of social benefits in a timely manner. Provide proper evaluations of the financial resources of the municipalities and allocate sufficient funds to cover the costs of social assistance programs.
- Apply the work requirement (in exchange for benefits) equitably, i.e. not on the basis of race.
- Make public facilities accessible to Roma. Do not discriminate against Roma as a group in retaliation for individual misbehavior.
- Do not force Roma to choose needlessly among nonexclusive types of

benefits when they are entitled to more than one. Do not compel Roma to accept poor quality food pantry benefits instead of cash.

- Do not impose time limits on the receipt of benefits. Provide benefits to all persons in need, regardless of their length of time in poverty.
- Ensure wide participation of Romani NGOs and individual Roma in the delivery of social services. Educate non-Romani social workers and public administration officials about Romani traditions, family structure, mobility patterns, etc.
- Create effective appeals mechanisms for persons who dispute social workers' assessments of wealth, income, and need. Review and improve the existing complaint mechanisms. Ensure effective remedies for the victims of social rights violations. Simplify accountability mechanisms, reduce judicial fees, and provide subsidized or free legal services to those in economic need.

3. Specific Recommendations for Improving Access to Health Care

- Generate and disseminate information that accurately assesses the health care needs of Roma. Analyze and monitor on a continuous basis the access of Roma to health care services.
- Ensure equal access of Roma to health insurance. Adopt adequate measures to facilitate the access of the very poor to noncontributory health insurance. Repeal criteria based on marital and citizenship status, family size, and level of educational achievement.
- Ensure that low-income individuals who need emergency medical treatment receive it, regardless of technical compliance with health insurance provisions.
- Encourage media outlets to portray Roma, their state of health, and their medical needs in a more realistic and unbiased manner.
- Investigate and punish claims of direct racial discrimination in the provision of health care services by medical facilities and personnel. Train doctors and nurses not to subject Romani patients to verbal abuse and degrading treatment. Promote cultural competence within the health care system.
- Ban segregation of patients on the basis of race.
- Ensure that victims of police brutality or racist attacks can obtain medical certificates documenting their injuries by removing existing obstacles and delays.
- Ensure Roma access to information on preventative health measures.
- Ensure the participation of Roma in all activities aimed to improve the

health of their community. Support the institution of Romani health mediators on a national scale.

- Ensure Roma access to safe drinking water, improve vaccination rates, adopt measures aimed to decrease the infant mortality rates and to increase Romani life expectancy.
- Create or relocate health care facilities in Romani neighborhoods. Provide transportation to existing medical facilities. Create a system of incentives for medical personnel to work in especially poor Romani neighborhoods.
- Advance integrated approaches to Romani health issues by underlining connections with housing, education, employment, municipal services, and social protection issues.

4. Specific Recommendations for Improving Access to Housing and Municipal Services

- Review and amend housing legislation to eliminate all discriminatory provisions. Adopt clear regulations on social housing, giving priority to the indigent, large families, and disadvantaged people. Incorporate specific antidiscrimination provisions, clear sanctions, effective complaint mechanisms, and effective remedies.
- Create monitoring systems to identify, document, and report on discriminatory practices in the field of housing at national and regional levels.
- Regard housing problems as human rights issues. Ensure appropriate training for lawyers and judges, NGOs and Romani leaders, on housing rights and discrimination issues. Ensure victims' access to justice by providing low cost or free legal assistance and speedy procedures.
- Include Roma in the fair and equitable distribution of agricultural land. Give the Roma the tools, training, and time they need to be effective tillers of the soil.
- Adopt measures for the legalization of Romani settlements. Develop new urban plans, survey Romani dwellings, and register Roma as legal residents in the places in which they actually dwell.
- Build only acceptable housing for Roma. Terminate programs to construct substandard accommodations for the Roma.
- Ensure effective legal protection against racial segregation and end involuntary segregation of Roma behind physical barriers, in pigsties, warehouses, garages, and garbage dumps.

- Provide equal access to electricity, public transportation networks, garbage collection, and clean water to Romani neighborhoods. Subsidize the cost of services for the truly poor.
- Investigate and punish intrusions and harassment by local authorities and private gangs.
- Mobilize public and private local, national, and international resources. Support local initiatives from national budgets. If insufficient resources exist at the national level, apply for special loans from international financial institutions and/or include Roma in all relevant projects prepared with the international financial community. Subsidize local efforts and educate local authorities to allocate, create, and seek funds for housing or for improving the infrastructure in disadvantaged communities.

"We are not repairing the buildings anymore. The water and sewage systems do not function. There are no lights on the streets. We already pulled out whites from there. But Gypsies will stay at least for two years. Where should I put them? Do you really think that I should place them among our normal people?"

DEPUTY MAYOR OF SLEZSKA, OSTRAVA

Supplement: Housing in the Czech Republic

1. The State's Obligations under International, Constitutional, and National Law

The Czech Republic is a party to all United Nations conventions relevant to the right to housing: the International Covenant on Civil and Political Rights (ICCPR),[1] the International Covenant on Economic, Social and Cultural Rights (ICESCR),[2] the Convention on the Rights of the Child (CRC),[3] the Convention on the Elimination of All Forms of Discrimination Against Women (CEDAW),[4] and the International Convention on the Elimination of All Forms of Racial Discrimination (ICERD).[5] At the European level, the Czech Republic has ratified the European Convention for the Protection of Human Rights and Fundamental Freedoms (ECHR),[6] the European Social Charter,[7] and the Framework Convention for the Protection of National Minorities.[8]

International conventions on human rights and fundamental freedoms are directly applicable and take precedence over national legislation.[9] Therefore, the prohibition against racial segregation laid down by Article 3 of the International Convention on the Elimination of all Forms of Racial Discrimination[10] is part of national law.

The enjoyment of constitutionally protected rights and freedoms are guaranteed to all "irrespective of sex, race, color of skin, language, faith, religion, political and other opinion, national or social origin, belonging to a national or ethnic minority, property, birth or other status."[11] However, little legislation has been adopted so far to implement this antidiscrimination clause.[12] The national housing law does not contain any other specific provisions explicitly outlawing racial discrimination by public institutions or private persons.[13] There is neither fair housing legislation nor any state institution that monitors equal access to housing.[14]

2. National Housing Strategies for Roma

In 1998, the new government stated that it would "do everything possible for the provision of accessible and acceptable housing for all citizens."[15] Its subsequent policy papers differ as to how to consider and address the discrimination and poverty faced by the Roma. First, there is the Concept of Government Policy Toward Members of the Romani Community, which advocates for antidiscrimination legislation and affirmative action, but fails to recognize the existence of de facto racial segregation and the ongoing ghettoization process.[16] Second, the Ministry of Regional Development prepared a new Housing Policy Concept that likens Roma to "handicapped groups of citizens" that are "unable to resolve their housing situation." It proposes to use social work methods to strengthen the "ability of handicapped groups of citizens to prevent their own marginalization." The Housing Policy Concept focuses on ensuring rent payment, deduction of debts from social benefits, and timely reporting on failures to pay. It calls for a "specific approach" to "problematic Romani families" based on "general principles used to deal with unadaptable persons" in a context of an "increased involvement of Romani counselors." The Housing Policy Concept also states that the government should "channel international aid from the relevant European structures to the problematic areas, and . . . observe international standards for resolving this situation that reflect the realistic possibilities of countries and self-governments as well as the specific culture of the Romani population."[17]

3. Romani Settlements in the Czech Republic

At the end of World War II, the Czech territory was virtually "Roma-free." By 1944, between 6,000 and 8,000 Czech Roma had been killed in concentration camps, predominantly Auschwitz. In total, approximately 95 percent of all Roma living in the Czech lands lost their lives during the war,[18] leaving fewer than seven hundred survivors.[19] Between 1950 and 1970, the government brought thousands of Roma from Eastern Slovakian settlements to industrialized Czech zones, where state enterprises needed a cheap labor force.[20] Roma received apartments in buildings or houses belonging to municipalities, mining companies, factories, or agricultural farms. The apartments were located throughout Czech towns, including central locations.

Today, Roma generally reside in low-quality municipal apartments, often with inadequate hygienic conditions,[21] lacking appropriate facilities such as clean water, functioning sewage systems, and legally supplied electricity. Chronically underfunded municipalities rarely repair the apartments, unless they intend to sell them to private owners.

The government is in the process of privatizing many of these apartments, a program which displaces tens of thousands of Roma. The new owners, eager to earn more money, often pressure tenants to give up their apartments. Due to widespread unemployment and poverty, only a small percentage of the Romani population can afford to buy and keep the apartments in which they live. If Romani residents cannot purchase their dwellings, then the municipalities or new private owners eventually evict them. Currently, tens of thousands of eviction cases are pending around the country.[22] The number of Romani evictees who live in degrading conditions is growing exponentially.

Roma who do not have valid lease agreements are particularly in peril. In Southern Bohemia, for example, the government brought many Roma from Slovakia to work in the factories. Their employers permitted them to stay in houses from which Germans were expelled, but they never signed formal lease agreements.[23] Technically, they are now illegal occupants, and the owners of the properties may evict them at any moment, without being required to provide residents with substitute accommodations.[24] A similar situation exists in Ovcari, a small Romani settlement near Kutna Hora, where several Romani families received apartments twenty years ago but the local archives contain no formal lease contracts.[25]

Many Roma who reside in rural areas in the Czech Republic face similar insecurity. Many years ago, the state sent part of the cheap Romani labor force displaced from Slovakia to rural areas to work in agriculture, animal farms, and sugar mills. Those workers also received accommodations, usually in houses situated close to the workplace, at the margins of the villages, outside the villages, or within agricultural complexes. Although a few concluded lease contracts with the owners, the majority stayed at their employer's discretion, without documentation. Today many of the farms and enterprises that once employed the Roma have closed. Some houses were sold to private persons who are intent on forcing the Roma out. Others were transferred to municipalities in terrible shape, because the local councils have not invested in repairs.

Housing conditions in some rural areas are as bad as, or worse than, in some cities. For example, in Vetrni, government officials have acknowledged that more than a hundred Roma "live in totally unbearable housing conditions" in the area called Stare Pecky.[26] In Prostejov district, it is reported that Roma "live in bad hygienic conditions, in overcrowded flats of low quality, without sanitary facilities" in the villages of Dobrobimilice and Vrbatky.[27]

Romani individuals and families are trapped among endless layers of discrimination. The ongoing process of ghettoization is part of the systematic policies of exclusion that national and local authorities carry out. The process started after the fall of communism and became acute after 1993 during a five-year period in which the government deprived tens of thousands of Roma of citizenship rights and pushed them into poverty.

Before 1989, the overwhelming majority of Romani men and many Romani women were employed. After 1989, the combined effect of economic crisis, privatization, and dismissal left the majority of Roma without jobs. Unemployment in the Romani community skyrocketed. While unemployment in the Czech Republic generally was around 5 percent, among the Roma it was approximately 70 percent, and in some places as high as 90 percent.[28]

Between 1990 and the end of 1992, the social safety nets and health insurance systems protected the Roma. Then, on 1 January 1993, the new Czech citizenship law went into effect,[29] and tens of thousand of Roma became foreigners. Without Czech citizenship and permanent residence permits, they lost the rights to work, health insurance, and social benefits enjoyed by nearly all citizens and residents.[30] Mothers no longer had maternity benefits, children lost child allowances, and families could not receive housing and rent support. As "illegal aliens," they had access only to the "life minimum," the last safeguard against starvation. Poverty exploded in the community.

Some individuals managed to start their own businesses. Others left the country. Some resorted to petty crime. When caught, the government expelled them to Slovakia, without the right to return. Many families were separated. Mothers and children remained in the Czech Republic, trying to survive alone.[31] The majority, however, stayed in their municipal apartments, and became poorer and poorer.

Private owners convinced Romani tenants to leave voluntarily by offering them money, suggesting cheaper accommodations, or harassing them. When impoverished families could not pay for rent, heat, or water, authorities quickly initiated legal action and the courts evicted the families. With no money to pay attorney's fees, Roma had little chance to defend themselves. They systematically lost their cases and their apartments.

Those evicted first moved into their relatives' already overcrowded spaces. The number of people sharing the same space became higher and higher until it became difficult to preserve the apartments. New rounds of evictions followed, this time based on deterioration and destruction of the apartments.

The evictees then moved into "holbyty" or "substitute accommodations" granted by the court to "nonpayers" or to people evicted on other grounds (for more on "holbyty," see 7.2.2). The "holbyty" include barracks, dormitories, shelters, and new housing units constructed for "socially unadaptable people." Municipal funds paid for the construction of some of these substandard houses, which have no facilities and are located at the margins of the cities, far from most schools, hospitals, and commercial centers. They foster de facto segregation.

The conditions in these substandard houses are poor. In some places, there is only cold water or no water at all. In other places, people share filthy bathrooms. Most residents have no easy way of washing their children and their clothing properly. Their dwellings are far from the special schools that Romani children attend. Either children travel for hours and pay for the transport, or transport does not exist and children do not receive a formal education. Not sending the children to school is a criminal offense, for which authorities occasionally prosecute parents.

4. Racial Segregation

4.1. Failure to prevent racial segregation

Polls and public statements reveal strong anti-Romani sentiments among a significant percentage of the Czech Republic population, politicians, and administrators. Surveys indicate that the majority of the population resists living with Roma as neighbors.[32] In a 1996 poll, 35 percent of Czechs said they favored "concentrating and isolating the Roma," and 45 percent indicated they supported "moving the Roma out of the Czech Republic if possible."[33] A more recent study from the Institute for Criminology and Social Prevention found that 80 percent of secondary school students said they would resent having a Romani family as a neighbor.[34]

In the last two years, residents in several areas have signed and circulated anti-Romani petitions, which urge local authorities to "solve the Romani problem." For example, in June 1999 approximately one hundred inhabitants of Krnov signed a complaint that said that Roma "are noisy on the street, listen to loud music, make messes, and spoil the neighborhood."[35] Inhabitants of Jihlava collected signatures for a petition on "The Solution of the Gypsy Question in the City."[36] Another anti-Romani petition—in the southern Moravian town of Znojmo—was reported in the spring of 1999.[37] These letters pressure local authorities to displace all Roma, when a more appropriate measure would be for authorities to investigate and address specific concerns about particular persons, regardless of their race.

In some cases, government officials have indicated support for the petitioners' demands to displace Romani neighborhoods. In June 2000, 180 residents of the south Moravian town of Prostejov complained about noise, disorder, and the danger of infectious diseases due to poor hygiene[38] and demanded that Prostejov officials rein in the inhabitants of the Saint Anna Romani neighborhood.[39] The local council organized a press conference at which it declared "support for the inhabitants" and a willingness to address the situation by organizing "reeducation experiments," integrating the "better" families into mainstream society, scattering the others, and demolishing the entire neighborhood.[40] Czech radio quoted local councilors as saying that they had "already started planning where families can be moved to, but haven't disclosed their plans in order not to cause panic in town."[41]

Other Czech politicians have aired similar sentiments. In an article published in 1997, Senator Klausner, mayor of Prague 4, a large district of the capital city, recommended to landlords to move Roma out of Prague.[42] Ostrava's deputy mayor described Klausner's suggestion as "a sensible solution."[43] After the 1997 summer floods, Liana Janackova, the mayor of Ostrava's district Marianske Hory, offered to help Roma emigrate by paying part of the cost of a plane ticket to Canada. Those who benefited had to give up tenancy of their municipal apartments.[44] "We have two groups of people—Gypsies and whites—that live together, but can't and don't want to. So why can't one group take the first step toward finding a solution?" Janackova told the press. "I don't think it's racist. We just want to help the Gypsies."[45]

A significant proportion of housing administration officials support these views. The government has recognized that one of every three housing department employees is "in favor of concentrating Roma,"[46] and almost 45 percent think that the state should punish Roma more severely than non-Roma when they commit crimes or fail to meet generally accepted norms.[47] The government appears not to have taken any measures to address the widespread prejudice within the administration in general and within the housing departments in particular.[48]

In some of its public statements to the international community, the government has ignored the existence of racial segregation.[49] In its February 2000 periodic report to the Committee on the Elimination of Racial Discrimination, the government stated that, with the exception of the "Usti wall," it was "not aware of any other efforts in the Czech Republic to subject Roma to certain forms of isolation."[50]

4.2. Failure to prohibit racial segregation

As a successor state of Czechoslovakia, the Czech Republic is a state party to the International Convention on the Suppression and Punishment of the Crime of Apartheid and to the International Convention for the Elimination of All Forms of Racial Discrimination, both of which prohibit racial segregation. The Czech Constitution states that ratified and promulgated international treaties on human rights and fundamental freedoms are directly binding and take precedence over national law.[51]

Nonetheless, national legislation does not offer effective legal protection against racial segregation. The Czech legal system does not define the notion of "racial segregation" and does not have any law or regulation expressly prohibiting it. Housing regulations do not provide legal protection against racial discrimination,[52] administrative procedures available in racial discrimination cases are ineffective,[53] and no legal aid is offered to indigent victims of discriminatory practices.[54]

The government claims that, in times of peace, the prohibition against supporting and promoting movements seeking to suppress citizens' rights and freedoms[55] and the prohibition against expressing public sympathy for fascism or other similar movements[56] may be used against racial segregation.[57] The Penal Code does incriminate "apartheid practices" and "inhuman acts arising from racial discrimination," but only if committed in wartime.[58] In practice, antifascist ordinances do not offer effective legal protection against the local administrations' racial segregation policies and practices.

4.3. Failure to eradicate racial segregation

In October 1999, Usti nad Labem authorities built the "Usti wall," a 65-meter-long reinforced concrete wall demarking the boundary between Czech and Romani areas.[59] Officials said that they constructed the wall to solve a dispute between Romani and Czech neighbors. The Czechs living on the other side allegedly considered the Roma noisy and dirty.[60]

Although the national government said that it did not agree with the construction of the wall, it refused to categorize the wall as a racial segregation issue. In a document transmitted to the Committee for the Elimination of Racial Discrimination in January 1999, the government argued that the construction of a 1.8 meter high fence, without gates, separating the apartments of 150 Romani people from Czech neighbors, did "not suggest physical isolation, much less segregation."[61] Human rights NGOs criticized the government for failing to prevent its construction despite having the legal mechanisms to delay or block the local council's decision to build the wall.[62] In November 1999, under heavy international pressure, officials dismantled the Usti wall. However, racial segregation prevailed because authorities helped the non-Romani inhabitants move out,[63] transforming the entire area into a Romani neighborhood and contributing to the deepening of racial segregation.[64]

5. Discrimination in the Allocation of Municipal Apartments

5.1. Administration of municipal apartments

Local officials have authority over the allocation of municipal apartments, which amount to approximately 25 percent of the entire housing stock today.[65] A significant number of subsidized apartments are occupied by medium- or high-income tenants, who before 1993 held leases that contained no time limits. Each municipality sets aside part of the lower quality housing units as substitute accommodations for entitled evictees and emergency cases. The local authorities distribute the remaining units.

Between 1948 and 1991, comprehensive laws governed the distribution of municipal apartments. Under the 1964 Law on Administration of Apartments, the last such law, the government allocated apartments according to housing lists that gave priority to families with the lowest income and the greatest number of children.[66]

After 1991, the law was cancelled and no substitute mechanism was put into place.[67] Local authorities seized the opportunity to direct the distribution of municipal apartments according to their own regulations. They now have an enormous amount of discretion in awarding apartments. Many do not appear to follow the current government's declared intention "to do everything possible to secure accessible and adequate housing for all citizens."[68] The function of municipal apartments is often unclear.[69] The eligibility requirements in several cities indicate that the municipalities want tenants who are educated or permanent residents of the city and who have stable employment in the same locality and no criminal record.[70]

In this context of scarce resources and unchecked local discretion, municipal governments often appear to discriminate against the Roma in the allocation of municipal apartments. The most recent report of the European Commission against Racism and Intolerance (ECRI) notes, "Roma/Gypsies are reported to be the least preferred neighbors compared to all nationalities and ethnic groups. This is reflected not only in the private housing market but also in the assignment of council flats. As a result, there are large concentrations of Roma/Gypsies on the outskirts of cities, where these people often live in poor hygienic conditions, far from work and educational opportunities, and where they are essentially separate from the rest of society."[71]

Direct discrimination in the assignment of municipal apartments appears in two forms: refusal to rent municipal apartments to Romani applicants, and refusal to offer Roma the same terms and conditions as other applicants. Indirect discrimination occurs when apparently neutral allocation systems or eligibility requirements have a disparate impact on the Romani community, effectively barring their access to municipal apartments.[72] Poverty does not allow Roma "to arrange housing from their own resources, making them completely dependent on the system of assigning municipal apartments."[73]

5.2. Direct discrimination

5.2.1. Refusal to rent municipal apartments to Romani applicants

Roma privy to governmental decision-making processes claim that officials discriminate against Roma on the basis of their race in the allocation of municipal apartments. They say that officials often know which applicants are Roma and do not give apartments to them so as to avoid protests by prejudiced non-Romani residents.

"Roma are frequently refused housing or apartments simply because they are Roma,"[74] said Ondrej Gina, a Romani leader and a member of the housing commission in Rokycany. In a discussion with Canadian officials, he accused the housing commission of racism. It is easy to identify a Romani applicant, he explained, especially in small cities where people know each other. For example, in Rokycany, there are only about eight Romani extended families, and therefore only eight surnames, making it a simple matter for local officials to know who is Romani.[75] "The commission would go down the list name by name in a smooth process," Gina said, "but when they came to a Romani applicant, they would stop and start looking for reasons to deny them the apartment, saying, for example, that the available apartment 'is not suitable' or is 'too small' for a Romani family."[76] Even if commission members sincerely had these concerns, they made no effort to find acceptable alternative accommodations, for the large Romani families. In his resignation from the housing commission, Gina listed thirteen cases in which the commission unjustifiably denied a Romani applicant a municipal apartment.[77]

Robert Olah, former advisor on Romani policy for the Olomouc Regional Government, makes similar allegations about the housing commission in Olomouc. Knowing or assuming the Romani ethnicity of the otherwise eligible applicants, members of housing commissions refuse to allocate them municipal apartments out of fear that non-Romani neighbors would protest, Olah said.[78]

5.2.2. Refusal to offer Roma the same terms and conditions offered other applicants

5.2.2.1. Romani applicants relegated to segregated or unsafe areas

Romani NGOs report that municipal officials offer Romani applicants substandard accommodations in segregated areas while non-Romani applicants receive apartments in other parts of the cities. The VIZE 97 foundation determined that at least five of the thirty-four Romani families who live on Maticni Street should have received a normal municipal apartment.[79] They applied through the common procedure, had good social standing, and paid their rent regularly.[80] However, the municipality allocated them apartments with minimum basic conveniences in buildings specially designated "for people evicted from their homes for not paying the rent."[81] The government acknowledged that it placed Romani families and non-Romani ex-convicts on Maticni Street.[82]

Officials allocate apartments in unsafe areas to the Roma. In Hrusov, Ostrava, floods destroyed or severely damaged dozens of Romani and non-Romani apartments in 1997. Authorities moved the non-Romani families into state-owned apartments in other parts of Ostrava. However, they allegedly offered Roma the choice between apartments in a zone officially declared unsafe[83] and no housing at all.[84] Petr Kudela, the deputy mayor of Slezska who had direct responsibility for housing these families, said, "We explicitly told Gypsies that they should not think that they will get apartments somewhere else than in Hrusov. . . . We are not repairing the buildings anymore. The water and the sewage systems do not function. There are no lights on the streets. We already pulled out whites from there. But Gypsies will stay at least for two years. . . . Where should I put them? Do you really think that I should place them among our normal people?"[85]

5.2.2.2. Disparate treatment of Roma in damaged apartments

Local authorities have refused to allocate equivalent accommodations to Romani families whose dwellings were damaged by forces beyond their control. Skinheads destroyed a Romani household in Krnov (Bruntal district) during the first week of February 1998. The victims, all members of the Kovaci family, lawfully occupied two rooms on the ground floor of a municipal building inhabited mainly by Roma. Skinheads threw Molotov cocktails into one of the rooms, burning everything inside to ashes.[86] The municipality, which according to the Civil Code had the obligation to give the tenants equivalent accommodations,[87] offered them a smaller apartment of only one room. The family refused and insisted on an equivalent apartment. "Their position," Deputy Mayor Vladimir Vocelka said, "creates strong anti-Romani attitudes in the majority population, because people believe that the Kovaci family is trying to benefit from their tragedy."[88] Markus Pape, the ERRC correspondent in the Czech Republic, notes that the municipality made efforts to help the family replace lost furniture and to repair the apartment. However, they never received an equivalent place to live.[89]

5.2.2.3. Disproportionate numbers of Roma with invalid leases

Landlords often offer Roma leases for limited periods of time while they give non-Roma indefinite contracts. Emil Scuka, a Romani lawyer who frequently deals with housing issues in his legal practice, says that landlords presume that Romani tenants are more likely than other tenants to destroy their apartments, to make noise, to breach the norms of coexistence, or to fail to pay the rent.[90]

Landlords also take advantage of Romani illiteracy and ignorance regarding contracts. For example, Brno municipality entrusted administration of municipal apartments to "Faster Realty," a local real estate agency. According to Andreea Rezkova, an Ecological Legal Service lawyer, "the agency takes advantage of their lack of legal awareness and gives Roma pieces of paper that may hardly be called contracts. They are not dated; they are missing other important formal requirements of a contract; the rights of the tenants are not stipulated; or notice terms are shorter than those provided by law. I saw a contract where the tenant's signature was missing. I saw contracts stipulating that, for a certain period of time, people would work instead of paying rent, and only after that would the lease go into effect. When it comes to eviction procedures, the agency contests the validity of the contract and argues that the family does not have tenancy rights and therefore no right to substitute accommodations. This is a systematic practice. The mistakes are too obvious, and there are too many Romani cases to believe that all are coincidences. Half of the Romani contracts I examined were not valid."[91]

5.3. Indirect discrimination

Indirect discrimination exists where apparently neutral allocation rules have a disparate impact on Roma, de facto barring their access to municipal apartments. Eligibility requirements such as a clean criminal record, permanent residence, permanent employment, and good morality effectively exclude Roma from competing for municipal housing. Point systems often systematically disadvantage or exclude certain Romani applicants.

Czech citizenship is the condition sine qua non for the allocation of a municipal apartment in virtually all Czech localities. Consequently, a significant segment of the Romani population, those affected by the exclusionary provisions of the Czech citizenship law, did not have access to municipal apartments in the period 1993–1998. In 1998, when the government amended the citizenship law, many of them acquired citizenship and could apply for municipal housing. However, eligibility requirements or the distribution systems hindered their access to apartments.

5.3.1. Clean criminal record requirement

Local authorities use at least three different methods of conditioning eligibility for municipal housing on a clean criminal record. Many studies have documented how such conditions have a disparate impact on Roma.[92] There is no justification for inclusion of such a requirement among the conditions for social housing.

In some cities, the clean criminal record requirement appears as such in the regulations that govern the rental of municipal apartments. The applicant who has a criminal record is automatically disqualified, regardless of the nature or the seriousness of the criminal offense. For example, in Teplice a couple cannot rent a place unless both spouses have clean criminal records.[93] In Jihlava, applicants "sentenced for an intentional crime" are not eligible for municipal apartments.[94] Both intentional and unintentional offenses bar access to municipal housing in Pardubice.[95] In Chomutov, municipal rules forbid the access of people with criminal records to damaged apartments, even if they are able and willing to pay repair costs.[96]

In other cities, a clean criminal record is not listed as a requirement, but the applicant has an obligation to submit information about his or her criminal background with his or her application. In Most, the clean criminal record requirement does not appear in the text of the relevant regulations, but it is listed in the appendix among the documents that have to be submitted together with the application. The chief of the Housing Administration Department of Most stated that "under our regulations, an applicant who does not have a clean criminal record cannot receive a municipal apartment."[97] The city of Vsetin goes even further: The obligation to submit a criminal record pertains not only to the applicant but also to all of his or her family members.[98]

Still other cities use a point system that heavily favors those with a clean criminal record.[99] In Chomutov, for example, those without a record receive ten points, while the "criminals" receive nothing[100] (see section 5.3.6).

5.3.2. Exclusion of unemployed applicants

Some municipalities exclude unemployed applicants from municipal housing. In Pardubice, access to municipal housing is permitted only to the employed, self-employed or students.[101] In Louny and Rokycany, only the employed and self-employed have access to these apartments.

In a situation where the unemployment rate for Roma is several times higher than for non-Roma, the disparate impact of a stable employment requirement is obvious. Such a requirement is not essential for the applicant's ability to pay the rent—unemployed families receiving social welfare should have enough money to fulfill their rental obligations. Therefore, the function of the requirement appears to be exclusion of certain types of people, rather than protection of the municipalities' coffers.

5.3.3. Exclusion of beneficiaries of social support

Louny disqualifies applicants if they received social benefits in the preceding six months.[102] A regulation that explicitly excludes beneficiaries of social support constitutes direct discrimination of this particular category of persons. The regulation has a disparate impact on the Roma, since they are much more likely than other ethnic groups to receive social support.

5.3.4. Permanent residence requirement

Local councils in Louny, Beroun, Trebic, Prague-Vychod, and Nymburk do not permit nonresidents to apply for municipal housing. In some cities, even permanent residents cannot apply for municipal housing if they have not formally registered for a certain period of time: five years in Chomutov[103] and Teplice,[104] and three years in Prague districts 3 and 6 and Pardubice.[105]

Although the condition affects all potential applicants, it has a disparate impact on the Romani community. Some Roma, although living for many years in the territory of the Czech Republic, had or still have permanent residence in Slovakia. Communist authorities may have allocated them substandard apartments where only "temporary residence" was permitted, or they may have occupied "uninhabitable" apartments, or they may have lived all their lives in overcrowded apartments exceeding the number of people legally allowed in the space.

The UNHCR has noted how these regulations have affected people such as Ladislav Kuruc, who lived for many years in a dilapidated apartment in Prague. Although he submitted a series of documents proving his long-standing de facto residence, the authorities never registered him because they considered the apartment "uninhabitable." Therefore, he did not qualify for permanent residence.[106]

The Bratinka Report noted local authorities' reluctance to register Roma and the difficulties encountered by Romani families in obtaining permanent residence. "Some municipalities fear another influx of Roma, and so they decline to concern themselves more thoroughly with the problems of the local Romani community, including housing, in order to prevent the locale from becoming a target for Roma from other places. As a result of this attitude, some Roma report that they have been unable to register for permanent residence. . . ."[107]

Young people who have been institutionalized also have serious problems in obtaining permanent residence and in accessing municipal apartments. Reports indicate that the Krupka, Podborany-Psov, Dlazkovice, Visnove, Melc, and Horni Marsov municipalities have prohibited directors of children's homes from registering children as permanent residents "in order to avoid potential claims for housing."[108] Since the percentage of Romani children institutionalized relative to the Romani population is larger than that for non-Romani children and the non-Romani population, these provisions have a disparate impact on the Roma.

Some municipalities waive the permanent residence requirement in a manner that explicitly excludes the unemployed and poorly educated applicants. For example, in Teplice, officials may waive the five-year permanent residence condition if the claimant has a university degree or a baccalaureate.[109] In Pardubice, authorities do not apply the three-year permanent residence requirement to those who have stable employment, are self-employed, or enrolled as students.[110]

5.3.5. Other requirements aimed at excluding Romani applicants

Some municipalities have other conditions that exclude Roma without referring to race or ethnicity. For example, in Rokycany the assignment of an apartment to a certain applicant depends on the local government's interest in having the applicant live in the city.[111] It also depends on the "presumption of proper behavior in relation to the apartment and to other tenants."[112]

Some officials consider "moral credit" in assigning housing. In May 2000, Petr Kudela, deputy mayor of Slezska (Ostrava), stated that distribution of municipal apartments to those affected by floods in the summer of 1997 was done taking into consideration, not only the age of the applicants, the extent to which their apartment was affected, and the number of children, but also the "moral credit" of the family. According to Kudela, an applicant was morally credited only if he had "good behavior" and did not have debts.[113] The deputy mayor declared to a former project coordinator of the Helsinki Citizens' Assembly[114] that he did not want to "concentrate" Roma in Hermanice, a neighborhood in Ostrava where the municipality was building new apartments: "Gypsies steal chickens and fruit from the gardens," he said. "Also, Hermanice is my neighborhood. I live there."[115]

In Chomutov, regulations prohibit access to municipal housing to applicants who "caused their own difficult housing situation."[116] Apart from those who have debts, this category includes people who had municipal apartments and sold them, such as Roma who emigrated and are now returning to the Czech Republic. It also incorporates people who have been evicted once, people who do not behave properly, or people who violated housing orders.[117]

Discrimination on the basis of marital status by some municipalities may also have a disparate impact on the Romani community. Teplice prohibits access to municipal apartments to couples not legally married[118] or to applicants married to a foreigner.[119] Given Romani traditions and citizenship issues, these regulations have a much greater impact on the Romani community.

5.3.6. Point systems

Some municipalities use point systems that have the effect of excluding Roma from city housing. These systems permit access to municipal apartments only to those who, after meeting all "general requirements," accumulate a sufficient number of points as a result of fulfilling other conditions. Local authorities establish the criteria and the number of points corresponding to each criterion. Emphasizing certain factors such as stable employment, permanent residence, existence of a savings plan, age, and absence of debts, and deemphasizing the number of children, the number of persons per square meter, and the income level per family member effectively excludes certain types of families, namely Romani families.

For example, to gain access to municipal accommodations in Chomutov, a family must have Czech citizenship, permanent residence for at least five years, no debts to the city, no other failures to fulfill tenants' obligations, and the family must not be responsible for their difficult housing situation.[120] Only applicants who meet these requirements have access to the next stage of the process, during which the merits of their application are evaluated on points. The employed receive four points; the unemployed, zero. Those who earn a salary get eight points; those who receive social support, two points. Those with a clean criminal record, ten points; anyone who ever committed a criminal offense, zero points. A certain number of points are given for each child, but only up to three children. If the applicants are legally married, the points associated with residence, employment, salary, and a clean criminal record are calculated and added for the spouse.[121] With all other variables equal, an employed, legally married couple will always win out over unemployed partners, even if the latter have more children and more difficult living conditions. Romani couples are much less likely than non-Romani couples to have a civil marriage.

5.4. Lack of information

Lack of information makes it difficult for Roma to secure and maintain access to public housing. Jan Smock, a street worker with the Kutna Hora District Office, alleges that authorities' failure to inform Romani claimants that housing applications must be renewed every year impedes their effective access to municipal apartments. "Roma do not know and nobody tells them that they have to confirm their housing requests every year. Without the annual confirmation, their original applications stay unprocessed in a file while non-Roma receive apartments."[122] In Chomutov, applications must be renewed every year within sixty days of the initial filing date.[123]

It is unclear whether municipal officials generally fail to fulfill their duties to properly inform applicants regardless of their ethnic background or whether lack of information has a greater effect on Romani applicants. What is obvious is that a significant number of Roma do not have all of the information that they need in order to gain access to housing.

6. Private Rental Sector

The private rental sector in the Czech Republic constitutes no more than 6 percent of the housing stock.[124] The absence of proper rent regulations and lack of funds for the repair of buildings have a significant effect on the sector. The majority of Romani families do not have money to rent a private apartment; they live in relatives' places or in cheap municipal apartments. Comparative data on differential treatment of Romani and non-Romani clients in the private rental sector do not exist.

Although the Czech Civil Code prohibits landlords from cutting off essential facilities such as water and electricity,[125] property owners often harass their tenants by limiting access to these utilities.[126] As early as 1996, a UNHCR report drew attention to the manner in which certain owners harassed Romani tenants. "The consultancy's experiences in visiting permanent residences," the report said, "have routinely included encountering overcrowding into small apartments and discovering that . . . the landlord of a newly privatized building is seeking to evict Roma tenants by turning off power and water."[127] In Ovcari, a small Romani settlement, situated in the village Nove Bory (Kutna Hora), the former owner, the local sugar factory Cukrovar Nove Bory,[128] cut the water and electricity in the entire house reportedly because some tenants had not paid their bills. For one year, the eighty-six adults and forty-five children living in the house burned candles to provide light at night and acquired water from a well eight kilometers away. The dearth of water exacerbated hygiene-related problems: In the spring of 2000, approximately 40 percent of the residents examined had dysentery.[129]

Reports indicate that some landlords have employed physical threats and actual violence to evict Romani families. Some Romani families living in a building near Jaromer in the South Moravian district of Trebic have suffered from two vicious attacks. Municipal authorities offered them the apartments they occupied as substitute accommodations several years ago. An influential businessman owns the rest of the apartments in the same building. On 20 April 1999, a group of young people, led by the son of the owner, attacked the Romani tenants. They injured three Roma and one non-Roma and destroyed several cars. The prosecutor charged the owner's son with disturbing public order, but later halted proceedings against him. However, the court gave the three Romani men who defended themselves suspended prison terms. On 27 August 1999, another group attacked the Romani families again. This time the authorities arrested and indicted twelve attackers, including the owner and his son. The case is pending.[130]

7. Evictions

Many local governments and state officials have adopted policies that target the Roma for evictions, isolation, and concentration in ghettoes. Governments have created special housing facilities designed to accommodate Roma and other "socially unadaptable citizens" who cannot afford their current living arrangements. The new units are situated far away from city centers. The result is that Roma are even more isolated from the cities in which they reside.

7.1. State policy to evict, isolate, and concentrate Roma in ghettoes

Targeting Roma for evictions, isolation, and concentration in ghettoes is neither a recent nor an isolated phenomenon in the Czech Republic. Discriminatory attitudes on the part of citizens, local authorities, and politicians and systematic attempts at "getting rid" of Roma were evident even before the dissolution of Czechoslavakia.

In October 1992, a decree in Jirkov, Northern Bohemia, enabled local authorities to evict, without court orders, tenants who did not observe local regulations or hygienic rules.[131] The town council stated that the decree was aimed at Roma.[132] Shortly after, at least eighteen towns around the country requested a copy of the ordinance; Duchcov, Krupka, Bludov, Dubi, and Brandys nad Labem adopted similar measures.[133] In Krupka (Teplice), the local council endorsed "administrative eviction," a procedure that permitted the administration to evict tenants without court orders. The Duchcov decree imposed so-called "technical controls," giving the administration the right to enter any apartment, anytime, to check on the condition of the apartment. "The Jirkov decree violates the Charter of Fundamental Rights and Freedoms," the general prosecutor said. "However, the town council's attempt at solving the problem of Romani migrants should be appreciated."[134] The prefect later stopped the implementation of the Jirkov decree. Two years later, the Constitutional Court struck down the provisions of the Duchcov[135] and Krupka[136] decrees as unconstitutional.

In November 1992, a group of mayors demanded that the Czech Parliament and the Ministry of the Interior give them laws and regulations to assist them in administering housing. Among the requested measures were granting Czech citizenship only to applicants with clean criminal records, reducing child allowances received by families with more than four children, and enabling the municipalities to carry out evictions without court orders.[137] Indeed, the Citizenship Law[138] adopted in that period barred access to citizenship to all applicants sentenced for a criminal offense in the previous five years.[139] In 1993, the rightwing Republican Party offered expensive sports cars to the local governments that could rid their communities of Roma.[140]

In 1994, the city of Prerov pioneered the development of "holobyty" for people who failed to pay rent, but had the right to state-provided accommodations under Czech law. The media described the accommodations as "single-story blocks of twelve one-room apartments containing only the most basic housing requirements—concrete floors, squat toilets, metal doors and window frames, non-flammable floor coverings, reinforced glass and wire mesh."[141] Local authorities came from all over the country to study Prerov's model. "They are visiting us from all corners of the republic," Ivan Tiser, chief of the city's housing administration department, declared. "They ask all sorts of questions, and usually they make videotapes or take photos."[142] The idea spread fast. "They all call me, from Usti nad Labem, from Teplice. They all want to start similar projects," declared architect Vasil Pjesak, the father of the first row of "holobyty," to the Dutch newspaper *de Volksrant* in 1994.[143]

Politicians and local authorities embraced the "holobyty" solution. In 1994, the Kladno local branch of ODS, the then-ruling party, deplored the fact that "civilized people [were] obliged to live in direct contact with asocial groups of citizens. . . . If we want to influence these [asocial] citizens positively . . . we need to concentrate them. . . . The advantage of this solution is the long-term influence on the same group using a concentration of means. It is not possible to change their life style in a positive way if they are scattered all over and not all of them are registered." The document, which was a poster plastered on local walls, asked for "alternative punishments" because "fines are paid only by civilized people," for modifying the eviction rules for those who "do not pay the rent or cause disturbances," and for establishing a "timetable of control aimed at asocial groups of citizens and the places where they live." To do all this, the party promised to obtain financial support from the state and other institutions and "to put pressure on the Parliament."[144]

Indeed, from that moment on, local authorities—including the deputy mayor who was found guilty in 1998 of incitement to ethnic and racial hatred against Romani children[145]—methodically created the conditions for de facto racial segregation. Between 1995 and 1999, the city organized three housing areas for "unadaptable" people: Prumyslov with seventeen housing units, Na Vysokem with fourteen housing units, and Lesik with eight housing units. On 20 June 2000, the local council approved the purchase of a former meat factory[146] for the relocation of the remaining asocial citizens. The new substitute accommodations, situated on the outskirts of Kladno, will have thirty-six units and some special features for "extended families."[147]

7.2. Overrepresentation of Roma in "holobyty," housing for "socially unadaptable" citizens

7.2.1. Legal provisions related to evictions

Under Czech law, at the termination of a rent contract, the evicted tenant is entitled to alternative accommodations (bytové náhrady), which might be a substitute apartment (náhradní byt), substitute accommodations (náhradní ubytování),[148] or only shelter. If the contract is terminated for reasons not attributable to the tenant,[149] the municipality owes him or her a "substitute apartment," which "according to its size and conveniences provides for the lessee and the members of his household accommodations for dignified human habitation."[150] When the rent contract has been terminated for gross breaches of proper morality,[151] failure to pay the rent or other apartment-related fees for more than three months,[152] having two or more apartments,[153] or failure to use the apartment,[154] then the tenant is entitled only to "shelter," which are temporary accommodations and storage for furniture until the lessee obtains proper housing.[155]

When the contract is terminated for a breach of morals or a payment failure and a family with young children is involved, the court may rule that the family is entitled to substitute accommodations or even to a substitute apartment, instead of shelter.[156] The court rules only on the entitlement; the municipality, which owns the property, decides on the location and facilities of the new accommodations.[157]

The majority of Romani families enter eviction procedures for failure to pay rent or for overcrowding. Since those affected usually live in extended families with many small children, the court grants them access to substitute accommodations or apartments. However, this is not much of a favor. The municipalities offer them new "holobyty" housing, governed by special regulations. The overwhelming majority of the tenants in these housing units are Romani.

Municipal authorities and private owners have additional means at their disposal to evict Roma. Owners threaten nonpaying tenants with court proceedings and tell them that the court will not award them anything. Then the landlords tell the Roma that the owners will stop the court proceedings if the Roma move into cheaper, smaller apartments with fewer facilities. They accept, but after they move in, they discover that the rent is much higher and the contracts limited to several months or one year. Eventually, at the end of the contractual term, the police evict those unable to pay the increased rent, throwing them out into the street without even bothering to obtain a court order. The families move in with their relatives, increasing the number of persons who live in one apartment, the potential for tensions, financial problems, and the likelihood of another eviction.

Authorities call the process "natural ghettoization." They say that Roma "voluntarily" stick together, because they do not care about housing conditions, because it is cheaper to live with each other, and because they prefer being with their relatives. At best, the authorities are willfully ignorant of their role in this process. At worst, it is an egregious example of racist behavior.

7.2.2. "Holobyty," their description, location, and facilities

The term "holobyty" has come to mean much more than the original Prerov definition of "substitute accommodations" especially constructed for "socially unadaptable" people. Local authorities, NGOs, and private citizens use the term for a range of housing granted by the court to "nonpayers" or to people evicted on other grounds, such as breaches of coexistence norms. The term may designate a normal apartment, a substandard one, a room in a dormitory, or even a living space in a barracks. It may refer to houses, apartments, or groups of apartments taken over by local authorities to serve as "substitute accommodations." In May 2000, Petr Kudela, the deputy mayor of Slezska (Ostrava) responsible for housing issues, said, "Holobyty is nothing more than an apartment with a common bathroom and toilets and nothing to steal, nothing to destroy."[158]

Most "holobyty" sit on the outskirts of cities, such as in Pelhrimov, Louny, Prachatice Benesov, Beroun Rakovnik, Tabor, and Nymburk. Some of them are outside towns, such as in Decin, where one house is approximately one kilometer from the city limits; in Tachov, where one house is approximately six kilometers away; and in Kadan-Prunerov, where three houses with a capacity of eighty people each are two kilometers from the city in a former railroad station. "Holobyty" also exist less frequently in more central locations in cities such as Prague, Kolin, and Trutnov.[159]

The authorities may place the "unadaptable" in several types of accommodations ranging from small apartments with showers and toilets to rooms without bathrooms, toilets, or water. The presence of hot water is a real luxury. In some places, individual apartments have squat toilets; in others, people can access shared showers and toilets after paying a fee to a manager to obtain the key to the facilities. Sometimes even cold water is scarce. For example, there is one source of water for an entire building in Dukelska in Chomutov,[160] Unimobunky in Ostrava, and Liscina; there is one source of water for one floor in Maticni in Usti. Electricity might be the only type of heating in the house, such as in Kadan. During the winter, the bills are exorbitant. People choose among using electricity that they cannot afford, improvising stoves in the rooms, or letting their children freeze inside unheated concrete walls.

7.2.3. Rent

As a rule, the state does not regulate rent, but municipalities establish rules, which, in some cases, impose absurdly high rates. Romani families, many of them evicted precisely for their inability to pay, are placed in even more difficult situations requiring them to pay rents several times higher than their previous rents for less space and fewer facilities. Indeed, a large family living in Mexiko (Slany) may pay as much as 4,000-6,000 crowns per month,[161] an amount three to five times higher than the average level of the state-subsidized rent of 1,183 crowns per apartment per month.[162] Electricity, water, and gas, if available, are paid separately. The use of facilities such as showers, toilets, and laundry rooms is not only expensive but sometimes unreasonably limited in a way that impinges on the private lives of the tenants. In Slany, the use of the bathrooms is reduced to two hours per day except on Sundays, when access is prohibited.[163]

In Chrastava, financial burdens are equally abhorrent: Tenants are obliged by contract to pay, for rent, water, electricity, and "other services," sums between 1,500 and 2,800 crowns per month per person.[164] For a family of five, the total bill may reach 7,500-14,000 crowns monthly, which is practically ten times more than a family would pay for a normal apartment. Families use all their social support for housing-related payments; to survive, they eat less, do not use electricity, and perhaps are forced to turn to illegal activities. If they do not pay, they have to leave.

7.2.4. Loss of permanent residence

Apart from losing the apartment, moving into a "holobyty" means that the evictee gives up his or her permanent residence and all the rights associated with it. The substandard housing units do not qualify as "apartments," so the inhabitants cannot register as permanent residents at new addresses. This is much more than a formality. A permanent residence is essential for exercising voting rights and accessing the health care and social protection systems. Czech citizens without permanent residence do not have these rights and have not had them for years. The new residency regulations might provide a way out by offering a fictive permanent residence in the localities where the residence was cancelled or in Brno, but the procedure, which allows for a temporarary gap during which the individual concerned is registered nowhere, will probably start by denying rights to hundreds of additional people.

7.2.5. Statistics on overrepresentation of Roma

In theory, the houses for the "socially unadaptable" are meant to ensure accommodations for certain categories of evictees regardless of their ethnic backgrounds. The obvious reality is that the percentage of Romani residents to non-Romani residents is much greater than the percentage of Roma in the overall population. If it is true that government officials do not target Roma for evictions and do not single them out to be moved to segregated areas, it is incredibly difficult to explain how Roma account for 60 percent, 80 percent, or even 100 percent of the "holobyty" tenants when they constitute less than 3 percent of the Czech population. A survey by the Counseling Center in June and July 2000 indicates Roma represent 60 percent of the residents in housing units for the socially unadaptable in Havlickuv Brod and Tachov, 70 percent in Chrastava, 75 percent in Prague-Vychod and Karvina, 79 percent in Beroun, 80 percent in Nymburk, 100 percent in Slany (Ouvalova Street), 100 percent in Prachatice, and also 100 percent in Rakovnic.[165]

7.3. Violations of the right to privacy and the sanctity of the home

Local authorities force socially unadaptable tenants to accept contractual conditions that violate their fundamental rights. For example, local authorities in Slany interfere with tenants' rights to privacy by prohibiting people who live in the complex from receiving visitors. Not even relatives are allowed. Officials threaten termination of leases and immediate homelessness.[166] In Liberec, visitors are permitted only if previously entered in the housing register, and only if they come between 8 a.m. and 5 p.m.[167] In Chrastava, only "extremely close persons" have permission to visit and only if the administrator has been previously informed.[168] Regulations adopted by local authorities in Slany[169] and Liberec[170] oblige tenants to allow authorities access into their apartments at any hour of the day or night.

These rules violate the right to respect for one's home protected by Article 8 of the European Convention on Human Rights, which is legally binding on the Czech Republic. Furthermore, the rules have been adopted, entered into force, and implemented despite the existence of a Constitutional Court decision which stipulated that forcing tenants to permit access into apartments may be imposed only according to the law. Such an obligation imposed by municipalities via regulations, not law, violates Article 12(3) of the Charter.[171]

8. Recommendations

- Adopt comprehensive antidiscrimination legislation in all fields, including housing, following the principles established by the EU Race Directive. Create a specialized body capable of addressing discrimination issues.
- Address social housing, discrimination, and racial segregation issues in the national Romani housing strategy.
- Create a specialized body for monitoring respect for housing rights. Generate and disseminate information on Romani living conditions.
- Prohibit racial segregation, and adopt adequate measures to stop the exclusion of Roma from the rest of the population, to eradicate the consequences of past segregationist practices, and to prevent them in the future.
- Adopt social housing legislation ensuring equal access to those in need.
- Undertake a systematic review of the legality of all local regulations governing the distribution of municipal apartments and eliminate the provisions that trigger indirect discrimination against certain groups.
- Thoroughly investigate and sanction cases of direct discrimination in the distribution of municipal apartments.
- End the practice of concentrating Roma in substandard housing in segregated areas. Review all regulations governing the lease of apartments in housing reserved for "socially unadaptable" persons and eliminate all rules that constitute human rights violations.

Appendix: Romani Neighborhoods in Romania

To produce this report, the author, a Romanian human rights activist, toured dozens of Romani neighborhoods to observe Romani living conditions and to interview Roma. The notes from her visits provide much of the material that appears in the main sections of this report. The body of the report describes the dearth of social protection, health care, and housing benefits for Roma in Romania, Bulgaria, and Macedonia, compares and contrasts the social programs in the countries, and makes recommendations for improving the delivery of social services to Roma. The supplement adds information about the housing situation for Roma in the Czech Republic.

The disadvantage of the analytic structure of the main body of the report is that it separates the various aspects of the life of the average Romani person. The typical Romani individual living in these three countries faces a lack of social support, a scarcity of medical care, and terrible living conditions each and every day. Tweaking or fixing a few aspects of a couple of these problems will hardly affect the massive dual problems of discrimination and poverty.

This appendix attempts to show what it is like to live in several types of Romani settlements in Romania. Apart from the lack of facilities and the wretchedness and discrimination that are common to all, each of these settlements has a series of specific problems that raise different types of legal issues and need to be addressed separately. These multilayered sets of housing, health, and social protection problems are what make the development of national strategies so complicated.

1. Mahalas: Neighborhoods Traditionally Inhabited by Roma

The mahala is a naturally developed area with a compact Romani population. As a rule, mahalas, or at least parts of them, are included in urban plans. The quality of the buildings is acceptable but the infrastructure has been neglected for years or simply does not exist.[1] In Romania, "mahala" has an almost cultural connotation, being different, smaller, more heterogeneous, and more integrated into the fabric of the city than the huge mahalas in Skopje, Macedonia, or Sofia, Bulgaria.

1.1. Buhusi: Libertatii Street

Libertatii Street in Buhusi is a typical small mahala in a small Romanian provincial town. Only Roma inhabit its two or three streets. Houses and fences are freshly painted, the trees are nicely pruned, and the streets are clean. However, the infrastructure, which city hall should have provided, is totally missing. There is no sewage system. The entire neighborhood uses two toilets improvised on one of the streets. There is no water, and the unpaved roads are full of holes.[2]

2. Abandoned Buildings: Spontaneous Urban Ghettoes

Small urban ghettoes in apartment buildings that state enterprises and municipalities abandoned have begun to appear with much greater frequency. These abandoned buildings are quickly taken over by homeless families seeking temporary shelter and become places of absolute poverty and despair existing in virtually all Romanian cities.

2.1. Cluj: The "NATO" block

At 21 Albac Street in the Gheorghieni District, there are two four-storied substandard apartment buildings, with a total of 140 one-room apartments, each ten square meters in size, and with one bathroom per floor for the common use of all tenants. One of the two buildings is empty. At the time of the author's visit on 14 October 1999, approximately 40 families, or about 200 persons, occupied the second building. Some families had lived there for ten years.

Residents reported that authorities had cut off water, electricity, and methane gas supplies in 1994.[3] Those living there carry water with buckets from a nearby source in a marketplace. They heat the apartments by burning wood. Petrol lamps and candles supply artificial light. The average occupancy per room is between four and five persons, with some rooms even more overcrowded. There is no functioning toilet in either building; residents use vacant rooms as toilets.

Roma told the author that virtually all of the men had lost their jobs when the construction company employing them closed down. The great majority of the children do not go to school. Many of them work at the marketplace, collecting cartons, scrap iron, or empty bottles.

According to the inhabitants, in recent years, no representative of the department for child protection showed any interest in the fate of the underaged from the NATO block of apartments. They claim that the neighborhood's Greek Orthodox church stopped giving them food and clothes.[4] The only authority involved with the area is reportedly the police department, whose officers conduct monthly raids and fine anyone not properly registered at their address, which is to say, just about every adult.[5] People say that they would rather starve than not pay the fine and risk going to prison.[6]

Initially, the Cluj city hall transferred ownership of the buildings to the Ministry of Defense, which gave them to the police. Not one of the owners allegedly made any improvements to the apartments.[7] The Roma Federation had asked the Cluj city hall to transfer ownership of the apartments to the federation, but city hall chose to pass the apartments on to the Ministry of Defense.[8]

2.2. Cluj: "Hotel NATO II"

Hotel NATO II is situated on 4 Taberei Street, Manastur district, the same district where mayor Gheorghe Funar lives.[9] The building, five stories high, has approximately fifty substandard one-room apartments. The Cluj Construction Trust built the facility and, until 1990, used it as a hostel for unmarried workers. In October 1999, the building belonged to the Ministry of Defense. In the winter of 1998, approximately forty Romani families occupied it. According to the neighbors, in the spring of 1999, police and army troops evicted the Roma.

2.3. Orastie: Buildings 7 and 8[10]

The author visited apartment buildings 7 and 8 on Muresului Street, Orastie. The buildings are situated in the middle of a district of normal looking buildings. Each of the buildings has eighty substandard one-room apartments, each room measuring twelve square meters. The buildings are former hostels for unmarried workers. Building number 8 belongs to Chimica Orastie; building number 7, which once belonged to the Construction Trust, now belongs to the Municipal Administration Enterprise.[11]

Approximately 250 people live in the two buildings. Out of thirty families from building 8, sixteen have small children. Some of them have lived there for more than ten years. Only a few have leases for the apartments. They received the apartments when working for the enterprises that owned them. After 1989 they lost their jobs but remained in the apartments because they did not have anywhere else to go. Since most of the inhabitants are squatters, they are not eligible for benefits from social support or the food pantry. Education officials do not admit their children to school, because they do not have appropriate clothes or school supplies and cannot meet minimum hygiene requirements. The utility authorities turned off the electricity and water services a couple of years ago,[12] although some families claim they were paying their bills on time. The central heating radiators have been missing since 1989.[13] The lighting consists of candles and gas lamps. The heating is from burning wood in improvised stoves. On every floor, people occupy only eight to ten apartments; the rest of the apartments have no windows or doors and are used as toilets. The smell is unbearable.

People carry water from a pump in the neighboring cemetery approximately 200 meters from the apartments. They pay a 10,000 lei contribution per month per family. Residents consider lack of water the most important problem of the community. Interviewees said they would pay the cost of reconnecting the buildings to the water system, which is only ten meters away.[14]

The situation in building 7, where another twenty-five to thirty Romani families live, is identical. Residents claim that the police make frequent raids and impose fines on people for living at an unregistered address. People living in these two buildings say they repeatedly asked municipal officials to repair and help clean the buildings and install water and electricity, but the officials never responded. They say that in the last ten years, no representative of the local authorities ever visited the place, not the social assistance department, the department for the protection of children, or the health department. A priest allegedly came once, saw the place, and never came back.[15]

2.4. Targu Mures: Rovinari

In the 1960s, in a period of heavy industrialization, the authorities brought large numbers of families—and among them, many Roma—from rural areas to Targu Mures to supply unskilled workers for the city's industrial zone. The companies gave Romani workers substandard apartments of one or two rooms in the Rovinari district. Romanian and Hungarian families also received apartments in that area, but moved as soon as they could to other parts of the city. As a result, in the 1980s, Roma inhabited 99 percent of the district. When the economy began to decline, the men gradually lost their jobs. Employers sent many of them to work in Ceausescu's palace in Bucharest or to the Danube Black Sea Canal.[16] Women and children remained home with little or no money to pay the bills. Gradually, because the bills were not paid, the utility departments cut off the electricity, heating, and water. The families improvised stoves and heated the apartments with wood fires. The buildings started to fall apart, and, by 1998, they looked as if a fire had swept through them.

At the beginning of the 1990s, many Romani families sold their leases and went to Western European countries. The construction trust transferred ownership of the apartment buildings to the Targu Mures city hall. The municipality forcibly evicted the remaining families, renovated the apartments, and sold them to Romanian and Hungarian families.[17] The evicted Roma left the city, moved into the homes of their relatives, or built shacks in the local Romani slum, Valea Rece.[18]

During the author's visit to the Rovinari district, there were only two buildings inhabited by Roma: buildings 24 and 26, in which approximately eighty families live. There is no water, no sewage system, no electricity, no heating, and no gas. The buildings sit on the outskirts of the district where the fields start. Behind the buildings is a stinking heap of garbage. Children look through the garbage for things to play with or to eat.[19] Residents expect to be evicted any moment: "When the municipality finds buyers for apartments, it will evict all of us, repair the buildings, and give them to Romanians."[20]

2.5. Turda: 8 Constructorilor Street

In Turda, the Romani community consists of approximately 1,500 to 2,000 people.[21] Forty or fifty families live at 8 Constructorilor Street in an apartment building that the glass factory owned. They have no running water, and they have improvised electricity and gas connections. There are no toilets, and the people use the space around the building. Near the building are several pigsties.[22]

2.6. Buhusi: "NATO" building

Section 4.1. in the Romania section of the housing chapter describes in detail the conditions in the NATO building in Buhusi—conditions that are similar to those of the other abandoned buildings portrayed in this section.

3. Ghettoes Built or Encouraged by Public Authorities

In some instances the local authorities respond to homeless Roma or the disastrous living conditions of Romani families by offering them segregated, humiliating, and highly unhealthy living quarters. Section 5.2. of the Romania section of the housing chapter describes in detail the former pigsties given to the Roma in Deva (Hunedoara), and section 5.3 paints a picture of life in the walled-off community of Geoagiu, Hunedoara.

4. Slums

Slums are areas of shacks and hovels, built on the outskirts of the city, where the majority of the inhabitants are Roma. Roma build the houses without authorization on municipal or private land. Many families ended up living in these slums after the communist authorities demolished their houses to build industrial parks. Everyone is poor. Water sources are scarce. Where there is no electricity, residents have diverted power from existing lines. The unpaved roads are full of holes. Slums exist, without exception, in all cities visited by the author. Their populations range from a couple of hundred to more than a thousand. In all cases, the slums are located in the immediate vicinity of non-Romani apartment buildings and neighborhoods, which have water, electricity, streetlights, and paved roads. The differences between the two communities are not only visible, but also shocking. The slums have existed for dozens of years. Many residents said that they are tired of protesting against the inhuman conditions.[23] As a rule, municipalities justify the lack of infrastructure within the slums by claiming that Romani dwellings are outside the city's jurisdiction, or that the residents do not have legal possession of the land, or that there is a lack of organization within the community, or, most simply, that there is no money in the local budget.[24]

4.1. Alba Iulia: "Lumea Noua" Industrial Zone

Alba Iulia is a Transylvanian city of 72,744 inhabitants, of which 93 percent are Romanians, 3 percent Hungarians, 2 percent Roma, and 1 percent Germans and Jews. In the 1970s, in Alba Iulia, as in many other Romanian cities, "Tsigania" (The Gypsy Land), was situated at the edge of the city. At that time, officials demolished the Romani houses to make way for factories and dormitory-style housing for their workers. The owners of large well-built houses received some financial compensation while the rest received nothing. Some families found work in the factories and lived in the newly built dormitories. Some went to work for a company in the next city and found housing there. The majority, however, moved to an empty field a few hundred meters away and started building Lumea Noua (The New World).[25]

After 1989, Romani families living in apartment buildings gradually lost their jobs. Because they could not pay their rent or bills, they were evicted, or they gave up their leases and found places to live with their relatives in Lumea Noua, or illegally improvised some dwelling in that area.

Lumea Noua is a slum made up of Crevei and Elesteului streets; all of the residents are Roma. On its east side are Romanian apartment houses; to the south and southwest, an empty field; in the northwest corner, a large factory; in front, a vacant asphalt lot. The community is relatively stable, with many families having lived there for more than fifteen years.

The paved street ends where the slum begins and then 400 meters later, on the other side, starts again. After a rain, the mud is ankle deep. A water pipe ends fifty meters before the first Romani house. Two or three families have wells in their yards, but they do not allow the others to use them. The two hundred remaining residents share one well of smelly, sandy, red-worm-filled water.[26] Five families have toilets in their yards. The rest of the community uses the empty field behind the settlement. A power line passes directly through the slum. Residents allege that the electric company refuses to connect homes because construction occurred without authorization.[27] They say that they dare not tap into the power line without authorization for fear of severe penalties.[28] There are no streetlights. There is no organized garbage collection and, although the nearby factory has dumpsters out front, it allegedly forbids residents from using them.[29] When the smell becomes unbearable, the people haul the garbage in wheelbarrows to a dump five kilometers away. Residents report that the police make regular raids, often before 6 a.m., pounding loudly on the doors of randomly chosen residents, who are then taken to the police station and fined for not having registered formally at the address where they live.

4.2. Targu Mures: Valea Rece

Valea Rece is located in the southern part of the city of Targu Mures. The first Romani houses appeared here at the beginning of the century. The one thousand residents, of whom approximately six hundred are children, live in 150 houses, built on two streets on the side of a hill. The majority of the families are settled Roma. There are also three or four poor Hungarian families. Ninety percent of the population is unemployed and unskilled. They survive by selling things on the streets, painting houses, doing odd jobs, and conducting semilegal transactions, often earning as little as 20-30,000 lei (under U.S. $1.50) a day.

The only source of water for the entire community is at the bottom of the hill. The city has installed gas pipes for the community and families can now heat their homes and cook. The steep incline of the hill does not permit access to vehicles, including ambulances, taxis, and public transportation.[30]

Endnotes

Legal Standards

1. Committee on Civil and Political Rights (CCPR), "Nondiscrimination," *General Comment* 18, 37th session (10 November 1989): par. 13.
2. Council of the European Union Directive 2000/43/EC of 29 June 2000, art. 2.1.2.a.
3. Ibid., art. 2.1.2.b.
4. See, for example, CCPR, "Nondiscrimination," par. 6 and 7.
5. International Convention on the Elimination of All Forms of Racial Discrimination (ICERD), art. 1.1.
6. See, for example, CCPR "Nondiscrimination." See generally Committee on Economic, Social and Cultural Rights (CESCR), "The right to adequate housing," *General Comment* 4, E/1992/23 (13 December 1991): note 3.
7. ICERD, art. 2.1.
8. International Covenant on Civil and Political Rights (ICCPR), art. 2.1.
9. International Covenant on Economic, Social and Cultural Rights (ICESCR), art. 2.2.
10. Committee on the Elimination of All Forms of Racial Discrimination (CERD), *General Comment* 14, A/48/18, 42nd session (11 May 2000): par. 2.
11. ICERD, art. 5.d.
12. Ibid., art. 5.e.
13. CESCR, "The right to adequate food," *General Comment* 12, 12 May 99, E/C. 12/1999/5, par. 18.
14. CESCR, "The right to the highest attainable standard of health," *General Comment* 14 (11 May 2000): par. 12(2)(i).
15. CESCR, "The right to adequate housing," par. 17.
16. CESCR, "The right to the highest attainable standard of health," par. 43.
17. Ibid., par. 47.

18. In *General Comment* 12 on the right to food, the Committee on Economic, Social and Cultural Rights states that "[v]iolations of the Covenant occur when a State fails to ensure the satisfaction of, at the very least, the minimum essential level required to be free from hunger . . . Should a State party argue that resource constraints make it impossible to provide access to food for those who are unable by themselves to secure such access, the State has to demonstrate that every effort has been made to use all the resources at its disposal in an effort to satisfy, as a matter of priority, those minimum obligations . . . Furthermore, any discrimination in access to food, as well as to means and entitlements for its procurement, on the grounds of race, colour, sex, language, age, religion, political or other opinion, national or social origin, property, birth or other status with the purpose or effect of nullifying or impairing the equal enjoyment or exercise of economic, social and cultural rights constitutes a violation of the Covenant." CESCR, "The right to adequate food," par. 17 and 18.

19. In *General Comment* 4 on the right to housing, the Committee on Economic, Social and Cultural Rights states, "The right to adequate housing applies to everyone. While the reference to 'himself and his family' reflects assumptions as to gender roles and economic activity patterns commonly accepted in 1966 when the Covenant was adopted, the phrase cannot be read today as implying any limitations upon the applicability of the right to individuals or to female-headed households or other such groups. Thus, the concept of 'family' must be understood in a wide sense. Further, individuals, as well as families, are entitled to adequate housing regardless of age, economic status, group or other affiliation or status and other such factors. In particular, enjoyment of this right must, in accordance with art. 2 (2) of the Covenant, not be subject to any form of discrimination." CESCR, "The right to adequate housing," par. 6.

20. ICERD, art. 1(2).

21. ICCPR, art. 2(1).

22. CCPR, "The position of aliens under the covenant," *General Comment* 15 (11 April 1986): par. 2.

23. CCPR, "Nondiscrimination," par. 13.

24. ICERD, art. 1(4).

25. CCPR, "Nondiscrimination," par. 10.

26. CERD, *General Comment* 20, 1996, 48th session, A/51/18, par. 1.

27. Romania ratified ICCPR on 9 December 1974, ICESCR on 9 December 1974, CRC on 28 September 1990, CEDAW on 7 January 1982, and ICERD on 15 September 1970. Bulgaria ratified ICCPR on 21 September 1970, ICESCR on 21 September 1970, CRC on 3 June 1991, CEDAW on 8 February 1982, and ICERD on 8 August 1966. The Former Yugoslav Republic of Macedonia succeeded to ICCPR on 18 January 1994, ICESCR on 18 January 1994, CRC on 2 December 1993, CEDAW on 18 January 1994, and ICERD on 18 January 1994.

28. Romania ratified the European Convention for the Protection of Human Rights and Fundamental Freedoms (henceforth: the European Convention for Human Rights) on 20 June 1994; Bulgaria ratified it on 7 September 1992; the Former Yugoslav Republic of Macedonia ratified it on 10 April 1997; and the Czech Republic ratified it on 18 March 1992.

29. European Convention for Human Rights, art. 14.

30. Ibid., art. 1.

31. *Abdulaziz, Cabales and Balkandali v. the U.K.*, Judgement of 28 May 1985, Series A, no. 94, par. 72, as cited in explanatory report to protocol 12, par. 18.

32. European Convention for Human Rights, Protocol no. 12, art. 1.

33. European Convention for Human Rights, Explanatory Report to Protocol no. 12, par. 22.

34. Ibid., par. 28.

35. See note 28.

36. European Convention for Human Rights, art. 13.

37. Ibid., art. 8.

38. Ibid., art. 4.

39. Council Directive 2000/43/EC of 29 June 2000, art 2.1.

40. Ibid., art. 2.1.2.a.

41. Ibid., art. 2.1.2.b.

42. Ibid., art. 3.1.a.

43. Ibid., art. 3.1.e.

44. Ibid., art. 3.1.h.

45. Ibid., art. 14.

46. Ibid., art. 2.4.

47. Ibid., art. 8.1.

48. Ibid., art. 8.2.

49. The Framework Convention for the Protection of National Minorities, which entered into force on 1 February 1998, was ratified by Romania on 11 May 1995; Bulgaria on 7 May 1999; and the Former Yugoslav Republic of Macedonia on 10 April 1997.

50. Framework Convention for the Protection of National Minorities, art. 4.

51. Ibid., art. 6.

52. Ibid., art. 17.

53. Ibid., art. 4.

54. Ibid., art. 24 and 25.

55. Organization for Security and Cooperation in Europe (OSCE), Istanbul Summit, par. 31.

56. OSCE, Charter for European Security, par. 20.

57. "Persons belonging to national minorities have the right to exercise fully and effectively their human rights and fundamental freedoms without any discrimination and in full equality before the law." 1990 Copenhagen Document, par. 31. Participating States "clearly and unequivocally condemn . . . racial and ethnic hatred . . . and discrimination against anyone," and recognized "the particular problems of Roma." 1990 Copenhagen Document, par. 40. See also *OSCE Report on the Situation of Roma and Sinti in the OSCE Area* (The Hague, 10 March 2000): 7-13.

58. At the 1992 Helsinki Meeting, participating states said they would "consider taking appropriate measures . . . to ensure to everyone on their territory protection against discrimination on racial, ethnic and religious grounds, as a well as to protect individuals . . . against acts of violence . . . Moreover, they will make full use of their domestic legal processes, including enforcement of existing laws in this regard." 1992 Helsinki Document, par. 33. They added that they "[r]eaffirm[ed], in this context, the need to develop appropriate programmes addressing problems of their respective nationals belonging to Roma and other groups traditionally identified as Gypsies . . ." 1992 Helsinki Document, par. 35.

59. *Report of the Geneva Meeting of Experts on National Minorities* (1991).

60. *Report to the Revised European Social Charter,* par. 136.

61. Revised European Social Charter, art. 2 and 3.

62. Ibid., art. 8.

63. Ibid., art. 12.

64. Ibid., art. 14.

65. Ibid., art. 16.

66. Ibid., art. 17.

67. Ibid., art. 19.

68. Ibid., art. 26.

69. Ibid., art. 30.

70. Ibid., art. 11.

71. Ibid., art. 13.

72. Ibid., art. 31.

73. Romania ratified the Revised European Social Charter on 7 May 1999, and Bulgaria ratified it on 29 March 2000. The Former Yugoslav Republic of Macedonia signed the European Social Charter on 5 May 1998, but had not ratified it as of 31 October 2000.

74. Romanian Constitution (1991), art. 16.

75. Bulgarian Constitution (1991), art. 6.

76. Macedonian Constitution (1991), art. 9.

77. Romanian Constitution (1991), art. 20(1).

78. Ibid., art. 20(2).

79. Bulgarian Constitution (1991), art. 5.

80. Macedonian Constitution (1991), art. 118.

81. *Ordinance on Preventing and Punishing All Forms of Discrimination,* no. 137/2000 adopted by the Romanian Government on 31 August 2000, *Official Monitor* no. 431 (2 September 2000). (henceforth: Antidiscrimination Ordinance).

82. Antidiscrimination Ordinance, art. 16, par. 1.

83. Ibid., art. 16, par. 2.

84. Ibid., art. 17, par. 1. This provision does not restrict the authorities' right to enforce urbanization or urban renewal plans, as long as the modifications are made according to the law, with fair compensation and the measures are not determined by the person's or group's appurtenance to a race, nationality, ethnic group, religion, social category, or to a disadvantaged category, by their beliefs, sex or sexual orientation. See Antidiscrimination Ordinance, art. 17, par. 2.

85. The ordinance entered into force in November 2000. However, it is of no practical use until the National Council for the Prevention of Discrimination is created and becomes fully operational. Moreover, the text of the ordinance might be modified by Parliament, which was discussing do so in January 2001.

86. Antidiscrimination Ordinance, art. 2, par. 1, 2 and 3.

87. Ibid., art. 12. Discrimination on the grounds of nationality, belief, sex or sexual orientation also constitutes an offense.

88. Ibid., art. 21, par. 1.

89. Ibid., art. 21, par. 2.

90. Ibid., art. 21, par. 3.

91. Ibid., art. 22, par. 1.

92. Ibid., art. 22, par. 2.

93. Ibid., art. 23.

Barriers to Social Protection

1. Universal Declaration of Human Rights (UDHR), art. 25, par. 1.

2. International Covenant on Economic, Social and Cultural Rights (ICESCR), art. 9.

3. ICESCR, art. 10 adds, "During such period working mothers should be accorded paid leave or leave with adequate social security benefits."

4. Convention on the Rights of the Child (CRC), art. 27.

5. CRC, art. 26(1). Article 26(2) adds, "The benefits should, where appropriate, be granted, taking into account the resources and the circumstances of the child and persons having responsibility for the maintenance of the child, as well as any other consideration relevant to an application for benefits made by or on behalf of the child."

6. For example, see the Revised European Social Charter art. 8: "The Parties undertake . . . to provide either by paid leave, by adequate social security benefits or by benefits from public funds for employed women to take leave before and after childbirth up to a total of at least fourteen weeks."; art. 12: "The Parties undertake . . . to establish or maintain a system of social security [and] to maintain the social security system at a satisfactory level at least equal to that necessary for the ratification of the European Code of Social Security."; and art. 16: "The Parties undertake to provide . . . such means as social and family benefits, fiscal arrangements, provision of family housing, benefits for the newly married and other appropriate means."

7. International Convention on the Elimination of All Forms of Racial Discrimination (ICERD), art. 5(e)(iv).

8. Convention on the Elimination of All Forms of Discrimination Against Women (CEDAW), art. 11(1)(e).

9. Committee on Economic, Social and Cultural Rights (CESCR), "The right to adequate food," *General Comment* 12, E/C.12/1999/5, par. 18.

10. "The enjoyment of the rights set forth in this Charter shall be secured without discrimination on any ground such as race, color, sex, language, religion, political or other opinion, national extraction or social origin, health, association with a national minority, birth or other status." Revised European Social Charter, art. E.

11. International Covenant on Civil and Political Rights (ICCPR), ratified by Romania on 9 December 1974.

12. ICESCR, ratified by Romania on 9 December 1974.

13. CRC, ratified by Romania on 28 September 1990.

14. CEDAW, ratified by Romania on 7 January 1982.

15. ICERD, ratified by Romania on 15 September 1970.

16. European Convention for the Protection of Human Rights and Fundamental Freedoms (ECHR), ratified by Romania 20 June 1994.

17. Romania ratified the Revised European Social Charter on 7 May 1999. Romania affirmatively bound itself to articles 1, 2 (1–2, 4–7), 3 (1–3), 4-9, 11, 12, 13 (1–3), 15 (1–2), 16, 17, 18 (3–4), 19 (7–8), 20, 21, 24, 26, 28, 27(2) and 29.

18. The Framework Convention for the Protection of National Minorities, which entered into force on 1 February 1998, was ratified by Romania on 11 May 1995.

19. Romanian Constitution (1991), art. 11, par. 1.

20. Ibid., art. 11, par. 2.

21. Ibid., art. 20, par. 1.

22. Ibid., art. 20, par. 2.

23. Ibid., art. 43, par. 1.

24. Constantinescu M., Deleanu I., Antonie Iorgovan A., Muraru I., Vasilescu F., Vida I., "The Constitution of Romania – Commented and Annotated," Regia Autonoma, *Monitorul Oficial* (Bucuresti, 1992): 107.

25. Romanian Constitution (1991) , art. 45, par. 1.

26. Ibid., art. 45, par. 2.

27. See *Report Submitted by Romania, Pursuant to Article 25 par. 1 of the Framework Convention for the Protection of National Minorities* ACFC/SR (99) 11 (24 June 1999).

28. The government bases its strategy on this estimate, rather than the 1992 census figure of approximately 400,000. See, for example, "Terms of Reference of PHARE Project for the Improvement of the Situation of Roma in Romania: Elaboration of Government Strategy," RO 98.03.01.01.

29. Vasile Burtea, *Romanies in the Romanian Socio-Economic Context,* (Bucharest University, 1998).

30. See World Bank, *Romania at a Glance,* available at: http://www.worldbank.org/html/extdr/regions.htm + "Romania" + Go + "Country Data.(pdf).

31. World Bank and National Commission for Statistics, *From Poverty to Rural Development* (1999): 32.

32. The Romanian Integrated Household Survey (RIHS), which has been implemented every year since 1994, is a large scale, nationally representative survey encompassing about 40,000 households. See Dena Ringold, *Roma and the Transition in Central and Eastern Europe: Trends and Challenges* (Washington, D.C.: The World Bank, 2000): 51.

33. Ibid., 11.

34. Governmental Decision 459/1998 established the Inter-Ministerial Commission with the following objectives: a) to provide information and support the activity of the Department for the Protection of National Minorities; b) to contribute to the elaboration of the strategy for the protection of national minorities and the strategy for the protection of Roma; c) to elaborate annual reports on the implementation of the Framework Convention for the Protection of National Minorities and other international documents ratified by Romania, as well as national programs for the protection of minorities. Governmental Decision No. 459/1998 concerning the establishment, organization and functioning of the Inter-Ministerial Commission for the National Minorities, art. 4, par. 1.

35. Government of Romania, *Report on the Progress in Preparing for Accession to the European Union since the Previous Report* (August 1999) (June 2000): 21.

36. In Romanian GLAR stands for Grupul de Lucru al Asociatiilor Roma—the Working Group of Roma Associations.

37. Recommendation on the general policy concerning the implementation of the governmental program, "Improvement of Roma situation," proposed by GLAR and approved by the Inter-Ministerial Subcommission for Roma, on 23-24 September 2000 and by the Inter-Ministerial Commission for National Minorities on 28 September 2000. (henceforth: GLAR Proposal to Subcommission for Roma).

38. Governmental decisions set the Monthly Basic Income (MBI). In 1999, HG 295/1999 established the following levels per month: a) 299,800 lei (U.S. $16.20) for two-member families; b) 418,500 lei (U.S. $22.62) for three-member families; c) 525,700 lei (U.S. $28.41) for four-member families; d) 625,300 lei (U.S. $33.80) for five-member families; e) 97,000 (U.S. $5.24) for each additional person who belongs to the family; f) for persons living alone: 166,500 lei (U.S. $8.94).

39. Romanian law permits NGOs' participation in social inquiries [HG 125/1996, art. 5(4)] (henceforth: HG 125/1996). In practice, however, there are no indications that local authorities or NGOs take advantage of the existence of this provision.

40. *Law on Social Support,* Law 67/1995, *Official Monitor* no. 131 (29 June 1995). (henceforth: Law 67/1995).

41. For example, such decisions include Governmental Decision HG 125/1996 on granting social support and completing the implementation norms of Law 67/1995, and Governmental Decision HG 173/1998 concerning measures applicable to pensions, child allowances, and other sources of income in 1998.

42. Law 67/1995, art. 21.

43. The right to assistance from a food pantry for this category is limited to ninety days per year. See Law on Food Pantries, Law 208/1997, art. 2, par. 2. (henceforth: Law 208/1997).

44. To qualify for food pantry assistance, persons must have a monthly income under the MBI for persons living alone. Law 208/1997, art. 2, par. 1.

45. Ibid., art. 4, par. 2.

46. Ibid., art. 15.

47. Ibid., art. 3.

48. See, for example, Buhusi in the region of Moldova where individuals who qualify for the food pantry receive one portion of bread a day. Ion Turcea, mayor, Buhusi, interview by author, 19 September 2000.

49. Harjob Nicolae, deputy mayor, Orastie, interview by author, 11 October 1999.

50. 413 persons are eligible for the food pantry in Buhusi. Turcea, interview, 2000.

51. Law 208/1997, art. 7.

52. Ibid., art. 8.

53. Ibid., art. 14.

54. The amount and extent of emergency support can vary widely. At one extreme, the city council in Bacau created a special fund for emergency help. Paustin Balan, Association Rom-Star, interview by author, Bacau, Romania, 18 October 1999. At the opposite pole, local NGOs report that for ten days a Romani family from Geoagiu had to keep a family member's corpse in the house, because they did not have money

for the funeral, and the mayor refused to grant emergency help under the "other justified reasons" category. Nicolae Bologa, Roma expert, OSF Roma Board, Employment and Vocational Training Agency, interview by author, Deva, Romania, 10 October 1999.

55. As of September 2000. Despite governmental efforts, the relationship between the average salary and child allowances has declined. In June 1998, child allowances represented only 6.2 percent of the average salary versus 9.7 percent in 1990. See United Nations Development Program (UNDP), *Poverty in Romania* 1995–1998 (Romanian edition) vol. 2 (1999): 174–5.

56. *Law on Child Allowances,* Law 61/1993, *Official Monitor* no. 233 (28 September 1993) (henceforth: Law 61/1993). Law 61/1993 as amended and completed by Law 261/1998, further extends the categories of beneficiaries. See also Decision of the Government no. 173/1998 concerning social protection measures through pensions, other social insurance rights, child allowances, and other sources of income for the year 1998, from 26 March 1998.

57. Law 61/1993, art. 1, par. 1.

58. Ibid., art. 1, par. 1 and 2.

59. Ibid., art. 5, par. 1.

60. Sanda Ghimpu, Alexandru Ticlea, and Constatin Tufan, *Social Security Law* (Editura All Beck, 1998): 401.

61. Child labor is present in very poor communities such as Pata-Rat, Calvini, Glina, Ocolna, and Mangalia. See International Workshop on Roma Children in Europe/Save the Children, *Roma Children in Romania Research Report Summary* (Bucharest, June 1998): 86. Beside financial needs, other factors such as lack of effective access to school due to discriminatory practices, teachers' hostility or indifference, long distances to the school, and lack of interest of the parents discourage Romani children from attending school.

62. French Catholic Committee against Hunger and for Development (CCFD), *Information for an Assistance Program in Favor of Romanian Roma* (April 1996): 13.

63. Law 61/1993, art. 4, par. 1.

64. Ibid., art. 4, par. 3.

65. Ibid., art. 10, par. 3.

66. UNDP, *Poverty in Romania 1995–1998,* 174.

67. International Workshop on Roma Children in Europe/Save the Children, *Roma Children in Romania Research Report Summary,* 14.

68. Law 119/1997 concerning additional benefits for families with children; Government Decision 443/1997 concerning the norms for the calculation and payment of additional benefits for families with children; and Governmental Decision 495/1997 concerning the contents, the issuing, and the updating of the family book.

69. For example, in 1998, 1,137,400 Romanian families received additional benefits.

70. UNDP, *Poverty in Romania 1995–1998,* 83–91.

71. See Elena Zamfir and Catalin Zamfir, *Gypsies: Between Ignoring Them and Worrying about Them* (Editura Alternative, 1993): 80.

72. Council of Europe-Katherine Duffy, *Final Report–Social Cohesion and Quality of Life–The Human Dignity and Social Exclusion Project—Research Opportunity and Risk: Trends of Social Exclusion in Europe* (April 1998) available at: http://www.coe.fr/DASE/EN/cohesion/strategy/discuss/HDSE/chapter4.htm.

73. The government sets the amount. In 1999, mothers collected 293,000 lei (U.S. $15.83).

74. Law 67/1995, art. 19.

75. Ibid., art. 20.

76. Ibid., art. 26.

77. Balan, interview, 1999.

78. HG 125/1996, Annex 2.

79. Ibid., Annex 2.

80. Mariana Georgescu, director, Social Assistance Department, Sector 2, interview by author, Bucharest, 22 October 1999.

81. See 5.4, Lack of identification documents.

82. See Lack of Adequate Housing, Romania.

83. Bologa, interview, 1999.

84. CCFD, *Information for an Assistance Program in Favor of Romanian Roma,* 28.

85. See Vasile Burtea, "Case Study–Mangalia," in *Identity Documents and Citizenship in the Roma Communities, Romania–Aleatory Research and Case Study* (forthcoming).

86. Lack of access to vocational training and certification is caused not only by the decisions of local authorities but also by the legislation itself: Unemployed persons who do not receive unemployment support or other employment-related forms of support are obliged to pay taxes for training and certification courses. This affects directly and disproportionately the low-income, long-term unemployed and those who were never able to enter the labor market, blocking their way out of the poverty cycle.

87. Nicolae Ficuta, leader, Roma Party, Buhusi branch, interview by author, 18 October 1999.

88. Ficuta, interview, 1999.

89. M.N., Romani woman, Buhusi, interview by author, 18 October 1999.

90. Georgescu, interview, 1999.

91. GLAR Proposal to Subcommission for Roma.

92. Many families complain that functionaries and social workers ask for bribes to do their jobs. The families do not have the money to pay the bribes, or refuse to do so out of principle, with the result that officials decline to perform legally mandated tasks. For example, Roma from the Modruzeni district (Marasesti) complain about abuses by a particular social worker, alleging that she refuses to register children if the parent wants to give them two names instead of one; or, if, in order to solve a claim, she must make phone calls from her city hall office, she forces claimants to pay the costs of the calls. Romani residents of Modruzeni district, interviews by author, 19 October 1999.

93. Burtea, "Case study–Mangalia."

94. Ibid. The state issues identification cards to persons fourteen years old and older.

95. Emilian Nicolae, president, Association of Roma Students, interview by author, 14 September 1999.

96. Burtea.

97. In order to prevent statelessness, the new citizenship regulation links the renunciation to Romanian citizenship to acquirement of the citizenship of another country.

98. General Dumitru Arghiroiu, deputy director of the Department for the Evidence of the Population, Romanian Ministry of Interior, interview by author, Bucharest, Romania, 22 October 1999.

99. In these cases, the police verify the identities of the suspects and issue provisional cards within 24 hours, according to an unpublished study. Arghiroiu, interview, 1999.

100. Ibid.

101. Project C-PA-9941-99-3106, registered on 16 June 1999, partial funding of U.S. $9,000, Open Society Foundation–Romania.

102. Bologa, interview, 1999.

103. Balan, interview, 1999.

104. Author visit to Orastie, 11 October 1999.

105. R.G., Romani woman from Orastie, interview by author, 11 October 1999.

106. The implementation guidelines issued by the Ministry of Labor and Social Protection indicate that social support and food pantries are complementary rights that do not exclude each other.

107. According to Aurel Rosianu, leader of the Roma Party local branch and member of the Cluj local council, this body adopted a formal decision approving this practice. Interview by author, Cluj, Romania, 13 October 1999.

108. Law on Social Health Insurance, Law 145/1997, art. 9 (d).

109. Bologa, interview 1999.

110. Ibid.

111. The study, financed by the World Bank, was conducted between July and September 1997 by a team from the Ministry of Labor and Social Protection, the Finance Ministry, the Department for Local Public Administration, the National Commission for Statistics, and Bucharest's local government. The team evaluated the implementation of Law 67/1995 in eight counties: Botosani, Dambovita, Dolj, Hunedoara, Maramures, Tulcea, Ilfov, and Bucharest. See *UNDP, Poverty in Romania 1995–1998,* 166.

112. Law on Public Administration, Law 24/1996, art. 20, par. 1(r), as subsequently amended.

113. HG 125/1996, art. 5, par. (2): "The right to social support is established according to the law, within the limits of the funds approved for this purpose."

114. Ficuta, interview, 1999.

115. Romani inhabitants of Modruzeni district, interviews by author, Marasesti, 19 October 1999.

116. Romani woman, interview by author, Alba Iulia, 10 October 1999.

117. The budget in 1999 included 1.5 billion lei (U.S. $81,000) for social assistance, but local tax revenues were insufficient to cover all municipal needs. Harjob Nicolae, interview by author, 1999.

118. Ibid.

119. The Ombudsman is, therefore, not competent to examine the opportunity of an administrative decision. See Ion Santai, "The Characteristics, Conditions and Effects of the Ombudsman's Activity on Violations of Human Rights and Freedoms Perpetrated by the Public Administration," *The Law* (August 1997): 19.

120. Committee on Civil and Political Rights (CCPR), *Summary Record of the 1766th Meeting: Romania,* CPR/C/SR.1766, 24/01/2000.

121. For more on the mayor's responsibilities, see Virginia Vedinas, "The Mayor, Executive Authority of Local Autonomy," *The Law* (June 1997): 7.

122. See Law 69/1991, art. 12, as amended by Law 24/1996 and Ordinance 22/1997.

123. ICCPR ratified by Bulgaria on 21 September 1970.

124. ICESCR ratified by Bulgaria on 21 September 1970.

125. CRC ratified by Bulgaria on 3 June 1991.

126. CEDAW ratified by Bulgaria on 2 February 1982.

127. ICERD ratified by Bulgaria on 8 August 1966.

128. ECHR ratified by Bulgaria on 7 September 1992.

129. Revised European Social Charter ratified by Bulgaria on 29 March 2000. Bulgaria affirmatively bound itself to articles 1, 2 (2, 4–7), 3, 4 (2–5), 5-8, 11, 12 (1,3), 13 (1–3), 14, 16, 17 (2), 18 (4), 20–2, 24–6, 27(2–3), 28 and 29.

130. The Framework Convention for the Protection of National Minorities, which entered into force on 1 February 1998, was ratified by Bulgaria on 7 May 1999.

131. Bulgarian Constitution (1991), art. 14 reads: "The family, motherhood, and childhood shall enjoy the protection of the state and society."

132. Bulgarian Constitution (1991), art. 51 (1) reads: "Citizens shall have the right to social security and welfare aid."

133. Bulgarian Constitution (1991), art. 51, (2): "The state shall provide social security for the temporarily unemployed in accordance with conditions and procedures established by law," and (3): " The aged without relatives and unable to support themselves, as well as the physically and mentally handicapped shall enjoy the special protection of the state and society."

134. Ibid., art. 5, par. 2.

135. Ibid., art. 5, par. 4.

136. European Commission, *1999–Regular Report from the Commission on Bulgaria's Progress Towards Accession* (October 1999): 15.

137. Council of Europe, *Information Report: Honoring of Obligations and Commitments by Bulgaria,* doc. 8180 (September 1998): par. 104, "In the 1992 census 3.69 percent of the population identified itself as Roma. The real figure is probably about twice that high, since many persons of Romani descent tend to identify themselves to the authorities as ethnic Turks or Bulgarians [...]"

138. Ibid., par. 106.

139. European Commission, *1999–Regular Report from the Commission on Bulgaria's Progress Towards Accession,* 18.

140. A. M. Lizin, *Human Rights and Extreme Poverty,* report submitted pursuant to Commission resolution 1998/25, E/CN.4/1999/48 (January 1999).

141. World Bank, Bulgaria: *Poverty During the Transition,* Report no. 18411 (June 1999): ii.

142. This poverty threshold is just a little bit lower than the World Bank's definition of extreme poverty as living with less than U.S. $1 per day.

143. Project on Ethnic Relations, *The Roma in Bulgaria: Collaborative Efforts between Local Authorities and Nongovernmental Organizations* (April 1998) available at:
http://www.websp.com/~ethnic/new/roma_bul.htm.

144. Ibid.

145. Framework Program for Equal Integration of Roma in Bulgarian Society, adopted by the Bulgarian Council of Ministers on 22 April, 1999, Part II. (henceforth: Framework Program, Part II).

146. Framework Program for Equal Integration of Roma in Bulgarian Society, adopted by the Bulgarian Council of Ministers on 22 April, 1999, Part I. (henceforth: Framework Program, Part I).

147. Framework Program, Part I.

148. Romani Baht Foundation, *Annual Report–1999* (January 2000): 1.

149. Human Rights Project, "Conference on Roma Integration Program," press release (27 March 2000).

150. Helsinki Commission on Security and Cooperation in Europe, "Antidiscrimination Laws Needed, Witnesses Testify at Helsinki Commission Hearing on Roma," press release (9 June 2000).

151. European Union, "EU support for Roma Communities in Central and Eastern Europe," *Enlargement Briefings* (December 1999): 14, Annex 5.1. "PHARE-funded Programmers for the Roma in Bulgaria."

152. The Bulgarian government targets social assistance through three types of programs: (i) an income based approach, aimed to ensure fulfillment of a person's basic needs; (ii) a group based approach, aimed to support certain vulnerable groups, such as the disabled and large families, and (iii) a specific needs approach, aimed to satisfy particular necessities, such as those for heating, water, electricity, and rent. United Nations Development Program (UNDP)- International Labor Office (ILO), *Bulgaria: Poverty in Transition* (Geneva: ILO, 1998): 45.

153. The percentages correspond to the year 1997. World Bank, *Bulgaria: Poverty During the Transition,* 47.

154. For example, if the person concerned worked less than three years she or he receives unemployment benefits for four months. For more than twenty-five years of work, the unemployed is entitled to receive benefits for twelve months.

155. See Denial of Health Care, Bulgaria.

156. *Social Assistance Act,* 7 May 1998, *Official Monitor* no. 56 (19 May 1998): 1-5 (henceforth: Social Assistance Act).

157. Decree no. 243, 5 November 1998, last amended by DV no. 13, 16 February 1999 (henceforth Decree no. 243/1998, as subsequently amended).

158. Bulgarian Helsinki Committee, *Human Rights in Bulgaria in 1998,* available at:
http://www.bghelsinki.org/frames-publications.htm.

159. Social Assistance Act, art. 3.

160. Up to 1999. See Committee on Economic, Social, and Cultural Rights (CESR), *Replies by the Government of Bulgaria to the List of Issues (E/C.12/Q/BUL/1) to Be Taken up in Connection with the Consideration of the Third Periodic Report of Bulgaria Concerning the Rights Referred to in Articles 1–15 of the International Convenant on Economic, Social and Cultural Rights* (E/1994/104/Add.16) (9 July 1999): par. 4.4.

161. Decree no. 243/1998, as subsequently amended, art. 9, par. 3.

162. Ibid., art. 9, par. 3.

163. Ibid., art. 9, par. 3, point 6.

164. Ibid., art. 9, par. 3, point 1.

165. Ibid., art. 9, par. 3, points 2, 3 and 4.

166. Ibid., art. 10, par. 3.

167. Ibid., art. 10, par. 4.

168. Ibid., art. 11, par. 7. The law exempts certain categories of persons provided that they register with the unemployment office within thirty days of the termination of the situation that determined the exception, such as discharge from military service, release from prison, or graduation from a special school.

169. Ibid., art. 11, point 2.

170. Ibid., art. 11, point 4.

171. Ibid., art. 11, point 7.

172. Ibid., art. 25, par. 1, point 1.

173. Ibid., art. 25, par. 1, point 2.

174. Governmental Decree 75/1999, 31 March 1999.

175. Georgi Petrov, director, Social Assistance Center, Plovdiv, Bulgaria, interview by author, 10 December 1999. Patyo Valchev, director, Social Assistance Center, Chrpan, Bulgaria, interview by author, 10 December 1999.

176. Decree no. 243/1998, as subsequently amended, art. 25, par. 3.

177. Nikolay Kirilov, chairman of Roma-Lom Foundation, interview by author, Sofia, Bulgaria, 12 December 1999.

178. Decree no. 243/1998, as subsequently amended, art. 14.

179. Ibid., art. 16.

180. World Bank, *Consultations with the Poor: National Synthesis Report Bulgaria* (May 1999): 72.

181. See information available at: http://europa.eu.int/comm/enlargement/pas/phare/pt/social.htm

182. The flat sum was 4 ECU per family member.

183. UNDP–ILO, *Bulgaria: Poverty in Transition,* 52.

184. The level of income was also calculated on a case by case basis, but as a rule, it was higher than the level of income required for qualification for monthly social support. See Decree no. 243/1998, as subsequently amended, art. 15, par. 1, 2, and 5.

185. Ibid., art. 15, par. 4.

186. Romani Baht Foundation, *Annual Report–1998,* 26.

187. Anastasia Ivanova, director of the Social Work Center, interview by author, Sofia, Krasna Poliana, 6 December 1999. Krasna Poliana is a district of Sofia that includes Fakulteta.

188. Decree on the Encouragement of Childbearing (DEC) 1968. This decree was published in DV no. 15 of 23 February 1968 and amended more than ten times. Last amendment published in DV no. 88 of 15 October 1993 (henceforth: Decree on Childbearing).

189. UNDP–ILO, *Bulgaria: Poverty in Transition,* 50.

190. The educational institutions' budget covers the costs if the mother is a student.

191. Decree on Childbearing, art. 2, par. 1.

192. Ibid., art. 2, par. 1. Because Bulgaria grants some support for the fourth child and each additional child but much less than the support granted for the third child, its approach to the relationship between the number of children and the level of support lies between the Romanian and Macedonian ones. The Romanian law grants equal support for all children while Macedonian law gives support to three children only.

193. Ibid., art. 3, par. 1.

194. Ibid., art. 2, par. 4.

195. "Family benefits are inherited from the pre-reform period and are comprised of ineffective schemes which are not adjusted to the needs of the families at risk, such as unemployed parents, single mothers, large families and so on. These family patterns are typical for the Gypsy population, and they do not receive adequate social protection." Theodora Noncheva, "Local Social Welfare Center-Lom, Bulgaria," in *Managing Multiethnic Communities,* available at: http://www.osi.hu/lgi/ethnic/csdb/html/csdb_64.html.

196. "The representative from the Ministry of Labor and Social Policy commented that . . . in addition, the Roma have some traditional characteristics that need to be taken into account. For example, there are a large number of single mothers among the Romani population." Project on Ethnic Relations, *The Roma in Bulgaria: Collaborative Efforts between Local Authorities and Nongovernmental Organizations, Lom, Bulgaria, 24–25 April 1998,* available at: http://www.websp.com/~ethnic/new/roma_bul.htm.

197. Irina Vandova and Varban Tomov, *Case Study of Bulgaria–Nikola Kochev District and Nadezhda Ghetto in the Town of Sliven, Villages of Sotirya, Topolchane and Gorno Alexandrovo* (forthcoming) available at: http://www.yale.edu/socdept/reports/vandova.html.

198. Romani Baht Foundation, *Annual Report–1999,* 22.

199. Decree on Childbearing, art. 3, par. 3.

200. Varban Tomov, "Roma from the Village of Topolchane," *Poverty and Ethnicity–Bulgarian Case Study* (forthcoming) available at: http://www.yale.edu/socdept/reports/tomov.html.

201. Forty percent of Romani girls get married before age 16 and the other 32 percent of them before age 18 while Bulgarian women tend to get married between ages 20 and 24. Ilona Tomova, *The Gypsies in the Transition Period* (Sofia: International Center for Minority Studies and Intercultural Relations, 1995): 41–2.

202. Members of Romani Baht, a NGO based in Fakulteta, Sofia, which, among other activities, assists Romani individuals to apply for social assistance, interview by author, 1999.

203. The local authorities do not keep ethnic-sensitive statistics; there is no separate information available concerning Stolipinovo. Therefore, it is difficult to know, out of 991 cases, how many mothers live in the Romani neighborhood (in Stolipinovo) and how many of them live in other parts of Istucen, or, how many of these cases are actually Romani women. Furthermore, the director of Plovdiv Social Work Center stated that the real number of families with children under the age of three is not known. Georgi Petrov, director of

Plovdiv Social Work Center, and Mariana Dimova, director of Istucen Social Work Center, interview by author, Plovdiv, Bulgaria, 10 December 1999.

204. Decree on Childbearing, art. 1, par. 4.

205. Ibid., art. 1, par. 1.

206. That is, mothers who were involved in education or employed for a determined period before the birth of the child (e.g. students, fellowship holders in the country and abroad, recently graduated mothers, women who gave birth or adopted a child within six months (180 days) after the termination of their labor or insurance contract).

207. Mothers who decide to take an additional year of unpaid leave are entitled to 10 leva per month until the child is three years old.

208. This applies to mothers who do not enter an employment relationship in the six-month period preceding the birth and are not insured.

209. Rumiana Panova, director of Triaditza Unemployment Office, interview by author, Sofia, Bulgaria, 13 December 1999.

210. Ringold, *Roma and the Transition in Central and Eastern Europe: Trends and Challenges,* 24.

211. Decree no. 243/1998 as subsequently amended, art. 10, par. 1, point 4.

212. UNDP–ILO, *Bulgaria: Poverty in Transition,* 56.

213. Ibid.

214. Noncheva, "Local Social Welfare Center–Lom, Bulgaria."

215. Romani Baht Foundation, *Annual Report–1998,* 26.

216. Ilona Tomova, researcher, interview by author, Sofia, Bulgaria, 7 December 1999.

217. Tomov, "Roma from the Village of Topolchane."

218. In 1998/1999, in Plovdiv, Rajon Jugen, the social assistance services distributed 8 kilos of beans, 3.5 kilos of flour and 3 kilos of cooking oil to 2,608 recipients of monthly social support. See World Bank, *Consultations with the Poor: National Synthesis Report Bulgaria,* 71.

219. V. B., a Romani woman in Nadezhda neighborhood, interview by author, Sliven, 11 December 1999.

220. Council of Europe, "Chapter 4: Exclusion from social protection," *Social Cohesion and Quality of Life Report* available at: http://www.coe.fr/dase/en/cohesion/strategy/discuss/HDSE/chapter4.htm.

221. Decree no. 243/1998 as amended, art. 11, par. 7.

222. The border police stamp the passport every time a person, citizen or noncitizen, leaves or enters Bulgaria.

223. Ivanova, interview, 1999.

224. So-called "suitcase commerce" has flourished in the Bulgarian border regions in recent years. The embargo against Serbia created a significant demand for otherwise unattainable goods. In the region of Lom, one of the areas with the highest unemployment, Roma, but also Bulgarians, buy goods in Bulgaria and sell them in Serbia. Those who developed successful (and sometimes illegal) businesses in the border regions need no longer apply for social protection. See Kirilov, interview, 1999. It has also been reported that Roma from small villages try to gain some income through "suitcase trade" over the border, in between seasons when they cannot find work in agriculture. See Varban Tomov "Roma from the Village of Gorno Alxandrovo," (forthcoming) available at: http://www.yale.edu/socdept/reports/tomov.html.

225. See Vandova and Tomov, *Case Study of Bulgaria–Nikola Kochev District and Nadezhda Ghetto in the Town of Sliven, Villages of Sotirya, Topolchane and Gorno Alexandrovo.*

226. Article 35, par. 1 of the Bulgarian Constitution provides: "Everyone is free to choose a place of residence and has the right to movement on the territory of the country and to leave the country. This right shall be restricted only by virtue of law for reasons of national security, public health, and the rights and freedoms of other citizens."

227. Article 32, par. 1 of the Bulgarian Constitution states: "Everyone is entitled to protection against any illegal interference in his private or family life."

228. Decree no. 243/1998, as subsequently amended, art. 12, par. 1.

229. Ibid., art. 12, par. 2.

230. Ibid., art. 12, par. 3.

231. See, for Lom, Noncheva "Local Social Work Center–Lom, Bulgaria."

232. Ibid.

233. A. N., a Romani woman in Nadezhda neighborhood, interview by author, Sliven, Bulgaria, 11 December 1999.

234. See Vandova and Tomov, *Case Study of Bulgaria–Nikola Kochev District and Nadezhda Ghetto in the Town of Sliven, Villages of Sotirya, Topolchane and Gorno Alexandrovo,* case 418.

235. "Send Jobless Gypsies to the Field by Lists," *Noshen Troud,* 14–15 July 1998, cited in Kamelia Anguelova's *Ethnic and Religious Minorities in the Bulgarian Press* (April 1998-September 1998) available at: http://www.access.online.bg/archive/bn/newsletter/bn-8/bulgaria2.htm.

236. Decree no. 243/1998, as subsequently amended, art. 10, par. 1, point 2.

237. Many companies are registered in the names of Romani women. "The women will even shoulder the financial responsibility—if they register a company, it will be in the woman's name—let her be accountable to the tax inspectors . . ." *World Bank, Consultations with the Poor: National Synthesis Report Bulgaria,* 70.

238. Anton Karagiozov, chairman of the Foundation for Regional Development, interview by author, Plovdiv, Bulgaria, 7 December 1999.

239. Decree no. 243/1998 as subsequently amended Article 10, par. 1/6. Some Social Work Centers interpret this provision in the strictest sense, others reportedly make an exception for the applicants who can prove they used the money from the sale of the first house to buy another one, in which they actually live. Ivanova, interview, 1999.

240. Ibid.

241. Tomova, *The Gypsies in the Transition Period,* 68.

242. Organization for Security and Cooperation in Europe (OSCE), *OSCE Report on the Situation of Roma and Sinti in the OSCE Area* (The Hague, 10 March 2000): 100.

243. Mihail Gheorgiev, "Fighting for Fakulteta: Advocating for Roma Housing Rights in Bulgaria," *Roma Rights–Newsletter of the European Roma Rights Center,* 2 (2000): 49.

244. Ibid.

245. Decree no. 243/1998, as subsequently amended, art. 10, par. 1, 1(a).

246. Ibid., art. 10. par. 1, 1(b).

247. Ibid., art. 10. par. 1, 1(c).

248. Ibid., art. 10. par. 1, 1(d).

249. Ibid., art. 10. par. 1, 1(e).

250. Social Work Center, Istucen (the district which includes Stolipinovo), visit by author, Plovdiv, Bulgaria, 10 December 1999.

251. P. B., Romani social support beneficiary, interview by author in the front of the Social Work Center, Istucen (Stolipinovo), Plovdiv, Bulgaria, 10 December 1999.

252. See Vandova and Tomov, *Case Study of Bulgaria–Nikola Kochev District and Nadezhda Ghetto in the Town of Sliven, Villages of Sotirya, Topolchane and Gorno Alexandrovo,* case 100.

253. Ibid., case 98.

254. Ibid., case 418.

255. Ibid., case 422.

256. Dimova, interview, 1999. According to Dimova, in 1997, when the heating program started, Roma behaved aggressively, obliging the authorities to take measures to ensure the social workers' security.

257. World Bank, *Consultations with the Poor: National Synthesis Report Bulgaria,* 70.

258. "Despite central subsidies, the Municipal Council votes the local budget and allocates all revenues . . . Priority is given to education and health, because they are a better link of tax payers and beneficiaries' interests. The social assistance system is often considered as a one-way transfer from the employed, economically active population to the low qualified, chronically poor. That is why the expenditures in social assistance are kept at the minimum level.

In more than half of the municipalities there is 'municipal debt' in social assistance. It comprises allowed benefits, which are delayed or paid in a reduced amount, due to the lack of resources in the social assistance budget. This deficit emerged for first time in 1993 and it reached 15 percent of the allowed benefits by 1997.

The financial difficulties and unpaid benefits enlarge the gap between the Gypsies, who perceive themselves as the main clients of social assistance and the group that suffers disproportionately from the underfunding of the social welfare system, and the rest of the population." From Theodora Noncheva, *Civic Council and Gypsies' Particiipation in Social Welfare Policy* (Sofia, Bulgaria, January 1999) available at: http://www.osi.hu/lgi/ethnic/csdb/html/csdb_33.html.

259. Vassil Chaprazov, president, United Roma Union, Sliven, interview by author, 11 December 1999.

260. Mityo Kemalov, Roma coordinator of the Human Rights Project in Stara Zagora, former mayor, former local council member, interview by author, 6 December 1999.

261. At present, the Social Work Center in Lom runs two food pantries for the poor, one in the Bulgarian-inhabited area and the other one in the Romani neighborhood. Both of them are organized with money from abroad.

262. Vesselin Lakov, HRP coordinator in Montana, interview by author, 10 December 1999.

263. Patyo Valchev, director, Social Work Center in Chirpan, interview by author, 10 December 1999.

264. World Bank, *Bulgaria: Poverty During the Transition,* Annex 3.

265. Ibid., 34.

266. Research for OECD countries suggests that unemployment is strongly correlated with benefit generosity.

267. Kirilov, interview, 1999.

268. Karagiozov, interview, 1999.

269. Petrov and Dimova, interview, 1999.

270. According to competent authorities an exception to this rule might be made by unemployment offices provided that the person concerned (under 18) asks the labor inspector for permission to work between the ages of 16 and 18 in a specific working place. Of course, the desire to work is not enough. The applicant has to prove that his/her family has a difficult financial situation and needs his or her work. If permission is obtained and the job is not available, the person might be registered as unemployed. However, this exception is never used in practice. Panova, interview, 1999.

271. Seventy-two percent of Romani girls get married before age 18. Bulgarian women tend to get married between ages 20 and 24. Tomova, *The Gypsies in the Transition Period,* 43–4.

272. Decree on Childbearing, art. 3, par. 3.

273. Decree no. 243/1998, as subsequently amended, art. 1, par. 3.

274. In which case, the child's birth certificate bears the notation "father unknown."

275. C. P., social worker from Romani Baht Foundation, interview by author, 3 December 1999.

276. Many Roma prefer traditional marriages to civil ones because they think that their traditional weddings are as valid if not more valid than civil ones. Civil marriages involve money and papers they often cannot obtain, and many of them marry before 16 which is the legal civil marriage age.

277. World Bank, *Consultations with the Poor: National Synthesis Report Bulgaria,* 73.

278. For example, the Social Work Center in Chirpan employs fourteen persons to carry out social work. Only three of them have a university degree in social work, while the rest are engineers or economists.

279. For example, during 1997, in Pazakdzhik and Plovdiv, the social welfare center denied social support to Romani families that owned a satellite antenna. The center abandoned the practice after Plovdiv representatives of the Roma Bureau repeatedly denounced it. Stefan Stefanov, executive director, Roma Bureau, interview by author, Sofia, Bulgaria, 6 December 1999.

280. World Bank, *Consultations with the Poor: National Synthesis Report Bulgaria,* 72.

281. Ibid. "The Ministry of Labour and Social Policy has decreed that all applicants who are caught cheating shall be disqualified. This has caused new problems—some applicants forgot to mention real estate, which did not bring them any revenue, but they were disqualified anyway. Also, some applicants find the procedure quite complicated, and claim that there have been several cases of misunderstanding. For example, the application form included a question about children, without specifying their age; the welfare office actually meant children under 18, but the applicants naturally listed all their children. One major problem comes from the absence of effective coordination among the tax administration, banks and the welfare office. For instance, the welfare office has no effective means of checking if an applicant owns real estate in other municipalities; it does not have access to bank accounts and therefore cannot check if an applicant has savings in the bank or has received bank transfers (except at the State Savings Bank)."

282. A small form-completing industry arose to help address this problem. In cities where Romani NGOs do not exist or are not active enough, Roma and non-Roma offer paid services to help applicants to fill out the forms.

283. Decree no. 243/1998, as subsequently amended, art. 29, par. 1 and 2.

284. Noncheva, *Civic Council and Gypsies' Participation in Social Welfare Policy.* "An important deficiency in the present decentralized system is the lack of administrative procedure for appeals. As local social work centers (LSWCs) are under the auspices of the local administration, not of the central government, the appeals could not be addressed to the relevant state authority. Formally, the mayor represents the top administrative level of the LSWC. However, the municipal administration has no independent expert in social welfare, no public commission that would be able to resolve the claims. The more complicated appeals have to be sent to the judiciary system, which is fairly ineffective and over-burdened with other

priorities, such as crime and black economy. Practically, it could not be used for the protection of the rights of poor people."

285. UNDP–ILO, *Bulgaria: Poverty in Transition,* 63.

286. Macedonia succeeded to ICCPR on 18 January 1994.

287. Macedonia succeeded to ICESCR on 18 January 1994.

288. Macedonia succeeded to ICERD on 18 January 1994. The Republic of Macedonia made the declaration under Article 14 of the Convention, recognizing the competence of the Committee on Elimination of Racial Discrimination to consider individual and group complaints, on 22 December 1999.

289. Macedonia succeeded to CEDAW on 18 January 1994.

290. Macedonia succeeded to CRC on 2 December 1993.

291. Macedonia ratified ECHR on 10 April 1997.

292. On 10 April 1997, Macedonia ratified the Framework Convention for the Protection of National Minorities, which entered into force on 1 February 1998.

293. Macedonia signed the European Social Charter on 5 May 1998. Macedonia had not ratified the Charter as of 31 October 2000.

294. Macedonian Constitution (1991), art. 118: "The international agreements ratified in accordance with the Constitution are part of the internal legal order and cannot be changed by law." Macedonian courts rule on the basis of the Constitution and laws and international agreements ratified in accordance with the Constitution (Article 98).

295. Ibid., art. 9: "Citizens of the Republic of Macedonia are equal in their freedoms and rights, regardless of sex, race, color of skin, national and social origin, political and religious beliefs, property and social status."

296. Ibid., art. 35, par. 1.

297. Ibid., art. 35, par. 2.

298. U.S. Department of State–Bureau of Democracy, Human Rights, and Labor, *1999 Country Reports on Human Rights Practices* (25 February 2000): section 5.

299. World Bank, *Former Yugoslav Republic of Macedonia–Focusing on the Poor,* vol. 1, Main Report (Report No. 19411-MK, 11 June 1999): ii.

300. World Bank, *Former Yugoslav Republic of Macedonia–Focusing on the Poor,* vol. 2, Statistical Annex (Report No. 19411-MK, 11 June 1999): 47.

301. European Commission DGIA, "Social and Economic Integration of Marginalized Roma," in *The Former Yugoslav Republic of Macedonia: A Future with Europe* (May 1999): 17.

302. UNICEF, *Situation Analysis of Roma Women and Children* (Republic of Macedonia, 1999): 22.

303. Nevzat Zekir, Romani member of the Council on Inter-Ethnic Relations, interview by author, Skopje, Macedonia, 18 November 1999.

304. European Commission DGIA, *The Former Yugoslav Republic of Macedonia: A Future with Europe,* 18.

305. Ibid., 16.

306. Ibid., 17.

307. World Bank, *Former Yugoslav Republic of Macedonia–Focusing on the Poor,* vol. 1, Main Report, 61

308. Council of Europe, "The Former Yugoslav Republic of Macedonia (1)," in *Report of the European Commission Against Racism and Intolerance,* par. 8.

309. Enver Jonuz, social worker, interview by author, Skopje, Macedonia, 13 November 1999.

310. See section 4.2.2.

311. World Bank, *Former Yugoslav Republic of Macedonia–Focusing on the Poor,* vol. 2, Statistical Annex, 66.

312. According to the government, 17,301 persons, including 3,000 refugees, live in Shuto Orizari. See Project of the Government of the Former Yugoslav Republic of Macedonia and UNDP, *Communal Water and Infrastructure Improvement Vizbegovo–Shuto Orizari* (2000): section B. 3.

313. Jonuz, interview, 1999.

314. Macedonian Constitution (1991), art. 9 (antidiscrimination clause) and art. 40 (family protection).

315. World Bank, *Former Yugoslav Republic of Macedonia–Focusing on the Poor,* vol. 1, Main Report, 65

316. World Bank, *Former Yugoslav Republic of Macedonia–Focusing on the Poor,* vol. 2, Statistical Annex, 64.

317. Ibid., 64.

318. Ibid., 65.

319. Ibid., 66.

320. Decision 23-715/1 from 16 March 1998, art. 16, implementing rules.

321. The social benefits of a divorced woman from Bitolia had been cut because somebody informed the Social Work Center that she lives with her husband. She appealed the decision, but the Center did give an answer for six months. After living all this time with no source of income she decided to send a request directly to Skopje. See case in World Bank, *Former Yugoslav Republic of Macedonia–Focusing on the Poor,* vol. 1, Main Report, 63.

322. Jonuz , interview, 1999.

323. World Bank, *Former Yugoslav Republic of Macedonia–Focusing on the Poor,* vol. 1, Main Report, 63.

324. UNICEF, *Situation Analysis of Roma Women and Children,* 22.

325. World Bank, *Former Yugoslav Republic of Macedonia–Focusing on the Poor,* vol. 2, Statistical Annex, 47.

326. Macedonian Constitution, (1991), art. 34 and 35.

327. In 1999, the government lowered the residence requirement from fifteen to ten years, in conformity with the Council of Europe Convention on Citizenship; the new residency requirements are to become effective within about one year, following the passage of enabling legislation. See U.S. Department of State–Bureau of Democracy, Human Rights, and Labor, *1999 Country Reports on Human Rights Practices.*

328. European Roma Rights Center (ERRC), *A Pleasant Fiction–The Human Rights Situation of Roma in Macedonia–Country Reports Series* 7 (July 1998): 17-28. See also: ERRC, *Written Comments of the European Roma Rights Center Concerning the Former Yugoslav Republic of Macedonia–for Consideration by the European Commission Against Racism and Intolerance in Strasbourg in June 1998* (4 June 1998): 5–9.

329. Council of Europe, "The Former Yugoslav Republic of Macedonia (1)," in *Report of the European Commission Against Racism and Intolerance,* par. 4 and 5.

330. Jonuz, interview, 1999.

331. ERRC, *A Pleasant Fiction–The Human Rights Situation of Roma in Macedonia–Country Reports Series 7*: 82.

332. Committee on the Rights of the Child (CRC), *Concluding Observations of the Committee on the Rights of the Child: The Former Yugoslav Republic of Macedonia (FYRM)* CRC/C/15/Add.118, (January 2000): par. 21.

333. Ibid., par. 22.

334. Senaj Osmanov, president of the Association for Protection of Human Rights of Roma in Stip, interview by author, 15 November 1999; Muharen Jasarovki, leader of Nevo Suno, Prilep, interview by author, 21 November 1999; and Memedali Rahmani, president of Mesecina, Gostivar, interview by author, 23 November 1999.

335. World Bank, *Former Yugoslav Republic of Macedonia–Focusing on the Poor,* vol. 1, Main Report, 67.

336. R. S., a Romani woman in Stip, interview by author, 15 November 1999.

337. Decision 23-715/1 from 16 March 1998, art. 14. To avoid possible abuses of the system, the government also decided that the person who voluntarily left the social assistance program may apply for another four-year term only if the interruption was longer than nine months. If the interruption was shorter than nine months, the new term picks up where the old term left off.

338. World Bank, *Former Yugoslav Republic of Macedonia–Focusing on the Poor,* vol. 1, Main Report, 64.

339. According to the International Helsinki Federation for Human Rights: "Roma were often the first to be fired and the last to be hired, and many said that they experienced discrimination in employment." See International Helsinki Federation for Human Rights, *Annual Report 1997–Macedonia* (1997).

340. The average household in Macedonia has approximately 4 members, while the Romani household has approximately 6.4. See UNICEF, *Situation Analysis of Roma Women and Children,* 21.

341. Decision 23-715/1 from 16 March 1998, art. 4. Family is understood as a group of people who live in the same housing unit.

342. Jonuz, interview, 1999.

343. World Bank, *Former Yugoslav Republic of Macedonia–Focusing on the Poor,* vol. 1, Main Report, 62.

344. Committee on the Rights of the Child (CRC), *Concluding Observations of the Committee on the Rights of the Child: The Former Yugoslav Republic of Macedonia* (FYRM), par. 16.

345. Ibid., par. 17.

346. Several NGOs currently provide legal assistance for Roma, including the Association for Protection of Roma Rights in Stip, the Civil Society Resource Center, and ARKA. The Association for Protection of Roma Rights in Stip receives between five and nine social support-related complaints every month. The legal department filed three appeals with the Ministry of Labor, but, over three months later, had received no answer, even though the law requires the Ministry to decide within thirty days. Another eight to nine discrimination claims are in preparation.

Denial of Health Care

1. Universal Declaration of Human Rights (UDHR), art. 25, par. 1.
2. International Covenant on Economic, Social and Cultural Rights (ICESCR), art. 12, par. 1.
3. Convention on the Rights of the Child (CRC), art. 27, par. 3.
4. International Convention on the Elimination of All Forms of Racial Discrimination (ICERD), art. 5(e)(iv).
5. Convention on the Elimination of All Forms of Discrimination Against Women (CEDAW), art. 11(1)(f) and art. 12.
6. Committee on Economic, Social and Cultural Rights (CESCR), "The right to the highest attainable standard of health," *General Comment* 14 (11 May 2000): par. 12(2)(i).
7. "The enjoyment of the rights set forth in this Charter shall be secured without discrimination on any ground such as race, color, sex, language, religion, political or other opinion, national extraction or social origin, health, association with a national minority, birth or other status." Revised European Social Charter, art. E.
8. Romanian Constitution (1991), art. 33: "The right to the protection of health. (1) The right to the protection of health is guaranteed. (2) The State shall be bound to take measures to ensure public hygiene and health. (3) The organization of the medical care and social security system in case of sickness, accidents, maternity and recovery, the control over the exercise of medical professions and paramedical activities, as well as other measures to protect physical and mental health of person shall be established according to the law."
9. Bulgarian Constitution (1991). Article 52 reads: "(1) Citizens shall have the right to medical insurance guaranteeing them affordable medical care, and to free medical care in accordance with conditions and procedures established by law. (2) Citizens' medical care shall be financed from the state budget, by employers, through private and collective health-insurance schemes, and from other sources in accordance with conditions and procedures established by law. (3) The state shall protect the health of citizens and shall promote the development of sports and tourism. (4) No one shall be subjected to forcible medical treatment or sanitary measures except in circumstances established by law. (5) The state shall exercise control over all medical facilities and over the production and trade in pharmaceuticals, biologically active substances, and medical equipment."
10. Macedonian Constitution (1991), art. 39: "Every citizen is guaranteed the right to health care. Citizens have the right and duty to protect and promote their own health and the health of others."
11. See Legal Standards section: National standards.
12. Convention on Human Rights and Biomedicine (Oviedo 4 April 1997). Article 3 reads: "Parties, taking into account health needs and available resources, shall take appropriate measures with a view to providing, within their jurisdiction, equitable access to health care of appropriate quality."
13. Romanian Constitution (1991), art. 33.
14. The strategy for improving Romani health is part of a White Paper that will define the Romanian government's national strategy for Roma.
15. Mariana Buceanu, "Answers of Public Health Directors Concerning the Health Situation of Romani Communities," (GLAR-Working Group of Roma Associations, unpublished).
16. GLAR, " Memorandum: Recommendation on the General Policy Concerning the Implementation of the Governmental Program: Improvement of Roma situation," approved by the Inter-ministerial Subcommission for Roma, on 23–24 September 2000 and by the Inter-ministerial Commission for National Minorities on 28 September 2000.
17. Kveta Kalibova, "The Demographic Characteristics of Roma/Gypsies in Selected Countries in Central and Eastern Europe," in *The Demographic Characteristics of National Minorities in Certain European States, Population Study* 31, vol. 2 (Council of Europe Publishing, 2000): 186–7.
18. Save the Children, "Roma Children in Romania. Research Report. Summary" in *Final Report to the International Workshop on Roma Children in Europe* (Bucharest 1998): 82.
19. Laurentiu Vircan, *Elements of a Strategy for Improving the Health in Romani Communities: Presentation of the Status of Health in Romani Communities on the Basis of Information Received from Public Health Directors* (Romanian Ministry of Health: 2000, unpublished).
20. Buceanu, "Answers of Public Health Directors Concerning the Health Situation of Romani Communities."
21. Ibid.
22. Adrian Streinu-Cercel, head of the National AIDS Committee, cited by Radio Free Europe/Radio Liberty (RFE/RL) Newsline, "Romania has the Most AIDS Infected Children in Europe," 24 November 1999, available at: http://www.rferl.org/newsline/1999/11/241199.html
23. Dana Robea, reporter, "Sentenced," TVR 2, 1 July 1999. File videotape.

24. Health Rehabilitation Project P008759 (closed) and the Health Sector Reform Project P008797 (active).
25. The Law on Social Health Insurance 145/1997 entered into force on 1 January 1998. The section concerning Health Insurance Houses as autonomous public institutions entered into force on 1 January 1999 (henceforth: Law 145/1997).
26. Law 145/1997, art. 4 (1) provides that all Romanian citizens domiciled in the country as well as foreigners and stateless persons legally residing in Romania are subjected to compulsory health insurance. Members of diplomatic missions accredited in Romania are excepted, art. 7.
27. Ibid., art. 3, par. 1.
28. Ibid., art. 53, par. 1 and 2.
29. Ibid., art. 54, par. 2.
30. Applies to children and students, handicapped people, and the wife, husband, parents or grandparents of the insured person if they have no income of their own. Other special categories of people are also insured without being obliged to pay the health insurance contribution. Law 145/1997, art. 6.
31. The eligibility conditions for social support are provided by Law 67/1995.
32. Law 145/1997, art. 9, (d).
33. Ibid., art. 52, par. 1.
34. Ibid., art. 6 and art. 55, par. 1.
35. Some Romanian journalists have already denounced the existence of "constant and persuasive editorial politics of incitement of the majority population against the Roma minority." See, for example, Valerian Stan,"Prejudices and Intolerance," *Cotidianul,* 27 December 1999.
36. In December, the daily *Evenimentul* reported a dramatic car accident in which six Romani adults and several children were wounded. The description of the arrival of the victims, including a woman in serious condition starts as follows: "A gang of Gypsies besieged the hospital disturbing the peace of the doctors and of the other patients." See Silvia Vrincean, "The Pea, Gypsy Woman from Laiesti, Poisoned Herself with Fire-Water," *Evenimentul,* 10 December 1999.
37. "Doctor Severely Beaten by Gypsies Because She Told Them to Stop Smoking Inside the Hospital," *Ziua,* 26 November 1999.
38. On 24 October 1999, PRO TV, one of the main Romanian television stations, broadcast a prime-time report on two health clinics in Ferentari and Rahova, both of them Romani dominated areas of Bucharest. The journalist reported that "some patients" (Roma were not named as such but Romani pedestrians were on the screen and the images were sufficiently suggestive) threaten the doctors, break windows and doors, and spray walls with graffiti, and that Ferentari clinic was "destroyed once a week." Narrating over images of empty rooms, the reporter described how "certain groups" slammed cabinet doors, insulted, and even attacked doctors. Old patients—the camera panned some elderly people on the street who were clearly non-Roma—are robbed while waiting to be seen by doctors. The same un-named groups of criminal offenders "steal old ladies' bags" and "pull the prescriptions for free medication out of their hands." A public health official declared that "indeed doctors are reluctant to practice medicine in Rahova and Ferentari" without providing any explanation. His statement seemed to confirm all the allegations of the journalist. No doctor, nurse or other patient, except an old lady from the neighborhood, was interviewed.
39. UNICEF Romania and Romani CRISS, *Improving Primary Health Care: Public Health and Cultural Research with Roma Communities in Romania* (April-May 1998): 9.
40. Ibid., 10.
41. Ibid., 26.
42. Ibid., 9-10.
43. Save the Children, "Roma Children in Romania. Research Report. Summary," in *Final Report to the International Workshop on Roma Children in Europe,* 19.
44. Doctor's Code of Ethics, art. 46.
45. Doctor's Code of Ethics, art. 32.
46. Law on Medical Profession, Law 74/1995, art. 4.
47. UNICEF Romania and Romani CRISS, *Improving Primary Health Care: Public Health and Cultural Research with Roma Communities in Romania,* 10. The authors were inclined to believe that this is a rather exceptional situation and that the refusal "should not be widespread and general throughout the country." To support this presumption, they cited a doctor from Stefanesti (a village in Moldova) saying that he had welcomed all Roma who wanted to register.
48. Vircan, *Elements of a Strategy for Improving the Health in Romani Communities: Presentation of the Status of Health in Romani Communities on the Basis of Information Received from Public Health Directors.* Asked to comment on the refusal of doctors to enroll Roma, the general director of the National Health Insurance Company argued that "these are isolated cases that cannot be generalized." In his view, "Gypsies are not at risk of being excluded because doctors have an economic interest in accepting them." (*Evenimentul,* 26 February 2000). Romani organizations argue that newly enacted legislation has a

devastating impact on the Romani community. In a 1999 memorandum addressed to the DPMN, the Foundation WASSDASS, an organization with extensive expertise on health issues, states that "as a result of the newly enacted legislation at least 60 percent of Roma remained without health care."

49. Committee on the Elimination of Racial Discrimination. Fifty-Seventh Session. Special Thematic Discussion on Roma Issues, Statement on Behalf of Roma Center for Social Intervention and Studies (August 2000, unpublished).

50. Romani CRISS organized the Roma Health Mediators—probably the most interesting health program in the region. Romani women were trained and subsequently employed to play an active role as mediators between the health care authorities and the communities. Their role is to educate, to mediate, and to facilitate Romani access to the health care system. They are also supposed to compile records of the health needs of the community, and serve as a valuable source of information for health-related research. The organization runs, inter alia, a health mediator project in Stefanesti.

51. Joyce Schoon, *Improving Primary Health Care: Public Health and Social-Cultural Research with Roma Communities in Romania — Description and Evaluation of the Local Primary Health Care Projects of Romani CRISS* (May 1998): 9.

52. Adrian Moldovan, president of Ramses-Dej, interview by author, 15 October 1999.

53. G. M., Romani, interview by author, Modruzeni, Marasesti, 19 October, 1999.

54. Sugar is said to help heart patients.

55. Ficuta N., Roma Party leader, Buhusi branch, interview by author, 18 October 1999.

56. A. S. and M. T., Romani women, interviews by author, Geoagiu, 11 October 1999.

57. Press reports appear to support this allegation. For example, in June 2000 the daily *Evenimentul* wrote about the Roma ghetto in Geoagiu: "Public health authorities are never visiting this place, let alone family doctors, whose number is by far too low for the commune." Lucian Stanciu, "The Roma Ghetto in Geoagiu, the Place Where Nobody Dares to Enter," *Evenimentul,* 16 June 2000.

58. Nicolae Bologa, Roma expert, OSF Roma Board, interview by author, 11 October 1999.

59. "Gypsies from Iasi Will Not Be Received in Hospitals Anymore," *Ziua,* 7 September 1999.

60. Ibid.

61. Human rights NGO based in Targu Mures.

62. PRO EUROPE League (Liga PRO EUROPA) immediately verified the situation in the field and reported that, at the League's requests, in October 1999, a Romani student from Iasi visited the hospital. The presence of several Romani patients in the hall of the hospital indicated that, at that date, they were still not permitted to enter. Istvan Haller, ERRC correspondent in Romania, *ERRC Report, 4-24 October 1999, Romania, Targu Mures* (unpublished).

63. Telephone conversation with Dan Oprescu, 9 August 2000, in the file.

64. *Report, 4-24 October, 1999, Romania, Targu Mures* (unpublished).

65. A. S., interview, 1999.

66. C. R., Romani woman, interview by author, Modruzeni, 19 October 1999.

67. M. C., Romani woman, interview by author, Modruzeni, 19 October, 1999.

68. P. A., Romani woman, interview by author, Buhusi, 18 October 1999.

69. Law on Social Support, Law 67/1995, art. 2.

70. Law 145/1997, art. 6(1).

71. Ibid., art. 5.

72. Mariana Buceanu, coordinator of Health Programs at Romani CRISS, interview by author, 7 September 1999.

73. See Barriers to Social Protection, Romania.

74. Aurel Rosianu, Roma Party, interview by author, Cluj, 13 October 1999.

75. Paustin Balan, president, Association Rom-Star, interview by author, Bacau, 18 October 1999.

76. See Barriers to Social Protection, Romania.

77. Law 145/1997, art. 9(d), provides that the state pays the health insurance contribution for beneficiaries of social support during the period when the individual concerned qualifies as beneficiary for this special form of support.

78. Law 145/1997, art. 12, par. (2) lit.e.

79. One of these efforts is the Health Sector Rehabilitation Project. The Ministry of Health, supported by the World Bank, set up a network of ninety-six new rural emergency centers and improved communication and transport systems.

80. F. F., Romani woman, interview by author, Geoagiu.

81. Schoon, *Improving Primary Health Care: Public Health and Social-Cultural Research with Roma Communities in Romania—Description and Evaluation of the Local Primary Health Care Projects of Romani CRISS,* 5.

82. Ibid., 11–2. Source: Lucan Mariana, health mediator.

83. Ibid., 14. Calin Florentina and Stanciu Carmen, health mediators, interviewed by author.

84. UNICEF Romania and Romani CRISS, *Improving Primary Health Care: Public Health and Cultural Research with Roma Communities in Romania,* 11.

85. Bulgarian Constitution (1991) Article 52 reads:

"(1) Citizens shall have the right to medical insurance guaranteeing them affordable medical care, and to free medical care in accordance with conditions and procedures established by law.

(2) Citizens' medical care shall be financed from the state budget, by employers, through private and collective health-insurance schemes, and from other sources in accordance with conditions and procedures established by law.

(3) The state shall protect the health of citizens and shall promote the development of sports and tourism.

(4) No one shall be subjected to forcible medical treatment or sanitary measures except in circumstances established by law.

(5) The state shall exercise control over all medical facilities and over the production and trade in pharmaceuticals, biologically active substances, and medical equipment."

86. For more on the Framework Program for Equal Integration of Roma in Bulgarian Society see Barriers to Social Protection, Bulgaria: National Strategies for Romani Integration and Social Support.

87. Ilona Tomova, *Ethnic Dimensions of Poverty in Bulgaria,* report commissioned for the Bulgaria Social Assessment, (Washington, D.C.: World Bank, 1998).

88. CESCR, *Replies by the Government of Bulgaria to the List of Issues (E/C.12/Q/BUL/1) to Be Taken up in Connection with the Consideration of the Third Periodic Report of Bulgaria Concerning the Rights Referred to in Articles 1–15 of the International Convenant on Economic, Social and Cultural Rights* (E/1994/104/Add.16) (9 July 1999): par. 4.1.

89. Ilona Tomova, *The Gypsies in the Transition Period* (Sofia: International Center for Minority Studies and Intercultural Relations, 1995): 49.

90. Project on Ethnic Relations, *The Roma in Bulgaria: Collaborative Efforts between Local Authorities and Nongovernmental Organizations* (April, 1998) available at: http://www.websp.com/~ethnic/new/roma_bul.htm.

91. Organization for Security and Cooperation in Europe (OSCE), *OSCE Report on the Situation of Roma and Sinti in the OSCE Area* (The Hague, 10 March 2000): 117.

92. Tomova, *The Gypsies in the Transition Period,* 50.

93. Ilona Tomova and team, "Bulgaria: 6 Case Studies," as cited in Dena Ringold, *Roma and the Transition in Central and Eastern Europe: Trends and Challenges* (Washington, D.C.: The World Bank, 2000): 21.

94. Ibid.

95. Ilona Tomova and team, "Bulgaria, 6 Case Studies." (2000).

96. Tomova, *Ethnic Dimensions of Poverty in Bulgaria.*

97. The World Bank's investment Program in Bulgaria "Health Sector Restructuring" available at: http://www.worldbank.bg/operations/HEALTH_1.pdf.

98. CESCR, *Replies by the Government of Bulgaria to the List of Issues (E/C.12/Q/BUL/1) to Be Taken up in Connection with the Consideration of the Third Periodic Report of Bulgaria Concerning the Rights Referred to in Articles 1-15 of the International Convenant on Economic, Social and Cultural Rights* (E/1994/104/Add.16) par. 36.1.

99. The World Bank's investment Program in Bulgaria "Health Sector Restructuring," Financing Plan in millions of U.S. dollars: IBRD: $26; Council of Europe Social Development Fund: $11; EU PHARE: $2.3; Government: $7.8. Total: $47.1. Available at: http://www.worldbank.bg/operations/HEALTH_1.pdf. For the period 2000-2005, see the "Health Insurance Project" (BG-PE-55157).

100. *Health Insurance Act, State Gazette,* no. 70, 19 June 1998. Last amended in *State Gazette,* no. 64, 4 August 2000 (henceforth: Health Insurance Act).

101. *Health Care Institutions Act, State Gazette,* no. 62, 9 July 1999. Last amended in *State Gazette,* no. 65, 8 August 2000.

102. *Professional Associations of Medical Doctors and Dentists Act, State Gazette,* no. 83, 21 July 1998.

103. *Public Health Act, State Gazette,* no. 88, 6 November 1973. Last amended in *State Gazette,* no. 36, 2 May 2000.

104. Health Insurance Act, art. 2 and art. 3, par. 1 and 2.

105. National Health Insurance Fund, *Health Reform in Bulgaria–Main Objectives and Achievements Up to Date–October 1999* (October 1999): 4.

106. Ibid.

107. Health Insurance Act, art. 37, par.1.

108. Ibid., par. 2.

109. Ibid., art. 33.

110. The Parliament substantially amended the Health Insurance Act on December 1999: DV no. 110 of 17 December 1999 effective as of 1 January 2000.

111. Health Insurance Act, art. 40, par. 1, sub-par. 11.
112. Before December 1999 the socially disadvantaged and all those registered with the unemployment offices, regardless of their eligibility for monthly social support, were supposed to be insured from municipal funds (see Health Insurance Act, art. 40, before being amended).
113. Health Insurance Act, art. 40, par. 1, sub-par. 9.
114. Ibid., art. 40, par. 1, sub-par. 9.
115. See Barriers to Social Protection, Bulgaria.
116. For example, out of approximately 7,000 families living in Fakulteta, Sofia's largest Romani neighborhood, less than 70 met the requirements for monthly social support. Anastasia Ivanova, head of the Social Work Center, Krasna Poliana Branch, interview by author, 6 December 1999. According to Romani Baht, a Romani NGO based in Fakulteta, 95 percent of these 7,000 families do not have regular sources of income and more than half of them live in severe poverty. Romani Baht Foundation, *Annual Report–1998* (January 2000): 5.
117. Romani Baht Foundation, *Annual Report–1999*, 25.
118. Irina Vandova and Varban Tomov, *Case Study of Bulgaria–Nikola Kochev District and Nadezhda Ghetto in the Town of Sliven, Villages of Sotirya, Topolchane and Gorno Alexandrovo* (forthcoming) available at: http://www.yale.edu/socdept/reports/vandova.html.
119. Varban Tomov, *Roma from the Village of Gorno Alxandrovo* (forthcoming) available at: http://w ww.yale.edu/socdept/reports/tomov.html.
120. Romani Baht in Fakulteta and Roma Bureaus operate in only three or four cities. According to the unemployment offices, the number of people registered as unemployed increases spectacularly in the localities where Romani NGOs are active.
121. Dr. Stefan Panayotov, chairman of The Health of Romani People Foundation, interview by author, Sliven, 11 December 1999.
122. Irina Vandova, *Roma from the Village of Sotirya,* case 505, (forthcoming) available at: http://www.yale.edu/socdept/reports/tomov.html.
123. Varban Tomov, *Roma from the Village of Topolchane,* case 612, (forthcoming) available at: http://www.yale.edu/socdept/reports/tomov.html.
124. Vandova and Tomov, *Case Study of Bulgaria–Nikola Kochev District and Nadezhda Ghetto in the Town of Sliven, Villages of Sotirya, Topolchane and Gorno Alexandrovo,* case 413.
125. Romani Baht Foundation, *Annual Report–1998,* 28-31.
126. Ibid., 28.
127. Kamelia Anguelova, "Ethnic and Religious Minorities in the Bulgarian Mainstream Press," *Balkan Neighbors, Newsletter of the Balkan Neighbors Project* (October 1996–March 1997).
128. "Yellow Visitor [Tuberculosis] Takes Us by Surprise," and "TBC Strikes Gypsies, Prisoners, Drunks and Poor," *24 Chassa,* 14 August 1997.
129. "Three Babies Die of Syphilis," *24 Chassa,* 6 August 1997.
130. "Gypsies Sell Infected Blood," *Standard,* 8 August 1997.
131. T., "Lice Suck Blood in Gypsy Neighborhoods," *Dneven Troud,* 8 July 1997.
132. NT, "Fakulteta Augurs Epidemics," *Noshten Troud,* 23–24 July 1997.
133. World Bank, *Consultations with the Poor, National Synthesis Report Bulgaria* (May 1999): 76.
134. Panayotov, interview, 1999.
135. Ilona Tomova, interview by author, Sofia, 7 December 1999.
136. Tomov, *Roma from the Village of Topolchane.*
137. *Roma (Gypsies) in Bulgaria,* available at: http://www.bsos.umd.edu/cidcm/mar/bulroma.htm.
138. "Snapshots from around Europe: Police Abuse of Roma in Bulgaria," *Roma Rights–Newsletter of the European Roma Rights Center* (Summer 1998): 17. Later, fifteen people eventually obtained forensic evidence, and they filed nine complaints with the Military Prosecutor's Office. U.S. Department of State–Bureau of Democracy, Human Rights, and Labor—*Bulgaria Country Report on Human Rights Practices for 1998* (26 February 1999).
139. Petar Malinov, "The Case of Todor Todorov from Sliven," *Roma Rights in Focus–Newsletter of Human Rights Project* (January–July 1999): 5.
140. Romani Baht Foundation, *Annual Report–1999,* 25.
141. The author did not find evidence that other types of hospitals segregate patients on a wholesale basis. It should also be acknowledged that segregation is not a universal practice in Bulgarian maternities: there are still places in the country such as Lom where Romani and non-Romani women reportedly share the same rooms in maternity wards.
142. Romani women, interviews by author, Nadezhda, Sliven, 11 December 1999.
143. S. D., Romani woman, interview by author, Nadezhda, Sliven, 11 December 1999.
144. Panayotov, interview, 1999.
145. P. G., coordinator of HRP, interview by author, Sliven.

146. Panayotov, interview, 1999.
147. Romani women in Nadezhda ghetto, Sliven, 11 December 1999.
148. Panayotov, interview, 1999.
149. Vandova and Tomov, *Case Study of Bulgaria–Nikola Kochev District and Nadezhda Ghetto in the Town of Sliven, Villages of Sotirya, Topolchane and Gorno Alexandrovo.*
150. Denitsa Sacheva-Atanassova, general director, National Health Insurance Fund, interview by author, Sofia, 13 December 1999.
151. Patyo Valchev, director Social Work Center, interview by author, Chirpan, 10 December 1999.
152. According to WHO, in 1997, BCG coverage was 97 percent; Polio, 96 percent; Diphtheria, 94 percent; Pertussis, 94 percent; Tetanus, 94 percent; and Measles, 93 percent (4,119 cases between 1993 and 1997). The Bulgarian Population in 1997 was 8,427,476. World Health Organization (WHO), *Immunization Profile–Bulgaria* (1997), available at: www.who.org.
153. Varban Tomov, *Poverty and Ethnicity: Bulgarian Case Study–Roma from the Village of Topolchane* (forthcoming) available at: http://www.yale.edu/socdept/reports/tomov.html.
154. OSCE, *OSCE Report on the Situation of Roma and Sinti in the OSCE Area,* 117.
155. Ilona Tomova and team, "Bulgaria, 6 Case Studies." (2000).
156. Committee on the Rights of the Child (CRC), *Initial Reports of States Parties due in 1993: Bulgaria,* CRC/C/8/Add.29 (12 October 1995): par. 176.
157. According to Romani Baht, nurses and doctors show up sometimes in Fakulteta with a mobile lab and insist on performing vaccinations. There is no Roma on the medical staff to explain to the community in its own terms the objective of the vaccination program. Under the circumstances, many Romani mothers refuse it. Mihail Georgiev, chairman of the board of directors of Romani Baht Foundation, interview by author, Sofia, 3 December 1999.
158. Doctors in the regional Hospital in Sliven as cited in Vandova, *Roma from the Village of Sotirya.*
159. Tomova, interview, 1999.
160. Ibid.
161. Dr. Ivailo Tournev, president, Ethnic Minorities Health Problems, interview by author, 7 December 1999.
162. In fact, according to Ivailo Tournev, an NGO president and doctor from the University Hospital, doctors identified three other specific disorders in Bulgarian Roma that have yet to be analyzed. The high number of specific disorders is because Romani groups tend to be rather closed communities that do not mix with the outside world. Different groups do not present the same disorder, but rather develop particular forms.
163. L. Kalaydijeva et.al, *Hereditary Motor and Sensory Neuropathy–Lom* (Oxford University Press, 1998). In Lom, the hardest hit area is Mladenovo, a Romani neighborhood where approximately 300 people are severely affected. Hundreds of children present "Lom Disease" symptoms. Romani leaders claim that up to 10 percent of that community might be sick. People are aware of the hereditary character of the disorder: conventional wisdom states that no Roma from outside would marry somebody from Mladenovo. In the last thirty years, only three marriages outside the group are known. The marriages within the neighborhood's borders and the lack of information about the disease threaten the very existence of the group. Nikolay Kirilov , chairman of the Roma-Lom Foundation, interview by author, 12 December 1999.
164. See Ivailo Tournev et al, "Congenital Cataracts Facial Dysmorphism Neuropathy Syndrome, a Novel Complex Genetic Disease in Balkan Gypsies: Clinical and Electrophysiological Observations," *Annals of Neurology,* vol. 45, no.6 (June 1999):
165. Muscular dystrophy is a type of hereditary neuromuscular disorder, which is among the most frequent causes for invalidity and death. The available data show an "extremely high frequency of the neuromuscular disorders and presence of new syndromes in the Gypsy population." See National Science Fund, Bulgaria, available at: http://www.minedu.government.bg/nsfb/BulgariaRTD/nfni-proj/v-735.htm. In one trial, health professionals tested 500 young Roma from Omurtag for muscular dystrophy and found that 10 percent were carriers of the disease. The community is relatively small and socially isolated. The probability that two carriers will marry is relatively high. Doctors informed the carriers about the risks if they marry and advised them to take pregnancy tests. Tournev, interview, 1999.
166. For comparison, the surgeon's salary at the University Hospital is 180 leva per month.
167. Tournev, interview, 1999.
168. For example, twenty-six-year-old Todora Schopova Alexandrova is a Roma with muscular dystrophy. Three years ago, officials placed her in a home for elderly people in Provadia. She cannot walk but her intellectual capacity is intact. She shares the room with six elderly women suffering from dementia. She never leaves the room because she does not have a wheelchair. She does not have any family to visit her. She does not even have a TV in her room. There is no therapy, no rehabilitation program, no attempt to assist her. The diagnosis is correct, the placement is wrong, and the treatment nonexistent. Case presented by Dr. Ivailo Tournev. According to Tournev, there is no place available for Todora in an adequate institution. Tournev, interview, 1999.

169. The Ordinance on Provision of Emergency Health Care no.25, 4 November 1999, regulates the organization of emergency health care (henceforth: Ordinance on Provision of Emergency Health Care no. 25).
170. Ibid., art. 3
171. Ibid., art. 1, par. 1.
172. Ibid., art. 9, par. 8.
173. Romani Baht Foundation, *Annual Report–1998*, 28.
174. Mihail Georgiev, chairman of the board of directors, Romani Baht Foundation, interview by author, Fakulteta, Sofia, 3 December 1999.
175. Vandova and Tomov, *Case Study of Bulgaria–Nikola Kochev District and Nadezhda Ghetto in the Town of Sliven, Villages of Sotirya, Topolchane and Gorno Alexandrovo*, case 403, 7.
176. Kirilov, interview, 1999.
177. Romani Baht Foundation, *Annual Report–1998*, 28.
178. Ibid., 5.
179. Vandova and Tomov, *Case Study of Bulgaria–Nikola Kochev District and Nadezhda Ghetto in the Town of Sliven, Villages of Sotirya, Topolchane and Gorno Alexandrovo.*
180. Ibid., case 599, 17.
181. Tomova, interview, 1999.
182. Macedonia succeeded to ICCPR on 18 January 1994.
183. Macedonia succeeded to ICESCR on 18 January 1994.
184. Macedonia succeeded to ICERD on 18 January 1994. The Republic of Macedonia made the declaration under art. 14 of the Convention, recognizing the competence of the Committee on Elimination of Racial Discrimination to consider individual and group complaints, on 22 December 1999.
185. Macedonia succeeded to CEDAW on 18 January 1994.
186. Macedonia succeeded to CRC on 2 December 1993.
187. As of 17 October 2000. The European Social Charter was signed on 5 May 1998.
188. Macedonian Constitution (1991), art. 118: "The international agreements ratified in accordance with the Constitution are part of the internal legal order and cannot be changed by law." Article 98 states that Macedonian courts rule on the basis of the Constitution and laws and international agreements ratified in accordance with the Constitution.
189. Ibid., art. 39: "Every citizen is guaranteed the right to health care. Citizens have the right and duty to protect and promote their own health and the health of others."
190. Ibid., art. 9: "Citizens of the Republic of Macedonia are equal in their freedoms and rights, regardless of sex, race, color of skin, national and social origin, political and religious beliefs, property and social status."
191. Council of Europe–European Commission Against Racism and Intolerance, *Report on the Former Yugoslav Republic of Macedonia* (1) (January 2000): par. 8.
192. Roma presence in the age groups over age 40 is two-thirds the rate of the national levels. For example, Macedonian participation in the age group 40–44 is 8.0 while Romani participation is 6.1; in the age group 45-49, 6.3 compared to 4.2; in the age group 50–54, 5.7 compared to 3.5. UNICEF, *Situation Analysis of Roma Women and Children* (Republic of Macedonia: UNICEF, 1999): 12.
193. In 1996. See *Statistical Yearbook of the Republic of Macedonia for 1997.*
194. UNICEF, *Situation Analysis of Roma Women and Children*, 11.
195. There is medium-level infant mortality in the Republic of Macedonia with 22.5 deaths per 1,000 live births in 1995. Committee on the Rights of the Child (CRC), *Initial Reports of States Parties due in 1993: The Former Yugoslav Republic of Macedonia*, CRC/C/8/Add.36 (27 July 1997): par. 155.
196. Ibid.
197. UNICEF, *Situation Analysis of Roma Women and Children*, 11.
198. Immunization is performed continuously for diphtheria, tetanus, whooping cough, polio, measles, mumps, and rubella, as well as for type B hepatitis and flu in cases with epidemiological indications. Liljana Ivanovska and Ilir Ljuma, *Health Sector Reform in the Republic of Macedonia*, vol.40, no. 2 (Skopje, Republic of Macedonia: Ministry of Health-Health Insurance Fund, March 1999): available at: http://www.vms.hr/cmj/1999/4002/400209.htm.
199. UNICEF, *Situation Analysis of Roma Women and Children*, 26.
200. Fifty-two percent of the mothers answered "yes" to whether their infants have had diarrhea in the past month. UNICEF, *Situation Analysis of Roma Women and Children*, 25. Approximately 36 percent of Romani women do not have access to adequate sanitation/waste disposal systems. UNICEF, *Situation Analysis of Roma Women and Children*, 29.
201. Approximately 39 percent of all Romani mothers surveyed by UNICEF indicated that at least one of their children under seven years of age had suffered a serious respiratory illness in the month preceding the survey. UNICEF, *Situation Analysis of Roma Women and Children*, 25.

202. *Health Insurance Law*, 29 March 2000, *Official Gazette* no. 25 (30 March, 2000): 1455-65. The law entered into force 2000-04-07 (henceforth: Health Insurance Law).
203. Health Insurance Law, art. 5, par. 1.
204. Ibid., art. 5, par. 2.
205. Ibid., art. 9.
206. Ibid., art. 6.
207. Ibid., art. 2.
208. Ibid., art. 74, par. 1.
209. Ibid., art. 2.
210. Ibid., art. 53 to 72..
211. Ibid., art. 28 par. 1: "The insured person has the right and the obligation to select a primary care general practitioner."
212. Ibid., art. 28 par. 4.
213. Ibid., art. 38, par. 2, point 1.
214. Ibid., art. 38, par. 2, point 5.
215. Ibid., art. 38, par. 2, point 2.
216. Ibid., art. 38, par. 2, point 4.
217. Ibid., art. 38, par. 2, point 3.
218. Ibid., art. 52.
219. Ibid., art. 32, par. 1.
220. Ibid., art. 76-a, par. 1, let. 1) of the Law on Health Care provides that children up to the age of fourteen are exempted from participation.
221. The regulations concerning the payment for participation by children entered into force in September 2000, six months after the entry into force of the new Health Insurance Law. Health Insurance Law, art. 94, par. 2.
222. Indigent persons are defined as insured persons who have total net monthly family income lower than the average net salary in the Republic of Macedonia in the previous year. Health Insurance Law, art. 34, par. 2.
223. Health Insurance Law, art. 34 par. 2,.
224. Ibid., art. 34, par. 1,.
225. Liljana Ivanovska and Ilir Ljuma, *Health Sector Reform in the Republic of Macedonia*, vol. 40, no. 2(Skopje: Ministry of Health-Health Insurance Fund, March 1999) available at: http://www.vms.hr/cmj/1999/4002/400209.htm.
226. Macedonian NGOs cannot provide any general assessment concerning health insurance coverage for the Romani community. They base their local, ad hoc estimates on indirect evidence, such as the number of people who request legal assistance to apply for Macedonian citizenship, or on information related to the number of persons who graduated primary school and number of children per family.
227. Two different sources estimate that 30 percent of the inhabitants of Shuto Orizari, Skopje's largest Romani neighborhood, do not have health insurance. Nijazi Elnazov, the vice president of Anglunipe, a Skopje based Romani Youth Organization, participated in a social survey organized in 1999 in a small area of Shuto Orizari. Out of the 200 Romani families he interviewed personally, approximately 70 did not have health insurance. Most of them had not obtained health insurance, because they did not graduate primary school. There were also several women without citizenship papers, several people who were unable to compile all the required documents, and a couple who declared that they were not interested in being insured. Nijazi Elnazov, interview by author, Skopje, 19 November 1999. Enver Jonuz, a social worker in Shuto Orizari, knows approximately 2,500 Romani families receiving social support and affirms that more then 800 of them do not have health insurance. Again, the main obstacle is the education requirement. Enver Jonuz, interview by author, Skopje, 13 November 1999.
228. Some 550 Romani families or approximately 6,500 persons live in Stip. The local Association for the Protection of Human Rights of Roma, an NGO that provides legal assistance in citizenship and social welfare cases, reports that 90 percent of these families do not have health insurance. Eighty percent of Roma from Stip do not fulfill the education requirement, another 3 to 4 percent do not have Macedonian citizenship, and the rest fail to fill out the applications or are not interested. Senaj Osmanov, president, Association for the Protection of Human Rights of Roma in Stip, interview by author, 15 November 1999.
229. According to its inhabitants, nobody has health insurance in Kvantasi, a small Romani settlement ten kilometers east of Skopje. The settlement has thirty adults and fifty children. Twenty adults are not citizens. Those who have Macedonian citizenship did not finish primary school. Kvantasi inhabitants, interview by author, 14 November 1999. All ten families living in Lisice, a small Romani area near Skopje, have no medical insurance because they lack the required education. Lisice inhabitants, interview by author, 14 November 1999. Twenty-five kilometers southwest of Skopje is the Romani settlement called Batinci, where seventy families or approximately 400 people live. Only three adults finished primary school, so only three

are eligible for health insurance. Batinci inhabitants, interview by author, 14 November 1999.
230. Before April 2000, under art. 17 of the of the Law on Health Care, all children who were not otherwise insured should have had health insurance without paying a contribution. However, it seemed that this regulation was not applied in Macedonia, or at least it was not applied systematically to Roma and their children. The majority of Romani applicants with the Center for Social Work for so-called "one time emergency help" in Shuto Orizari want help paying for surgery or hospitalization for their children. Jonuz, interview, 1999.
231. Health Insurance Law, art. 6 and 7.
232. Dr. Andrej Arsovski, member of the Advisory Committee of the Health Program of OSI–Macedonia, interview by author, Skopje, 11 November 1999.
233. Law on Health Care, art. 76 and 76(a).
234. Case reported by Senaj Osmanov, interview, 1999.
235. A. D., Romani woman in Stip. She does not have any kind of papers, not even an expired ID. Her child does not have a birth certificate and is not otherwise registered. From an administrative point of view, he might as well not exist. There are approximately ten similar cases in Stip. Osmanov, interview, 1999.
236. Romani women, interviews by author, Radanski Pat, Stip, 15 November 1999.
237. Committee on the Rights of the Child, *Concluding Observations of the Committee on the Rights of the Child: The Former Yugoslav Republic of Macedonia (FYRM)* CRC/C/15/Add.118 (January 2000): par. 21.
238. According to a recent UNICEF study, 97.7 percent of Romani women have no regular or temporary jobs. UNICEF, *Situation Analysis of Roma Women and Children,* 22.
239. Forty-six percent of Roma did not finish their primary education and cannot read. Ibid., 22.
240. Memedali Rahmani, president of Mesecina Gostivar, interview by author, 23 November 1999.
241. Health Insurance Law, art. 5, par. 1, let. 11.
242. In 1999, the 15-year residence requirement was lowered to 10 years, in conformity with the Council of Europe Convention on Citizenship. U.S. Department of State–Bureau of Democracy, Human Rights, and Labor *Former Yugoslav Republic of Macedonia, 1999–Country Reports on Human Rights Practices* (25 February 2000) available at: http://www.state.gov/www/global/human_rights/1999_hrp_report/macedoni.html.
243. Ibid.
244. European Roma Rights Center (ERRC), *Written Comments of the European Roma Rights Center Concerning the Former Yugoslav Republic of Macedonia–for Consideration by the European Commission Against Racism and Intolerance in Strasbourg in June 1998* (4 June 1998): 5–9.
245. International Helsinki Foundation (IHF), Report by the International Helsinki Federation, OSCE Review Conference: Human Dimension Issues, Vienna–Istanbul 1999.
246. See Macedonian government statistics in *Third Periodic Report Submitted to the UN Committee on the Elimination of Racial Discrimination,* CERD/C/270/Add.2 (13 March 1997): 57.
247. In Kumanovo, for example, 30 percent of approximately 5,000 Roma were not citizens; similar percentages were reported in Skopje. In Tetovo, between 500 and 1000 Roma are not citizens. ERRC, *Written Comments of the European Roma Rights Center Concerning the Former Yugoslav Republic of Macedonia–for Consideration by the European Commission Against Racism and Intolerance in Strasbourg in June 1998,* 5.
248. Council of Europe–European Commission Against Racism and Intolerance, *Report on the Former Yugoslav Republic of Macedonia* (1), par. 5.
249. Health Insurance Law, art. 5, par. 1, let. 7).
250. Officials throughout the country apply the requirement unevenly. In Skopje, Stip, Gostivar, and other smaller Romani settlements, all persons interviewed—Romani leaders, social workers, and Roma families—declared that a primary school diploma is a necessary prerequisite for health insurance. In Prilep, however, several Romani women said that they registered with the unemployment office and received health insurance, although they did not finish primary school. Ahmet Jasarovski, the president of DROM, says that officials in Kumanovo do not impose the education requirement.
251. According to art. 15 of the Unemployment Law, an "unemployed" person is someone registered by the unemployment office as a person seeking employment. Such a person: (1) cannot provide himself and his family with enough resources to live; (2) accepts any kind of employment suitable to his/her professional background, working abilities, and family circumstances; (3) registers regularly with the unemployment office; (4) accepts additional training which might increase his/her chances of employment.
252. Nikolina Cvetkovska, deputy director, National Unemployment Agency, interview by author, Skopje, 24 November 1999.
253. Jordan Misovski, lawyer, counselor of the Minister of Health, interview by author, Skopje, 22 November 1999.
254. Elnazov and Jonuz interviews, 1999.
255. Osmanov, interview, 1999.
256. Batinci inhabitants, interview, 1999.

257. Osmanov, interview, 1999.
258. Many of them, however, have the potential to organize such programs. For example, DROM in Kumanovo has a database of all Romani families in the city with information on citizenship, number of children, social support, and sometimes even health insurance status, but does not yet have any information on why a family does not possess health insurance.
259. Committee on the Rights of the Child, *Concluding Observations of the Committee on the Rights of the Child: The Former Yugoslav Republic of Macedonia (FYRM)*, 16–17.
260. Law on Health Care, art. 64, lit. 3.
261. This contribution was calculated every year and equaled 70 percent of the lowest salary as determined by the Collective Labor Agreement. Law on Health Care, art. 65, final paragraph.
262. In 1999, the additional compulsory insurance was 2 percent of 9,000 denars for each "additional" child. According to Nikolina Cvetkovska, deputy director of the National Employment Agency: "We pay for five members, no more. The rest is the business of the family—they have to pay directly to the Health Insurance Fund. Our expenditure is already huge—there are almost 200,000 unemployed persons in Macedonia. This year we paid 105,000,000 denars for their health insurance." Nikolina Cvetkovska, interview by author, Skopje, 24 November 1999.
263. R. S., Romani woman, interview by author, Skopje, Shuto Orizari, 14 November 1999.
264. Rahmani, interview, 1999.
265. Romani man, interview by author, Gostivar, 23 November 1999.
266. Health Insurance Law, art. 6 and 7.
267. Ibid., art. 6.
268. Health Insurance Law, art. 9, par. 1, let. a(3).
269. Law on Health Care, art. 46 par.4.
270. Ibid., art. 182, par.1, lit.3 and par.2.
271. Rahmani, interview, 1999.
272. Ibid.
273. Batinci inhabitants, interview by author, 1999.

Lack of Adequate Housing

1. Universal Declaration of Human Rights (UDHR), art. 25, par. 1.
2. International Covenant on Economic, Social and Cultural Rights (ICESCR), art. 11, par. 1.
3. International Convention on the Elimination of All Forms of Racial Discrimination (ICERD), art. 5(e)(iii).
4. Convention on the Elimination of All Forms of Discrimination Against Women (CEDAW), art. 14(2)(g) and (h) and art. 16(1)(h).
5. Convention on the Rights of the Child (CRC), art. 27(3).
6. For example, "[p]arties undertake . . . to take measures within the framework of an overall and co-ordinated approach to promote the effective access of persons who live or risk living in a situation of social exclusion or poverty, as well as their families, to, in particular, employment, housing, training, education, culture and social and medical assistance; to review these measures with a view to their adaptation if necessary." Revised European Social Charter, art. 30; "The Parties undertake to provide . . . such means as social and family benefits, fiscal arrangements, provision of family housing, benefits for the newly married and other appropriate means." Revised European Social Charter, art. 16; "The enjoyment of the rights set forth in this Charter shall be secured without discrimination on any ground such as race, color, sex, language, religion, political or other opinion, national extraction or social origin, health, association with a national minority, birth or other status." Revised European Social Charter, art. E.
7. Romanian Constitution (1991) art. 11(2); Bulgarian Constitution (1991), art. 5(4); Macedonian Constitution (1992) art. 118.
8. See Legal Standards section.
9. For an overview of antidiscrimination legislation, see European Commission Against Racism and Intolerance (ECRI), *Legal Measures to Combat Racism and Intolerance in the Member States of the Council of Europe* (Laussane, Strasbourg: Swiss Institute of Comparative Law 1996).
10. International Covenant on Civil and Political Rights (ICCPR), ratified by Romania on 9 December 1974.
11. ICESCR, ratified by Romania on 9 December 1974.
12. CRC, ratified by Romania on 28 September 1990.
13. CEDAW, ratified by Romania on 7 January 1982.
14. CERD, ratified by Romania on 15 September 1970. However, Romanian citizens cannot address complaints to the Committee on the Elimination of Racial Discrimination because Romania did not recognize the competence of the relevant Committee to receive individual or group complaints related to racial discrimination under art. 14 of the Convention.
15. European Convention for the Protection of Human Rights and Fundamental Freedoms (ECHR), ratified by Romania, 20 June 1994.
16. Romania ratified the Revised European Social Charter on 7 May 1999. Romania affirmatively bound itself to art. 1, 2 (1–2, 4–7), 3 (1–3), 4–9, 11, 12, 13 (1–3), 15 (1–2), 16, 17, 18 (3–4), 19 (7–8), 20, 21, 24, 26, 28, 27(2) and 29.
17. The Framework Convention for the Protection of National Minorities, which entered into force on 1 February 1998, was ratified by Romania on 11 May 1995.
18. Romanian Constitution (1991), art. 11, par. 1.
19. Ibid., art. 11, par. 2.
20. Ibid., art. 20, par. 1.
21. Ibid., art. 20, par. 2.
22. Ibid., art. 43, par. 1.
23. Constantinescu M., Deleanu I., Iorgovan A., Muraru I, Vasilescu F., Vida I., "Constitution of Romania–Commented and Annotated," *Official Monitor* (Bucharest 1992): 107.
24. *Housing Law,* Law 114/1996, adopted 11 October 1996, *Official Monitor* no. 254 (21 October 1996). (henceforth: Law 114/1996).
25. Law 114/1996, art. 21-33
26. Ibid., art. 38-50.
27. Ibid., art. 55 and 56.
28. Emergency Ordinance no. 40, 10 July 1997, modification and completion of Law 114/1996.
29. *Ordinance on Preventing and Punishing All Forms of Discrimination,* no. 137/2000, adopted by the Romanian Government 31 August 2000, *Official Monitor* 431, 2 September 2000. (henceforth: Antidiscrimination Ordinance).
30. The ordinanace entered into force in November 2000.
31. Antidiscrimination Ordinance, art. 2, par. 1, 2 and 3.
32. Discrimination on the grounds of nationality, religious beliefs, sex or sexual orientation also constitutes an offense. Antidiscrimination Ordinance, art. 12

33. See: PHARE, *Project for the Improvement of the Situation of Roma in Romania RO98.03.01.01. Elaboration of Government Strategy* (PHARE 1998).
34. Wassdas Foundation, "Memorandum of Roma from Romania–The Contribution of Wassdas Foundation to the Elaboration of the Strategy for the Protection of the Roma Minority," (1999, unpublished).
35. Romani Working Group (GLAR), " Memorandum–General Policy Recommendation Concerning the Implementation of the Governmental Programme: Improvement of the Situation of Roma," submitted to the Inter-Ministerial Subcommission for Roma, 23–24 September 2000 (unpublished).
36. Committee on the Elimination of Racial Discrimination (CERD), *Romania: Fifteenth Periodic Reports of States Parties due in 1999,* CERD/C/363/Add.1 (17 May 1999): par. 137.
37. For more on mahalas, see Vladimir Macura, *Housing, Urban Planning and Poverty: Problems Faced by Roma (Gypsy) Communities with Particular Reference to Central and Eastern Europe* CoE MG-S-ROM (99)1 (Beograd: Council of Europe, January 1999): 12.
38. Romani residents, interviews by author, Valea Rece (Targu Mures), 16 October 1999, Lumea-Noua/Zona Industriala (Alba Iulia), 10 October 1999, and Strada Coastei (Cluj), 13 October 1999.
39. Maria Ionescu, GLAR expert, Together Agency, interview by author, 13 September 1999. Ionescu notes, however, that there are also cases of mayors who applied for funding with international agencies and installed electricity and water (e.g. the village of Cerat in Salaj) or water and gas (e.g. Sacalaseni in Baia Mare) in Romani settlements.
40. Elena Zamfir and Catalin Zamfir, *Gypsies: Between Ignoring Them and Worrying about Them* (Editura Alternative 1993): 139.
41. Ibid.
42. Ibid.
43. Author visit, NATO building, Buhusi, on 16 October 1999.
44. Dena Ringold, *Roma and the Transition in Central and Eastern Europe: Trends and Challenges* (Washington, D.C.: The World Bank, 2000): 13.
45. Zamfir and Zamfir, *Gypsies: Between Ignoring Them and Worrying about Them,* 41.
46. Ioana Gligor, "Roma from Cluj Are Not Satisfied with the Attitude of Gheorghe Funar," *Adevarul de Cluj,* 30 November 1996.
47. Lia Valendorfer, "140 Apartments Abusively Occupied," *Romania Libera,* 15 June 1999, 10.
48. Romani men living in building 7, interviews by author, Orastie, 11 October 1999.
49. B. N., Romani woman, interview by author, Rovinari, Targu Mures, 16 October 1999.
50. World Bank and the National Commission for Statistics, *From Poverty to Rural Development* (1998): 1.
51. Ibid., 23.
52. Ibid., 25.
53. Ibid., 27.
54. Ibid., 27.
55. CERD, *Romania: Fifteenth Periodic Reports of States Parties due in 1999,* par. 59.
56. Antidiscrimination Ordinance art. 2: "(4) Measures taken by public authorities or by legal entities under private law in favor of a person, a group of persons or a community, aiming to ensure their natural development and the effective achievement of their right to equal opportunities as opposed to other persons, groups of persons or communities, as well as positive measures aiming to protect disfavored groups, shall not be regarded as discrimination under the ordinance herein. (5) In accordance with the ordinance herein, the elimination of all forms of discrimination shall be achieved by means of affirmative action in favor of persons and groups of persons belonging to national minorities, of the communities of national minorities, when they do not enjoy equal opportunities."
57. Valendorfer, "140 Apartments Abusively Occupied."
58. B. N., interview, 1999.
59. Nicolae Ficuta, Roma Party, Buhusi branch, interview by author, 18 October 1999.
60. Romani men, interview by author, Buhusi, NATO building, 18 October 1999.
61. Ficuta, interview, 1999.
62. M. C., Romani woman, resident of NATO building, interview by author, Buhusi, 18 October 1999.
63. Ficuta, interview, 1999.
64. Maria Ionescu, GLAR expert, Together Agency, interview by author, 13 September 1999.
65. *Land Law,* Law 18/1991, 19 February 1999, *Official Monitor* 37 (20 February 1991 as amended). (henceforth Law 18/1991).
66. Council of Europe–Rapporteur: Mr. Gunnar Jansson, Finland, *Honoring of Obligations and Commitments by Romania–Report* (1), doc. 7795, (11 April 1997).
67. European Union–Committee on Foreign Affairs, Human Rights, Common Security and Defense Policy, Rapporteur: Baroness Nicholson of Winterbourne, *Report on Romania's Application for Membership to the European Union and the State of the Negotiations* A5-0247/2000 (21 September 2000): 10.
68. Law 18/1991, art. 18.

69. Gabriel Troc, *Rural Roma Communities: Brazilia and Boghis (Transylvania)* (Cluj, Romania: Babes-Bolyai University, 26 July 2000, forthcoming).

70. Ringold, *Roma and the Transition in Central and Eastern Europe: Trends and Challenges,* 13.

71. GLAR, " Memorandum - General Policy Recommendation Concerning the Implementation of the Governmental Programme: Improvement of the Situation of Roma."

72. Vasile Burtea, *The Process of Marginalization of the Roma Population* (Bucharest University, 1998): 114.

73. CERD, *Romania: Fifteenth Periodic Reports of States Parties Due in 1999,* par. 65.

74. CERD, *Concluding Observations of the Committee on the Elimination of Racial Discrimination: Romania* A/54/18 (19 August 1999): par. 272-290.

75. CERD, "Racial Segregation and Apartheid (Article 3)," *General Recommendation XIX* (18 August 1995): par. 1.

76. Ibid., par. 3.

77. Gruia Bumbu, program manager, Romani CRISS, Alba Iulia, 10 October 1999.

78. Nicolae Bologa, Romani expert, OSF Roma Board, Employment and Vocational Training Agency, interview by author, Deva, October 10, 1999.

79. "Gypsies in Deva Sleep in Vaults in the Graveyard," *Evenimentul Zilei,* 29 May 1998, 13.

80. Residents A.R and F.T, interview and visit by author, 10 October 1999.

81. Bologa, interview 1999.

82. Paustin Balan, Association Rom-Star Bacau, interview by author, 18 October 1999.

83. Gheorghe Andronic, city hall secretary, interview by author, Geoagiu, 11 October 1999.

84. The non-Romani owner of the neighboring land recently built another wall, to protect his property. Visit by author, Geoagiu, 11 October 1999.

85. M.G., Romani man, interview by author, Lumea Noua/Zona Industriala, 10 October 1999.

86. Stealing electricity is a criminal offense under the Romanian Penal Code, art. 208.

87. Romani inhabitants, interview by author, Cluj, NATO Block, 13 October 1999.

88. Istvan Haller, program officer for Human Rights, PRO EUROPE League, interview by author, Targu Mures, 16 October 1999.

89. World Bank and the National Commission for Statistics, *From Poverty to Rural Development,* 26.

90. Zamfir and Zamfir, *Gypsies: Between Ignoring Them and Worrying about Them,* 141.

91. Valea Rece, Targu Mures, visit by author, 16 October 1999.

92. Romani residents of Lumea Noua/Zona Industriala, interviews by author Alba Iulia, 10 October 1999.

93. United Nations Development Program (UNDP), *Romanian Human Development Report 1996,* available at: www.undp.org/rbec/nhdr/1996/romania/.

94. Zamfir and Zamfir, *Gypsies: Between Ignoring Them and Worrying about Them,* 141.

95. Glina is a village near Bucharest, situated in close proximity to a huge garbage dump.

96. Save the Children, *Roma Children in Romania* (Bucharest 1998): 43.

97. Florin Cioaba, Romani leader, member of Sibiu local council, interview by author, 9 October 1999, Sibiu.

98. Doctors Without Borders, *Assistance for the Most Disadvantaged Roma Communities in Transylvania, Romania—Final Report 1991–1997,* 47.

99. Save the Children, *Roma Children in Romania,* 44.

100. Pata Rat, Cluj, visit by author, 13 October 1999.

101. Cioaba, interview, 1999.

102. Joyce Schoon, *Improving Primary Health Care: Public Health and Social-Cultural Research with Roma Communities in Romania—Description and Evaluation of the Local Primary Health Care Projects of Romani CRISS* (May 1998): 14.

103. Save the Children, *Roma Children in Romania,* 43.

104. Valea Rece, Targu Mures, visit by author, 16 October 1999.

105. Romani woman living in building 8, interview by author, Orastie, 11 October 1999.

106. Visit by author, 10 October 1999.

107. Visit by author, 16 October 1999.

108. Visit by author, Cluj, NATO block, 13 October 1999.

109. Visit by author, Orastie, 11 October 1999.

110. Visit by author, Buhusi, NATO building, October 1999.

111. Romania ratified ECHR on 20 June 1994.

112. Romanian Constitution (1991), art. 11, par. 1.

113. Romania ratified the First Protocol to ECHR on 20 June 1994.

114. Article 27 of the Romanian Constitution (1991) reads: "Inviolability of domicile.

(1) The domicile and the residence are inviolable. No one may enter or remain in the domicile or residence of a person without consent.

(2) Derogation from provisions under paragraph (1) is permissible by law, in the following circumstances:

a) for carrying into execution a warrant for arrest or a court sentence;

b) to remove any danger against the life, physical integrity or assets of a person;

c) to defend national security or public order;

d) to prevent the spread of an epidemic.

(3) Searches may be ordered only by a magistrate and carried out exclusively under observance of the legal procedure.

(4) Searches at night time shall be prohibited, except in cases of flagrante delicto."

115. Romanian Constitution (1991), art. 41: "Protection of private property.

(1) The right of property, as well as the debts incurring on the State are guaranteed. The content and limitations of these rights shall be established by law.

(2) Private property shall be equally protected by law, irrespective of its owner. Aliens and stateless persons may not acquire the right of property on land . . ."

116. European Roma Roma Rights Center (ERRC), "Fact Sheet: Roma in Romania," available at: http://errc.org/publications/factsheets/romania.shtml.

117. Amnesty International, "Romania: Publication of a New Summary of Human Rights Concerns," News Release, EUR 39/12/98, 21 April, 1998.

118. ERRC, "Fact sheet: Roma in Romania."

119. Istvan Haller, "Lynching is Not a Crime: Mob Violence Against Roma in Post-Ceaucescu Romania," *Roma Rights–Newsletter of the European Roma Rights Center* (Spring 1998).

120. Franz Remmel, *The Roma of Romania: People Without a Country* (Vienna: Picus Verlag, 1993): 103.

121. Haller, "Lynching is Not a Crime: Mob Violence Against Roma in Post-Ceaucescu Romania."

122. Ibid.

123. Branimir Plese, "ERRC Files Against Romania," *Roma Rights–Newsletter of the European Roma Rights Center* no. 1 (2000).

124. Ibid.

125. ECHR, art. 8.

126. Ibid., art.1 of Protocol 1.

127. Ibid., art.13.

128. Ibid., art. 14. See also, Plese , "ERRC Files Against Romania."

129. Indictment, case no. 1/P/1993, 12 August 1997, Prosecutor's Office, Court of Appeal–Targu Mures, Romania.

130. For more on Hadareni incident see, inter alia, The Romanian Helsinki Committee, *Report on the APADOR-CH Fact-Finding Mission to Hadareni and Targu-Mures* (5–7 October 1993); Amnesty International, *Romania: Broken Commitments to Human Rights* (May 1995): 28–33; Human Rights Watch/Helsinki, *Lynch Law: Violence Against Roma in Romania* vol. 6, no. 17 (November 1994): 22–8.

131. ERRC, *Cases of Relevance to the International Convention on the Elimination of All Forms of Racial Discrimination in Romania,* submitted by the ERRC for consideration by the United Nations Committee on the Elimination of Racial Discrimination at its 55th Session, 2–27 August, 1999.

132. In a similar vein, research conducted by the International Federation of Human Rights Leagues (FIDH) in 1994 concluded that although the chief prosecutor had identified the killers of the three Roma, he refrained from arresting them due to the high risk of agitation or retaliation from the Romanian/Hungarian side. FIDH, *Mission d'Enquête sur les Suites Judiciaires Données aux Meurtres, Incendies et Destructions de Maisons Appartenant à des Roms (Tziganes), 28 février–5 mars 1994* (1994).

133. Indictment no. 1/P/1993, issued by Prosecutor Liviu Moica of the Targu Mures Court of Appeal, 12 August 1997.

134. While the first verdict (also criticized for not being commensurate with the crimes committed) sentenced all eleven defendants to prison sentences ranging from one-and-a-half to seven years, the second accorded clemency to six of them who did not need to serve prison time. See ERRC, "Appeals Court Hands Down Verdict in Hadareni Case, Romania," *Roma Rights–Newsletter of the European Roma Rights Center* no. 1 (1999). The case is currently pending in the Supreme Court.

135. Manuela Stefanescu, Romanian Helsinki Committee (APADOR-CH), cited in "Sudden Rage at Dawn, Violence Against Roma in Romania," *European Roma Rights Center–Country Reports Series* no. 2 (September 1996).

136. ERRC, letter to the OSCE High Commissioner for National Minorities, Max van der Stoel, 15 April 1997.

137. ERRC, "Sudden Rage at Dawn, Violence Against Roma in Romania," 17.

138. Ibid., 18.

139. Haller, "Lynching is Not a Crime: Mob Violence Against Roma in Post-Ceaucescu Romania."

140. ERRC, "Police Raid in Sarulesti, Romania," *Roma Rights–Newsletter of the European Roma Rights Center* (Summer 1998).

141. ERRC, "Police Abuse of Roma in Romania," *Roma Rights–Newsletter of the European Roma Rights Center* no. 2 (2000).

142. Ibid.

143. T.B., Romani woman who lives in Cluj, NATO block, interview by author, 13 October 1999.

144. Romani inhabitants, interview by author, 13 October 1999.

145. Romani men living in building 7, interview by author, October, 1999.

146. Romani men living in Lumea Noua- Zona Industriala, interview by author, Alba Iulia, 10 October, 1999.

147. Bulgaria ratified ICESCR on 21 September 1970.

148. Bulgaria ratified ICERD on 8 August 1966.

149. ICERD, art. 5 (e)(iii).

150. Bulgaria ratified the Revised European Social Charter on 29 March 2000.

151. Bulgarian Constitution (1991), art. 5, par. 4.

152. Committee on Economic, Social and Cultural Rights (CESCR), *Third Periodic Report: Bulgaria* E/1994/104/Add.16 (18 October 1996): par. 197.

153. Ibid., par. 197 and 200–2.

154. European Commission Against Racism and Intolerance, *Second Report on Bulgaria, Adopted on June 1999* CRI (2000) 3 (Strasbourg: 21 March 2000): par. 15.

155. Ibid., par. 29.

156. For more on the Framework Program for Equal Integration of Roma in Bulgarian Society, see Barriers to Social Protection, Bulgaria.

157. Framework Program for Equal Integration of Roma in Bulgarian Society, adopted by the Bulgarian Council of Ministers on 22 April 1999, Part I/(1): Legislation changes for the protection from discrimination.

158. Framework Program for Equal Integration of Roma in Bulgarian Society, adopted by the Bulgarian Council of Ministers on 22 April 1999, Part II/(3): Land distribution.

159. Framework Program for Equal Integration of Roma in Bulgarian Society, adopted by the Bulgarian Council of Ministers on 22 April 1999, Part IV: Territorial Structure of the Roma neighborhoods.

160. European Commission, *1999 – Regular Report from the Commission on Bulgaria's Progress Towards Accession* (21 October 1999).

161. Specialist Group on Roma/Gypsies, Eighth meeting, Meeting Report MG-S-ROM (99) 11 (Sofia: 20–23 September 1999): Appendix 4–Hearing with Officials Responsible for Roma Issues and Romani Representatives and Organizations.

162. Commission on Security and Cooperation in Europe-testimony of Rumyan Russinov, "Human Rights of the Romani Minority," 8 June 2000, available at: http://www.house.gov/csce/RumyansTestimony.htm.

163. Elena Marushiakova, Veselin Popov, *The Gypsies of Bulgaria* (Lang: Frankfurter am Main 1997).

164. In new buildings, Bulgarians were reportedly put on the first three floors, and Roma on the fourth floor. See: David Olah, "Plovidv: Huts and Satellites," Roma Press Center article published in *Nepszabadsag* (Hungary), 18 August 1997, available at: http://www.romapage.c3.hu/rsk/engrs014.htm.

165. "Potential homeless" describes persons living in overcrowded conditions where there are three or more persons in a room, in primitive housing units or in condemned buildings. The number of individuals characterized as potentially homeless in Bulgaria in 1994 was approximately 300,000. At that time, the

government claimed that the country did not have "homeless" persons, in the sense of persons without accommodation or shelter. CESCR, *Third Periodic Report: Bulgaria,* par. 188.

166. The highly urbanized character of the inhabitants of the large Romani mahalas applies not only to Bulgaria, but is a common feature of mahalas in the Balkans. See Macura, *Housing, Urban Planning and Poverty: Problems Faced by Roma (Gypsy) Communities with Particular Reference to Central and Eastern Europe,* 1.

167. In rural areas, Christian Bulgarian Roma and Muslim Turkish Roma live on the outskirts of villages.

168. CESCR, *Replies by the Government of Bulgaria to the List of Issues: Bulgaria* 09/07/99, 21st session (Geneva: 15 November–1 December 1999): par. 4.1.

169. Ibid.

170. UNDP, *Bulgaria: Human Development Report 1996,* available at: http://www.undp.org/rbec/nhdr/1996/bulgaria/contents.htm.

171. "The Jungle" is the name of the poorest part of Nikola Kochev neighborhood, also inhabited by Roma.

172. Irina Vandova and Varban Tomov, *Case Study of Bulgaria–Nikola Kochev District and Nadezhda Ghetto in the Town of Sliven, Villages of Sotirya, Topolchane and Gorno Alexandrovo* (forthcoming), available at: http://www.yale.edu/socdept/reports/vandova.html.

173. Ibid.

174. Varban Tomov, *Roma from the Village of Topolchane* (forthcoming), available at: http://www.yale.edu/socdept/reports/tomov.html.

175. Ilona Tomova, *The Gypsies in the Transition Period* (Sofia: International Center for Minority Studies and Intercultural Relations, 1995): 68.

176. Ibid.

177. Mihail Gheorgiev, "Fighting for Fakulteta: Advocating for Roma Housing Rights in Bulgaria," *Roma Rights–Newsletter of the European Roma Rights Center* no. 2 (2000): 50.

178. Open Society Foundation–Sofia, *Habitat for Everyone – Urban Building for Citizens in Need in Fakulteta–Sofia and Istok-Pazardzhik* (1999): 73.

179. According to art. 173, par. 3 of the Law on Territorial and Urban Development, illegal structures may be demolished on the initiative of the Directorate of National Building Control or the municipality: "In cases of illegal construction on a plot, where construction is not allowed by a person who is not permitted to build, if such buildings are not in conflict with the regulation plans and current laws and could be used, they are to be confiscated by the state or the municipality by penal act of the mayor or on the initiative of the Directorate of National Building Control." Gheorgiev, "Fighting for Fakulteta: Advocating for Roma Housing Rights in Bulgaria," 50.

180. Gheorgiev, "Fighting for Fakulteta: Advocating for Roma Housing Rights in Bulgaria," 50.

181. Michal Shafir, "Radical Politics in East-Central Europe–Part VII: Bulgaria's Radical Transfigurations," *Radio Free Europe/Radio Liberty (RFE/RL),* vol. 2, no. 15 (2 August 2000), available at: http://www.rferl.org/eepreport/2000/08/15-020800.html.

182. Moreover, legalization efforts must be based on the principal of minimum interference with the existing situation. Framework Program for Equal Integration of Roma in Bulgarian Society, Part IV: Territorial Structure of the Roma neighborhoods.

183. In these neighborhoods, the density of buildings is high, the streets are narrow and the distances between houses are small. Open Society Foundation–Sofia, *Habitat for Everyone–Urban Building for Citizens in Need in Fakulteta–Sofia and Istok–Pazardzhik,* 74.

184. Gheorgiev, "Fighting for Fakulteta: Advocating for Roma Housing Rights in Bulgaria," 50.

185. Romani Baht, a Fakulteta based organization, which initially engaged in litigation on behalf of Romani clients, abandoned this option in favor of lobbying activities. Gheorgiev, "Fighting for Fakulteta: Advocating for Roma Housing Rights in Bulgaria," 50. However, litigation was more than needed at the beginning of the process, in order to identify the legal, procedural and financial barriers. Mihail Gheorghiev, interview by author, Sofia, 3 December 1999.

186. According to the 1992 census, private persons owned 98.7 percent of houses in villages. UNDP, "Settlement Network, Settlements and Housing Policy," Chapter 5, *Bulgaria: Human Development Report 1996.*

187. CERD, *Fourteenth Periodic Report of States Parties due in 1996: Bulgaria* CERD/C/299/Add.7 (8 May 1996): par. 104.

188. "List of issues: Bulgaria," E/C. 12/Q/BUL/1 (19 June 1998): par. 4.

189. CESCR, *Replies by the Government of Bulgaria to the List of Issues: Bulgaria* 09/07/99, par. 4.1 final.

190. Stefan Stefanov, executive director, Roma Bureau, interview by author, Sofia, 6 December 1999.

191. Ibid.

192. Ibid.

193. CERD, *Concluding Observations of the Committee on the Elimination of Racial Discrimination: Bulgaria,* par. 8

194. As of the end of 1999. See, for example, *The Main Guidelines of the Bulgarian Government Policy Concerning Minority Groups,* a document in which the Bulgarian Government describes the agreements signed with various ministries during 1999 for the implementation of the Framework Program. No land distribution activity is mentioned. Council of Europe, *Honoring of Obligations and Commitments by Bulgaria,* Parliamentary Assembly, doc. 8616, Addendum II (17 January 2000): 48-51.

195. Tomova, *The Gypsies in the Transition Period,* 65.

196. Olah, "Plovdiv: Huts and Satellites."

197. Gheorgiev, "Fighting for Fakulteta: Advocating for Roma Housing Rights in Bulgaria," 50.

198. World Bank, *Consultations with the Poor, National Synthesis Report Bulgaria* (25 May 1999): 37.

199. "Is There Racism in Bulgaria? – 72% of Nation Want Segregation and Gypsy Ghettoes," *24 Chassa,* 26 May 1998.

200. CERD, *Fourteenth Periodic Report of States Parties Due in 1996: Bulgaria,* par. 106.

201. Olah, "Plovdiv: Huts and Satellites."

202. World Bank, *Consultations with the Poor, National Synthesis Report Bulgaria,* 53.

203. According to a Romani Foundation for Regional Development a Plovdiv representative was quoted by the Project on Ethnic Relations as saying: "For six months now, there has been no water and electricity in the eight-story tenement buildings. The same problems exist in the Nadezhda neighborhood in Sliven and in hundreds of other towns and villages in Bulgaria." Project on Ethnic Relations, *The Roma in Bulgaria; Collaborative Efforts Between Local Authorities and Nongovernmental Organizations, Lom, Bulgaria* (24–25 April 1998).

204. B. N., Romani inhabitant of Nicola Kochev neighborhood, interview by author, Sliven, December 1999.

205. Vesselin Lakov, project coordinator of the Human Rights Project in Montana, interview by author, 10 December 1999.

206. Although the mayor of Lom reportedly opposed the installation of electrometers, the electricity companies installed them. Nikolay Kirilov, chairman, Roma-Lom Foundation, interview by author, 12 December 1999.

207. Lakov, interview, 1999.

208. Iztocen is a part of Plovdiv that includes Stolipinovo, one of the largest Romani neighborhoods in the country.

209. Liubomir Domakinov, city hall secretary, Iztocen, Plovdiv, interview by author, 10 December 1999.

210. Fakulteta, Sofia, visit by author, 3 December 1999.

211. World Bank, *Consultations with the Poor, National Synthesis Report Bulgaria,* 38.

212. Lakov, interview, 1999.

213. Tomova, *The Gypsies in the Transition Period,* 66.

214. World Bank, *What the Poor Say: Trends and Traps,* available at: http://www.worldbank.org/poverty/data/trends/traps.htm.

215. See Barriers to Social Protection, Bulgaria.

216. Kirilov, interview, 1999.

217. Bulgaria ratified the ECHR on 7 September 1992.

218. Bulgarian Constitution (1991), art. 33.

219. Bulgaria ratified the First Protocol to ECHR on 7 September 1992.

220. Bulgarian Constitution (1991), art. 17, par. 1 and 3.

221. International Helsinki Federation for Human Rights, *Annual Report 1999: Bulgaria.*

222. U. S. Department of State–Bureau of Democracy, Human Rights, and Labor, *Bulgaria Country Report on Human Rights Practices for 1998* (26 February 1999).

223. On harassment by private groups and positive obligations of the state, see, inter alia, *Whiteside v. the UK,* no. 20357/92, 76 A DR 80 (1994).

224. International Helsinki Federation for Human Rights, *Annual Report 1999: Bulgaria.*

225. U.S. Department of State–Bureau of Democracy, Human Rights, and Labor, *Bulgaria Country Report on Human Rights Practices for 1998*.

226. The attack took place on 25 February 1994. Amnesty International, *Bulgaria: Turning a Blind Eye to Racism* (15 April 1994) available at: http://www.amnesty.org/ailib/aipub/1994/EUR/150494.EUR.txt.

227. Michal Shafir,"Radical Politics in East-Central Europe - Part VII: Bulgaria's Radical Transfigurations."

228. Macedonia succeeded to ICCPR on 18 January 1994.

229. Macedonia succeeded to ICESCR on 18 January 1994.

230. Macedonia succeeded to ICERD on 18 January 1994. The Republic of Macedonia made the declaration under art. 14 of the Convention, recognizing the competence of the Committee on Elimination of Racial Discrimination to consider individual and group complaints, on 22 December 1999.

231. Macedonia succeeded to CEDAW on 18 January 1994.

232. Macedonia succeeded to CRC on 2 December 1993.

233. As of 17 October 2000. The European Social Charter was signed on 5 May 1998.

234. Macedonian Constitution (1991), art. 118: "The international agreements ratified in accordance with the Constitution are part of the internal legal order and cannot be changed by law." Macedonian courts rule on the basis of the Constitution and laws and international agreements ratified in accordance with the Constitution (art. 98).

235. Macedonian Constitution (1991), art. 9: "Citizens of the Republic of Macedonia are equal in their freedoms and rights, regardless of sex, race, color of skin, national and social origin, political and religious beliefs, property and social status."

236. Resolution 1424 (97) of the Administrative Council defines the fields of action for which the Fund can grant loans. Priority fields of action are aid to refugees and migrants and aid to regions affected by natural or ecological disasters. Other fields of action: small and medium-sized enterprises; social housing; health; education, vocational training; protection of the environment; rural modernization; improvement in the quality of life in disadvantaged urban areas; and protection and rehabilitation of the historic heritage.

237. However, the Macedonian government maintains that no racial segregation or discriminatory policies or practices exist in Macedonia and that "no cases of segregation have been registered". See CERD, *Third Periodic Report Submitted to the UN Committee on the Elimination of Racial Discrimination* CERD/C/270/Add.2 (13 March 1997): par. 23 and 76.

238. *Statistical Yearbook of the Republic of Macedonia for 1997 and 1998*, as cited by the Helsinki Committee for Human Rights in the Republic of Macedonia's *Report on Minority Rights in the Republic of Macedonia* (September 1999).

239. World Bank, *Former Yugoslav Republic of Macedonia—Focusing on the Poor*, vol. 1, Main Report (Report no. 19411-MK, 11 June 1999): 14, box 1.4: Gypsies.

240. Shuto Orizari was created in 1996, together with another approximately 85 new municipalities. However, the ability of these municipalities to solve the problems of local communities was undermined by the absence of support measures. See Council of Europe–Rapporteur: Jean-Claude Frecon, France, *Situation of Local Democracy in the Former Yugoslav Republic of Macedonia* CPL (7) 8 (Strasbourg: 23–25 May 2000) available at: http://www.coe.fr/cplre/session7/reports/cpl(7)8e.htm.

241. Georgi Hadzi Vaskov, counselor, Ministry for Urban Affairs, interview by author, Skopje, 16 November 1999.

242. Project of the Government of the Former Yugoslav Republic of Macedonia and UNDP, "Communal Water, Infrastructure Improvement Vizbegovo – Shuto Orizari," Section B.3. Available at: http://www.undp.org.mk/nivogore/mcd99006.htm.

243. "Volunteers for Social Reconstruction in Balkans – Macedonia: Shutka," (2 April 2000) available at: http://www.ddh.nl/org/balkansunflower/00/projects4.htm.

244. A community theater was recently organized by a nongovernmental organization. See "Volunteers for Social Reconstruction in Balkans – Macedonia: Shutka."

245. Shuto Orizari, Skopje, visit by author 10 November 1999.

246. Nezdet Mustafa, mayor, Shuto Orizari, interview by author, 16 November 1999.

247. "Communal Water, Infrastructure Improvement Vizbegovo - Shuto Orizari," Annex III.

248. "The first readmission agreement signed between a western and an eastern administration in response to problems emerging in connection with post-1989 migrations specifically targeted a group of Romani refugees: The repatriation agreement for Roma negotiated in December 1990 between the province (land) of North Rhine Westphalia and 'the Former Yugoslav Republic of Macedonia.'" Although the

agreement does not mention Roma explicitly, but merely refers to "unsuccessful asylum applicants," it was introduced under the heading "New Refugee Policy" as an alternative to an earlier policy represented by a decree issued by the Minister of the Interior in February 1990. The decree allowed "de facto stateless Roma" to apply for a residence permit, even if their applications for political asylum had already been rejected. The target group included in the readmission agreement was based on the subsequent applications of 1,500 Roma, most of whom had originated from the then Yugoslav Republic of Macedonia. These persons were sent letters during 1991 informing them that it is intended to reject the application filed in accordance with the Roma-decree of 01.02.1990, and offering them instead voluntary participation in a reintegration program in Shuto Orizari, a district near Skopje with a large Romani population. The government of North Rhine Westphalia offered to pay for the costs of travel and removal of the returnees, and to guarantee them a basic allowance during the first six months after their return. It also financed prefabricated housing and, in cooperation with the Catholic welfare organization Caritas, it provided for social and vocational consultation. According to the government of North Rhine Westphalia, altogether 602 persons agreed to participate in the program and were returned to the "Former Yugoslav Republic of Macedonia" between 1991 and November 1993. See Yaron Matras' report to the European Committee on Migration, *Problems Arising in Connection with the International Mobility of the Roma in Europe* CDMG (98) 14 (University of Manchester, 1998): par. 41.

249. According to the 1994 census, Gostivar has only 40,012 inhabitants. See " Geographical Location: Europe, the Balkans, Macedonia" available at: http://www.unet.com.mk/mian/geograph.htm.

250. For example, a dozen families live in Baraki, a Romani street in the city center, twenty families in Pitarnika, and between 100 and 120 families in Bajnica-Grudajci. Fifteen families reside in Fazanerija the poorest of all the settlements, where none of the sixty children go to school. Maleardi is a mixed neighborhood where between seventy and eighty families live along two or three streets. Another small group resides in Ciflik, in the center near the river; 120 families stay in Makedonski Malo, also in the center; and ninety families have shelter in Balindoska. Memedali Rahmani, president, Mesecina, interview by author, Gostivar, 23 November 1999.

251. Balindoska is the chic Roma neighborhood. Some of the houses were built twenty years ago when Roma still had good jobs. Some of them belong to people who returned from Germany. In Balindovka there are even several shops run by Roma.

252. Rahmani, interview, 1999.

253. ERRC, *A Pleasant Fiction—The Human Rights Situation of Roma in Macedonia–Country Reports Series 7* (July 1998): 77.

254. Vaskov, interview, 1999.

255. Ibid.

256. The practice appears to result from a legal rule according to which if the local authorities do not have money, the claimant may "offer" to pay the related costs. Vaskov, interview, 1999.

257. Administratively Batinci belongs to the Kisela Voda municipality.

258. F.T., Romani woman from Batinci, interview by author, 14 November 1999.

259. Batinci, visit by author, 14 November 1999.

260. N.M., and F.T., Romani women from Batinci, interview by author 14 November 1999.

261. Azbija Memedova, president, Roma Center, interview by author, 13 November 1999.

262. The author assisted in such an operation during a visit to Batinci, 14 November 1999.

263. Inhabitants of Batinci, interview by author, 14 November 1999.

264. Kvantasi, visit by author, 14 November 1999.

265. Ibid.

266. Since November of 1999 the Roma Center has been working to install three water pumps for the settlement. Memedova, interview 1999.

267. World Bank, *Former Yugoslav Republic of Macedonia – Focusing on the Poor,* vol. 1, Main Report, 13, box 1.3: Living Conditions of the Poor.

268. Case described in the World Bank report: *Former Yugoslav Republic of Macedonia – Focusing on the Poor,* vol. 1, Main Report 14, Box 1.4: Gypsies.

269. Bavce, Kumanovo, visit by author, 20 November 1999.

270. ERRC, *A Pleasant Fiction—The Human Rights Situation of Roma in Macedonia – Country Reports Series* 7, 76.

271. The local NGO told the author that the electricity company would not install the power line close to Romani houses in order to prevent them from stealing electricity and would not connect them to the electrical system because the Romani shacks are illegally built and because they were afraid that Roma would not pay the bills.

272. ERRC, *A Pleasant Fiction—The Human Rights Situation of Roma in Macedonia —Country Reports Series* 7, 80.

273. The government developed a solid waste management strategy with the financial support of PHARE Co-operation Program, which is still to be implemented. See Ministry of Urban Planning, Construction and Environment, *State of the Environment in Republic of Macedonia* (25 May 1998) available at: http://www.soer.moe.gov.mk/otpad_a.htm.

274. Illegal landfills emerge in the settlements not covered by organized communal waste gathering. *State of Environment in Republic of Macedonia.* Ministry of Urban Planning, Construction, and Environment, available at: http://www.soekmoe.govmk/otpad_a.htm.

275. Valerie J. Brown, "Wrought by War," *Conservation Matters 2000* (Boston: Conservation Law Foundation) available at: http://www.clf.org/pubs/cmnow.htm.

276. Mustafa, interview, 1999.

277. Ibid.

278. Muharem Jasarovski, president, Nevo Suno, interview by author, Prilep, 21 November 1999.

279. Dabnicky Zavoj, Prilep, visit by author, 21 November 1999.

280. M.S., Romani inhabitant of Dabnicki Zavoj, interview by author, 21 November 1999.

281. Jasarovski, interview, 1999.

282. M.S., interview, 1999.

283. Matthew Gatrell, water- sanitation coordinator, International Rescue Committee, interview by author, Skopje, 17 November 1999.

284. ERRC, *A Pleasant Fiction—The Human Rights Situation of Roma in Macedonia – Country Reports Series* 7, 81.

285. Dilbera Kamberovska, president, Daja Kumanovo, interview by author, 12 November 1999.

286. Ministry of Urban Planning, Construction and Environment, *State of the Environment in Republic of Macedonia.*

287. Asmet Elezovski, president, Drom–Kumanovo, interview by author, 20 November 1999.

288. Jivkova Karpa-Bavce, Kumanovo, visit by author, 20 November 1999.

289. Rahmani, interview, 1999.

290. Baraki, Gostivar, visit by author, 23 November 1999.

291. A.M., Romani woman from Baraki, Gostivar, interview by author, 23 November 1999.

292. Relations between NGOs and Gostivar city hall representatives are reportedly very tense, reaching hostility: "Here NGOs are the declared enemy," says Memedali Rahmani, president of Mesecina Gostivar. Rahmani, interview, 1999.

293. Ahmet Jasarovski, vice president of Drom–Kumanovo, interview by author, 20 November 1999.

294. Elezovski, interview, 1999.

295. Kamberovska, interview,1999.

296. See International Rescue Committee, *Macedonia* available at: http://www.intrescom.org/whatwedo/balkans/macedonia.cfm.

297. "Communal Water, Infrastructure Improvement Vizbegovo – Shuto Orizari."

298. Gatrell, interview, 1999.

299. UNICEF, *Situation Analysis of Roma Women and Children* (Republic of Macedonia, 1999): 23.

Supplement: Housing in the Czech Republic

1. International Covenant on Civil and Political Rights (ICCPR), succeeded to by the Czech Republic on 22 February 1993.

2. International Covenant on Economic, Social and Cultural Rights (ICESCR), succeeded to by the Czech Republic on 1 January 1993.

3. Convention on the Rights of the Child (CRC), succeeded to by the Czech Republic on 28 September 1990.

4. Convention on the Rights of the Child (CEDAW), succeeded to by the Czech Republic on 22 February 1993.

5. International Convention on the Elimination of All Forms of Racial Discrimination (ICERD), succeeded to by the Czech Republic on 22 February 1993.

6. European Convention for the Protection of Human Rights and Fundamental Freedoms (ECHR), ratified by the Czech Republic, 18 March 1992.

7. The Czech Republic ratified the European Social Charter on 3 November 1999. The Czech Republic affirmatively bound itself to art. 1 (1–3), 2, 3, 4 (2–5), 5–8, 11–14, 15 (2), 16, 17, 18 (4), and 19 (9). It is worth noting that art. 16, "The right of the family to social, legal and economic protection," states that "[w]ith a view to ensuring the necessary conditions for the full development of the family, which is a fundamental unit of society, the Contracting Parties undertake to promote the economic, legal and social protection of family life by such means as social and family benefits, fiscal arrangements, provision of family housing, benefits for the newly married, and other appropriate means."

8. The Framework Convention for the Protection of National Minorities, which entered into force on 1 February 1998, was ratified by the Czech Republic on 18 December 1997.

9. Czech Republic Constitution (1992), art.10.

10. See note 5.

11. The Charter of Fundamental Rights and Freedoms (1992), art. 3, par. 1.

12. The European Commission against Racism and Intolerance (ECRI), *Second Report on the Czech Republic* (Strasbourg: 21 March 2000): 5, par. 2.

13. Ibid., par. 9–10.

14. Many of the Czech lawyers whom the author spoke with noted the country's lack of comprehensive housing legislation and monitoring agencies.

15. Government of the Czech Republic, *Policy Statement of the Government of the Czech Republic* (Prague: August 1998).

16. Concept of Government Policy Towards Members of Romani Community Facilitating their Integration into Society, adopted by Government Resolution no. 279, from 7 April 1999.

17. Ministry for Regional Development of the Czech Republic, *Housing Policy Concept*, based on Government Resolution of 18 October 1999 (1999): 23.

18. Human Rights Watch, *Roma in the Czech Republic – Foreigners in Their Own Land,* vol. 8, no. 11 (D) (June 1996) available at: http://www.igc.org/hrw/reports/1996/Czech.htm#P437_60488.

19. Jirina Siklova and Marta Miklusakova, "Law as an Instrument of Discrimination – Denying Citizenship to the Czech Roma," *East European Constitutional Review,* vol. 7, no. 2. (Spring 1998).

20. Resolution of the Czechoslovak Government, no. 502/1965, 13 October 1965, on guided displacement and dispersion of Roma.

21. Government of the Czech Republic, *Report on the Situation of the Romani Community in the Czech Republic and Government Measures Assisting its Integration in Society* no.686 (Prague: 29 October 1997): 28. (henceforth: Bratinka Report),

22. According to the authorities, in the city of Kladno, with a total population of 72,325 persons, as many as 2500 cases of eviction are pending. "Another accommodation for non-payers – the only solution for 'civilized' tenants", 28 July 2000, Kladno city hall web page, available at: http://www.vismo.obce.cz/kladno/dokumenty2.

23. According to Emil Scuka, the president of the International Romani Union, the communist authorities wanted to keep control while at the same time having flexibility in allocation of flats. Knowing that Romani families were often traveling to Slovakia they did not want to complicate the process too much by signing contracts or issuing formal decisions. Emil Scuka, interview by author, Prague, 18 May 2000.

24. In case of eviction only certain tenants are protected against homelessness; those considered squatters (persons who do not have tenancy rights) are not.

25. Counseling Center for Citizenship, Civil and Human Rights, *Report on the Situation in the Complex Nove Bory–Ovcary: Legal Evaluation of the Situation* (21June 2000).

26. Letter issued by the Prefect of the Ceske Krumlov District,KP, 70/00min, 17 March, 2000.

27. Letter issued by the Department of Social Affairs, District Office of Prostejov, 15 March 2000.

28. Bratinka Report, 25.

29. Law on Acquisition and Loss of Czech Citizenship, Law No. 40/1993 Coll., 29 December 1992, entered into force on 1 January, 1993 (henceforth: Czech Citizenship Law).

30. U.S. Department of State, *Czech Republic Human Rights Practices, 1995* (March 1996).

31. Tolerance Foundation, "Part I: Judicial Expulsion," in *From Exclusion to Expulsion: the Czech Republic's New Foreigners* (Prague: November 1996).

32. Bratinka Report, 29.

33. U.S. Department of State–Bureau of Democracy, Human Rights, and Labor, *Country Reports on Human Rights Practices for 1996: Czech Republic* (30 January 1997).

34. Czech Committee for UNICEF, *Situation Analysis of Children in the Czech Republic* (1998): 73.

35. U.S. Department of State–Bureau of Democracy, Human Rights, and Labor, *Country Reports on Human Rights Practices for 1999: Czech Republic* (February 2000).

36. European Roma Rights Center (ERRC), "Snapshots from Around Europe: Czech Minister of Justice Will Not File a Complaint for 'Breach of Law' in Racially Motivated Killing; Skinheads Attack Witnesses During Trial; More Racial Discrimination and Violence Against Roma in the Czech Republic," *Roma Rights–Newsletter of the European Roma Rights Center* no. 3 (1999) available at: http://errc.org/rr_nr3_1999/snap01.shtml.

37. U.S. Department of State–Bureau of Democracy, Human Rights, and Labor, *Country Reports on Human Rights Practices for 1999: Czech Republic.*

38. Brian Hannon "British Judges Send Slovak Roma Home," *The Prague Post,* 19 July 2000, available at: http://www.praguepost.cz/news071900e.html.

39. Brian Hannon "The Problem with Prostejov," *The Prague Post,* 26 July 2000, available at: http://www.praguepost.cz/news072600c.html.

40. Minutes of telephone conversation with the deputy mayor of Prostejov, Ing. Vyslouzilova, 20 July 20 2000, provided by the Counseling Center for Citizenship, Civil and Human Rights.

41. "Anti-Roma Petition Circulated in Prostejov," Roma News of Radio Prague, June 30th, 2000, available at: http://www.romove.cz/roma/00-06.html. As of November 2000, there is no additional information in either the English or Czech language press as to the situation in Prostejov.

42. *Tucnak,* July 1997 as cited by European Roma Rights Center, *Written Comments of the European Roma Rights Center Concerning Czech Republic for Consideration by the United Nations Committee on the Elimination of Racial Discrimination at its Fifty-second Session, 6-9 March 1998* (23 February 1998).

43. *Mlada Fronta Dnes,* August 1997. See also, *Written Comments of the European Roma Rights Center Concerning Czech Republic for Consideration by the United Nations Committee on the Elimination of Racial Discrimination at its Fifty-second Session, 6-9 March 1998.*

44. Michele Legge and John Chipman, "Romanies Awaken to the Canadian Dream," *The Prague Post,* August 20, 1997, 1.

45. Ibid.

46. Bratinka Report, 28.

47. Ibid., 76, 77.

48. Ibid., "V. Recapitulation of fulfillment of the government's resolutions concerning the Romani community," 1-17.

49. See, for example, the manner in which the Government reports on the fulfillment of its obligations under art. 3 of ICERD in *Report of the Czech Republic on Performance of the Obligations Arising from the Convention on the Elimination of All Forms of Racial Discrimination—Periodic Report III and IV in a Single Volume* (4 November 1999): par. 54 and 55.

50. Committee on the Elimination of Racial Discrimination (CERD), *Additional Information Pursuant to Committee Decision: Czech Republic,* CERD/C/348, (21 January 1999): par. 1.

51. Czech Republic Constitution (1992), art. 10,

52. ECRI, *Second Report on the Czech Republic adopted on 18 June 1999,* par. 9-10.

53. The Counseling Center for Citizenship/Civil and Human Rights, *Comments to the Report of the Czech Republic on Performance of the Obligations Arising from the Convention on the Elimination of All Forms of Racial Discrimination* (Prague: July 2000).

54. ECRI, *Second Report on the Czech Republic Adopted on 18 June 1999*, 4, par. 11.

55. Czech Penal Code, art. 260 stipulates that the person who supports and promotes any movement which conclusively seeks suppression of the rights and the freedoms of citizens or who proclaims national, racial, class or religious hatred shall be punished by imprisonment for one to five years. Aggravating circumstances are: committing the act through mass media; committing it as a member of an organized group; and committing it when the country is in the state of emergency.

56. Czech Penal Code, art. 261 provides that those who publicly express sympathy to fascism or any other similar movements shall be punished by imprisonment for six months up to three years.

57. CERD, *Fourth Periodic Report of State Parties due in 2000: Czech Republic* CERD/C/372/Add.1 (14 April 2000): par. 54-55.

58. Czech Penal Code, art. 263, let. a).

59. Decision of Municipality and the City Council of District Nestemice (Usti nad Labem), from September 15, 1998.

60. See, inter alia, Paul Goble, "East/West: Analysis From Washington–New Walls in a Europe Whole and Free," 18 October 1999, *Radio Free Europe/ Radio Liberty* and Alexandra Poolos,"Czech Republic: A Wall Divides the Country," 21 October 1999, *Radio Free Europe/Radio Liberty*.

61. CERD, *Additional Information Pursuant to Committee Decision: Czech Republic*, par. 3.

62. The Counseling Center for Citizenship/Civil and Human Rights, *Comments to the Report of the Czech Republic on Performance of the Obligations Arising from the Convention on the Elimination of All Forms of Racial Discrimination.*

63. The government released 10 million CZK to help resolve the neighborhoods' problems. The local authorities used part of the money to purchase the houses inhabited by non-Roma who wanted to move out from Maticni. See: *Additional Information on Compliance with the Principles Set Forth in the Framework Convention for the Protection of National Minorities, under Article 25 of the Convention*. Available at: http://www.vlada.cz/1250/vrk/rady/rnr/dokumenty/ramcuml/dopl/eng.htm.

64. The Counseling Center for Citizenship/Civil and Human Rights, *Comments to the Report of the Czech Republic on Performance of the Obligations Arising from the Convention on the Elimination of All Forms of Racial Discrimination.*

65. Ministry for Regional Development of the Czech Republic, *Housing Policy Concept*, 4.

66. The national committees in charge with the distribution of these apartments, were also compiling special lists, for privileged state functionaries and artists. Czech Helsinki Committee, *Report on the State of Human Rights in the Czech Republic in 1997* (Prague 1998): 127.

67. Ibid.

68. Government of the Czech Republic, *Government Policy Statement of the Government of the Czech Republic.*

69. Ministry for Regional Development of the Czech Republic, *Housing Policy Concept*, 4.

70. See 5.3.1 and 5.3.2 in this section.

71. ECRI, *Second Report on the Czech Republic Adopted on 18 June 1999*, par. 40.

72. The apparently neutral eligibility requirements include a clean criminal record, permanent residence, permanent employment, morality, the city's interest to allocate the apartment to the applicant, and presumption of proper behavior of the applicants in relation to the flat and other tenants. (See 5.3.: Indirect discrimination).

73. Bratinka Report, 28.

74. Research Directorate Immigration and Refugee Board, *Roma in the Czech Republic: Selected Issues* (Ottawa, Canada: December 1997).

75. Research Directorate Immigration and Refugee Board, *Roma in the Czech Republic: Identity and Culture* (Ottawa, Canada: November 1997).

76. Research Directorate Immigration and Refugee Board, *Roma in the Czech Republic: Selected Issues.*

77. Nine Roma families in house no. 90/I in street ve Spilce, the case of family Kincovi in house no. 451/II in Soukenicka street (a family of four living in one room); case of Jana Ginova, permanent residence at Nerudovo square no. 13 (parents), temporarily at Soukenicka 451/II, request filed in 1991; case of Josef and

Eva Ginovi who lived in one room at Soukenicka 451/II; case of Jiri Mika and his family, street J. Knihy 114/I., where nine persons, out of whom two were disabled, were living in a 2+1 flat. The Counseling Center for Citizenship, Civil and Human Rights, Prague.

78. Robert Olah, interview by author, Prague, 23 May 2000.

79. The families are a single mother of two, a couple without children, another couple with four children, a couple with six children who were given two rooms only after paying a deposit of 8,000 Kc, and a divorced woman. VIZE – Foundation Dagmar and Vaclav Havel, *Final Project Report: Analysis of the Creation, Actual Situation and Possible Solutions of the Problems Faced by the Inhabitants of Maticni Street*, 97.

80. Ibid.

81. The designation of these apartments is clearly defined by the state in the *Report Submitted by the Czech Republic Pursuant to Article 25, paragraph 1 of the Framework Convention for the Protection of National Minorities* ACFC/SR (99) 6, (1 April 1999): Appendix no. IIIb.

82. "Between 1994 and 1998 these flats were provided to about 35 families, most of them Roma. Today, 30 Romani families live in the flats, about 130 persons in total, and also four non-Romani families and individuals, for example ex-convicts." See: *Additional Information on Compliance with the Principles Set Forth in the Framework Convention for the Protection of National Minorities, under Article 25 of the Convention.*

83. The zone was unsafe because flooding had destroyed the basements and the water and gas systems.

84. Romani families in Hrusov, interviews by author, 22 May 2000.

85. Hana Capova, "The Last Station: Hrusov. Slezka, Ostrava is Looking for a Ghetto for its Roma," *Respekt*, 1998.

86. The police arrested three skinheads and charged them with arson. The prosecutor did not charge them with a race/hate crime because the boys allege that they acted out of jealousy towards one of the young Romani boys. The lower court acquitted them on the arson charge, but the prosecutor appealed. Markus Pape, ERRC correspondent in Prague, interview by author, 23 May 2000.

87. If the apartment needs renovation and repair and cannot be used for a longer period of time, the tenant has the right to a substitute apartment. Czech Civil Code, sections 711, par. 1(e) and 712, par. 2.

88. *Mlada Fronta Dnes*, cited by Radio Prague in "The Situation of the Roma in the Czech Republic, 1998," 7 February 1998, available at: http://www.romove.cz/romove/jan98.html.

89. Pape, interview, 2000.

90. Emil Scuka, interview by author, Prague, 25 May 2000.

91. Andreea Rezkova, lawyer, Ecological Legal Service–Brno, interview by author, Prague, 24 May 2000.

92. See more on the manner in which the criminal record requirements affect the Romani community (in the context of the Czech citizenship law and expulsion regulations) in Research Directorate Immigration and Refugee Board, *Roma in the Czech Republic: Selected Issues.*

93. Rules on Renting Flats, Decision no. 68/1997, adopted by Teplice City Council, 5 February 1997, as amended by Decision no. 435/99, 23 June 1999, art. 3, par. 3. (henceforth: Rules on Renting Flats, Teplice).

94. Rules for the Administration of Municipality Flats of the City Jihlava, 10 February 2000, art. 3.

95. Regulation of the Pardubice City Council on the Lease of Municipal Flats, adopted by the City Council, entered into force on 1 March 2000, art. 6, par. 3(a). (henceforth: Regulation on the Lease of Municipal Flats, Paradubice).

96. Rules for Renting Municipal Flats, Decision no. 119/99, adopted by the Chomutov City Council, 8 March 1999. (henceforth; Rules for Renting Municipal Flats, Chomutov).

97. Minutes from telephone conversation between the Counselling Center for Citizenship, Civil and Human Rights, Prague and Ms. Urminska, chief of the Housing Administration Department, Most, 26 July 2000.

98. City of Vsetin Decree no. 11/1995, adopted on 19 December 1995: "Eligibility requirements for municipal flats are established by article 3, paragraph 2 as follows: . . . The applicant is struck off the list if they did not submit criminal record for himself and for his family members."

99. The points system permits access to municipal apartments only to those who, after meeting all the "general requirements" accumulate a sufficient number of points as a result of fulfilling other conditions.

100. Annex 1 of the Rules for Renting Municipal Flats, Chomutov. See translation in Annex 1 to this chapter.

101. Regulation on the Lease of Municipal Flats, Paradubice, art. 3, par. 2.

102. Rules of City Council in Louny no. P2/99, adopted by Decision 417/99 from 27 September 1999, art. 5, par. 4.

103. Rules for Renting Municipal Flats, Chomutov.

104. Rules on Renting Flats, Teplice.

105. Regulation on the Lease of Municipal Flats, Paradubice.

106. Jeffrey L. Blackman, *Statelessness in the Czech Republic: the Czech Citizenship Law and Its Application – the UNHCR Consultancy on Czech Citizenship Laws, A Final Report* (August 1996): 74, par. 20.14.

107. Bratinka Report, 29, par. 8.4.

108. Pavla Bouckova, head of the Counseling Center for Citizenship, Civil and Human Rights. Between 1997 and 1999, acting as head of the Citizenship Counseling Center of the Czech Helsinki Committee, Bouckova worked on individual cases of citizenship for institutionalized children. In this context she carried out interviews with municipalities and children's home agencies.

109. Rules on Renting Flats, Teplice, art. 3.

110. Regulation on the Lease of Municipal Flats, Paradubice, art. 3(2).

111. Rules on Management of the Housing Fund of the City of Rokycany, adopted by the City Council on 27 October 1998, art. 4 (1)b. The interest of the city and its good reputation is preserved not only by denying Roma access to housing but also prosecuting Romani leaders who protest the discriminatory practices. For example, Ondrej Gina, a prominent Romani leader who published information about the discrimination against Roma in Rokycany was accused by the mayor and the city council of "defamation of the Czech nation" and "harm to the reputation of the city of Rokycany at home and abroad." The police turned the case over to the prosecutor, charging Gina with slander, assault on a public office, and inciting racial discord. See U.S. Department of State– Bureau of Democracy, Human Rights, and Labor, *Country Reports on Human Rights Practices for 1999: Czech Republic.* (henceforth: Rules on Management of the Housing Fund, Rokycany).

112. Rules on Management of the Housing Fund, Rokycany, art. 4 (1), (d).

113. Petr Kudela, deputy mayor of Slezska (Ostrava), interview by author, May 22, 2000.

114. Eva Sobotka is former project coordinator of Helsinki Citizens' Assembly – Roma Section in Brno, Czech Republic. She is presently a researcher at the Richardson Institute for Peace Research (UK) and is undertaking a comparative research on Romani minority policy in the Czech Republic, Hungary, Slovakia and Yugoslavia.

115. Eva Sobotka, "Life Under the Bridge: Ghettoising Roma in Lower Hrusov Ostrava, Czech Republic," *Roma Rights–Newsletter of the European Roma Rights Center,* no. 2 (2000).

116. Rules for Renting Municipal Flats, Chomutov, art. 3, par. 2(d).

117. Mrs. Palisakova, an employee of the housing department of municipality of Chomutov , explained the manner in which the department interprets the rules. Telephone transcript with the Counseling Center on 4 August 2000.

118. Rules on Renting Flats, Teplice, art. 3(1).

119. Ibid., art. 3(3).

120. Rules for Renting Municipal Flats, Chomutov.

121. Ibid.

122. Jan Smock, street worker, interview by author, Kutna Hora, May 19, 2000.

123. Rules for Renting Municipal Flats, Chomutov, art. 3(2), (i).

124. Ministry for Regional Development of the Czech Republic, Housing Policy Concept, 4.

125. Article 127 (1) of the Czech Civil Code states: "The owner of a thing must refrain from anything that would cause annoyance to an unreasonable extent to another person or seriously jeopardize the latter's exercise of his rights." Article. 687 (1) of the Czech Civil Code stipulates that: "The lessor is obliged to hand over the flat to the lessee (tenant) in a condition suitable for its proper use and to ensure that the lessee is able to exercise the rights related to the use of the flat in full and without disturbance."

126. Czech Helsinki Committee, *Report on the State of Human Rights in the Czech Republic in 1997,* 130.

127. Blackman, *Statelessness in the Czech Republic: the Czech Citizenship Law and Its Application – the UNHCR Consultancy on Czech Citizenship Laws, A Final Report,* 71, par. 20.2.

128. In June 2000, the company sold the house to a private person.

129. Dr. Dombrasová, District Hygienic Station, Kutna Hora, interview by author, 19 May 2000.

130. Trebic, case 1T 71/99.

131. The Czech Center of New York "Dialogue Forum: Roma in the Czech Republic," conference, 17 April 1999, available at: http://www.czechcenter.com/RomaDialogue.htm.

132. Human Rights Watch, *Roma in the Czech Republic – Foreigners in Their Own Land.*

133. At that time, officials of Brandys nad Labem, told the press that the decrees were aimed to regulate the influx of Asian immigrants. See U.S. Department of State, *Czech Republic Human Rights Practices: 1993* (31 January 1994).

134. Ina Zoon, *Notes on the Citizenship Law's Background* (Prague: Tolerance Foundation, 2 February 1995).

135. Constitutional Court Decision 119/1994 (finding of the Constitutional Court of the Czech Republic of 26 April 1994 in the matter of the motion to repeal art. 3(6), art. 4(1) and art. 5(1) of generally binding regulation of the town Duchcov to ensure order in management of apartments held by the town, adopted on 10 December 1992), available at: http://www.sbirka.cz/ANGL1994/view5.htm.

136. Constitutional Court Decision 95/1994. "Finding of the Constitutional Court of the Czech Republic of 5 April 1994 in the matter of the motion to repeal generally binding regulation of the town of Krupka to ensure order in management of apartments held by the town," available at: http://www.sbirka.cz/ANGL1994/view5.htm.

137. Jiri Pehe, "Law on Romanies Causes Uproar in the Czech Republic, " *Radio Free Europe/Radio Liberty (RFE/RL) Research Report* vol.2, no.7 (12 February 1993).

138. The Czech Citizenship Law entered into force on 1 January 1993.

139. Jirina Siklova and Marta Miklusakova , "Law as an Instrument of Discrimination—Denying Citizenship to the Czech Roma," *East European Constitutional Review* vol.7, no. 2 (Spring 1998).

140. U.S. Department of State, *United States Department of State's 1993 Human Rights Report—Czech Republic* (Prague: 4 February 1994).

141. Kathleen Fox, "Indestructible Flats for Home Wreckers," *Prague Post,* 21–27 September 1994, 1.

142. Ibid.

143. Cees Zoon, "Czech Republic Puts Anti-Socials in 'Bare-Flats'," *de Volkskrant* (Netherlands), 19 November 1994.

144. "Security and Order in the Town of Kladno viewed by the Local Organization of ODS Kladno," publicly posted statement, October 1994. Translation on file.

145. Regional Court Prague, decision from 19 February 1998. Unofficial translation from Czech to English of the text of the decision on the European Roma Rights Center webpage, available at: http://errc.org/rr_aut1998/notebook-cases.shtml.

146. The name of the factory was Masokombinatu, Kladno.

147. "Another Accommodation for Non-Payers—the Only Solution for 'Civilized' Tenants," 28 July 2000, available at: http://www.vismo.obce.cz/kladno/dokumenty2.

148. Substitute accommodation means a one-room apartment, or a room in a house for single persons, or the sub-lease of a furnished or unfurnished part of another lessee's flat. (See Civil Code, Section 712, par. 4.)

149. Czech Civil Code, section 711, par. 1 (a), (b), (e), (f), and (i).

150. Ibid., section 712, par. 2.

151. Ibid., section 711, par. 1(c) stipulates that "the lessor may give notice terminating the lease of a flat with the consent of the competent court if the lessee or those who live with him, despite a written warning, grossly breach proper morality in the house."

152. Ibid., section 711, par. 1(d): "the lessor may give notice terminating the lease of a flat with the consent of the competent court if the lessee grossly breaches his obligations arising from lease of the flat, especially by not paying the rent or charges for services related to use of the flat, for a period longer than three months."

153. Ibid., section 711, par. 1(g): "the lessor may give notice terminating the lease of a flat with the consent of the competent court if the lessee has two or more flats, unless he cannot justly be required to use only one flat."

154. Ibid., section 711, par. 1(h): "the lessor may give notice terminating the lease of a flat with the consent of the competent court if the lessee fails without serious reasons to use the flat or if he uses the flat without serious reasons only occasionally."

155. Ibid., section 712, par. 5.

156. Ibid.

157. Law 102/1992, law on certain issues related to Law 509/1991 amending the Civil Code, provides some guidance on the administration of substitute accommodations. However, local authorities are completely free to chose the location.

158. Petr Kudela, interview, 2000.

159. The Counseling Center for Citizenship, Civil and Human Rights, *Holobyty Survey* (Prague: June-July 2000).

160. Dukelska, Chomutov, visit by author, 20 May 2000.

161. The Counseling Center for Citizenship/Civil and Human Rights, *Comments to the Report of the Czech Republic on Performance of the Obligations Arising from the Convention on the Elimination of All Forms of Racial Discrimination.*

162. In 1999. Ministry for Regional Development of the Czech Republic, *Housing Policy Concept,* Appendices: Housing Situation in the Czech Republic, 4.

163. According to Barbora Kvocekova, from the Prague based Counseling Center for Citizenship, Civil and Human Rights, this clause is included in the Housing Order annexed to each lease contract. Interview by author, Prague, 26 May, 2000.

164. Attachment to lease contracts for tenants in Frydlantska Street 111 and Soudni Street 453, as approved by the City Council on 15 March 2000.

165. The Counseling Center for Citizenship, Civil and Human Rights, *Holobyty Survey.*

166. The Housing Order, par. 2, which is attached to the standard renting contract concluded with each tenant in Mexico, Slany (henceforth: Housing Order, Slany).

167. The Housing Order for Non-Payers in the Complex Katerinki, Liberec, approved by the Liberec City Council by Decision no. 484/1997, 11 November 1997, art. 12. (henceforth: Housing Order for Non-Payers, Liberec).

168. Statute of the Accommodation Units in Soudni Street 453, Chrastava. Article 3/5 reads: "Tenants are not allowed to receive visitors, except immediate family members and close friends upon previous notification of the administrator."

169. Housing Order, Slany.

170. Housing Order for Non-Payers, Liberec, art. 20.

171. Constitutional Court Decision 119/1994.

Appendix: Romani Neighborhoods in Romania

1. For more on mahalas, see Prof. Vladimir Macura, AIA, *Housing, Urban Planning and Poverty: Problems Faced by Roma (Gypsy) Communities with Particular Reference to Central and Eastern Europe*, CoE MG-S-ROM (99)1 (Beograd, January 1999): 12.
2. Visit by author, Buhusi, 16 October 1999.
3. Romani inhabitants, interviews by author, Cluj, NATO block, 13 October 1999.
4. Ibid.
5. T. B. Romani woman, interview by author, Cluj, NATO block, 13 October 1999.
6. Romani inhabitants, interview, 1999.
7. Lia Valendorfer, "140 Apartments Abusively Occupied," *Romania Libera*, 15 June 1999.
8. Ioana Gligor, "Roma from Cluj Are Not Satisfied with the Attitude of Gheorghe Funar," *Adevarul de Cluj*, 30 November 1996.
9. Valendorfer, "140 Apartments Abusively Occupied."
10. Visit by author, Orastie, 11 October 1999.
11. Harjob Nicolae, deputy mayor, Orastie, interview by author, Orastie, 11 October 1999.
12. Ibid.
13. Romani residents of buildings 7 and 8, interviews by author, Orastie, 11 October 1999.
14. Romani woman living in building 8, interview by author, Orastie, 11 October 1999.
15. Romani men living in building 7, interviews by author, Orastie, 11 October 1999.
16. Istvan Haller, program officer, Human Rights PRO EUROPE League, interview by author, Targu Mures, 16 October 1999.
17. Ibid.
18. Rudolf Moca, member of regional council, Targu Mures Casrom Foundation, interview by author, 16 October 1999.
19. Visit by author, Rovinari district, Targu Mures, buildings 24 and 26, 16 October 1999.
20. B. N., Romani woman, interview by author, Rovinari, Targu Mures, 16 October 1999.
21. Aurel Rosiianu, president, Roma Party, Cluj Branch, interview by author, Cluj, 13 October 1999.
22. See also Elena Vaida, "Should Roma Make the First Steps?" *Adevarul de Cluj*, 16 May 1999.
23. Romani residents, interviews by author, Valea Rece (Targu Mures), 16 October 1999, Lumea-Noua/Zona Industriala (Alba Iulia), 10 October 1999, and Strada Coastei (Cluj), 13 October 1999.
24. Maria Ionescu, GLAR expert, Together Agency, interview by author, 13 September 1999. Ionescu notes that there are also cases of mayors who applied for funding from international agencies and did install electricity and water (e.g. the village of Cerat in Salaj) or water and gas (e.g. Sacalaseni in Baia Mare) in Romani settlements.
25. Gruia Bumbu, program manager, Romani CRISS, interview by author, Alba Iulia, 10 October 1999.
26. Visit by author, Lumea Noua/Zona Industriala, 10 October 1999.
27. M. G., Romani man, interview by author, Lumea Noua/Zona Industriala, 10 October 1999.
28. Stealing electricity is a criminal offense under the Romanian Penal Code, art. 208.
29. Romani residents, interviews by author, Lumea Noua/Zona Industriala, Alba Iulia, 1999.
30. Visit by author, Valea Rece, 16 October 1999.